A Guide to Good Money

Brendan Brown · Robert Pringle

A Guide to Good Money

Beyond the Illusions of Asset Inflation

Brendan Brown
Hudson Institute
Washington, USA

Robert Pringle
Central Banking Publications
London, UK

ISBN 978-3-031-06040-3   ISBN 978-3-031-06041-0   (eBook)
https://doi.org/10.1007/978-3-031-06041-0

Cover credit: Andrey Lobachev/shutterstock
Cover credit: MPanchenko/shutterstock

This Palgrave Macmillan imprint is published by the registered company Springer Nature Switzerland AG
The registered company address is: Gewerbestrasse 11, 6330 Cham, Switzerland

To my late mother, Irene Brown

—Brendan Brown

To my wife

—Robert Pringle

Preface

This book has been written primarily for people who are interested in knowing about the world's monetary problems but who may not have enough basic knowledge to follow the comments on TV, online or in the newspapers. It is a guide to how the money system works today and how it might work in the future. Our guide should also appeal, as a quest for truth amidst so much contemporary obfuscation, to specialist readers usually more at home with journal articles.

It focuses on the big issues—why the money system matters to all of us, how inflation spreads round the world, how financial crises occur and why governments' efforts to patch things up end in failure—causing far-reaching economic, social and geopolitical damage. We, the authors, present a point of view. We take sides. There is good money and there is bad money; good regimes treat everyone equally, bad regimes are easily manipulated by a minority. We devote one part to "the essence of good money" and another part to analysing bad money and the grip it seems to have on us.

Bad money has huge costs for people everywhere. Over four chapters, we show that it is based on a faulty and quite recent concept—the state theory of money, that it generates episodes of sustained asset inflation and has other dire consequences. These include a shortening of investment horizons, skewing the allocation of capital to get-rich-quick projects which hot speculative markets overrate and detaching money prices from the real value of goods or services. It levies several forms of taxation without the normal checks and balances of a legislative process. It causes widening inequality alongside reduced general prosperity. So we should avoid it like the plague.

Yet, most monetary regimes in the world now are, we judge, "moderately bad". If true (and we present the evidence), what keeps such inferior and dangerous systems in power? We have a chapter on that. What difference has the pandemic made? Many governments have been claiming that with their help, we "won" the battle with the virus. We argue on the contrary that official policies were far from optimal—that the so-called "victory" over Covid was indeed Pyrrhic.

The final part—"Reform, Idealism and Prosperity" is all about implementation, i.e. the reforms needed to instal good money regimes and the obstacles reformers will face. Good money needs a solid anchor. We discuss what features it should have and review candidates for this key function. Central banks have tried to put one in place—"inflation targeting". We take a different path. Money should be tied to the real world.

We also discuss the politics of reform. Which states or currency areas will lead the world on to good money? The status quo is defended by a "moat of consensus". Reformers need to cross it before seizing the castle, which, like Kafka's, looms ominously over us.

The authors would like to thank William White for having so meticulously and constructively read our whole volume in manuscript form. His stimulus and encouragement meant so much to us both at the inevitable moment of doubt and re-casting which marks the end-phase of book-writing. We also acknowledge the critical nurturing of the project from its start by our editor, Tula Weis.

Washington, USA   Brendan Brown
London, UK   Robert Pringle
March 2022

Introduction

All of us would like to live in a good society. Yes, people have differing ideas of what exactly that means. Yet most of us would agree that it would have certain basic features. These would include—in no particular order—the rule of law, an independent judiciary, freedom from arbitrary arrest and imprisonment, respect for human rights and the rights of minorities, secure property rights, absence of ethnic or gender discrimination, plus freedom of speech and of religious belief. The key questions that we pose in this book are the following: what kind of money and financial system would foster/nourish and protect such a society best and how would it differ from our present system? Money may not appear as fundamental a matter as some of the other features of a good society already mentioned, but we believe it is pretty basic. We argue that our money system is deeply flawed, and that, it imperils our enjoyment of the other properties of a good society. So what is wrong and how can we fix it?

To address these questions, we need to answer a prior question: what is money and the money system for? The answer might seem obvious enough: we need money to buy and sell things with. If you want to sell, unless the person buying your service has exactly what you want and you are both ready to do a barter deal, you would both do better doing the deal at an agreed price in money. We need it to compare prices offered by different vendors and to compare the profits of a company or the accounts of a charity over time. It is also helpful in many other ways—for instance if we decide to wait before we buy something, we can keep the sum in money. So money is not only whatever is accepted in payment in a society but is also potential purchasing power. But money is even more than that—it is an essential ingredient that lets markets operate. Only through functioning markets can we have any confidence in being able to buy or sell what we want when we want to. Only with money or access to it can we plan our lives with confidence. A supply of money is thus crucial to the attainment of personal liberty.

We should, however, pay attention not just to the supply of money but also to its quality. A high-quality money is a good from which we all derive benefits, both as individuals and as a society. It is critical to the proper operation of the modern market economy, which has been called the most complicated piece of machinery in history. There, it is a foundation of a social structure that supports high ethical standards, while a poor-quality money undermines those standards. There is no discrimination in the provision of good-quality money. Those without power or connections do not have to put up with an inferior good. It does not favour the monopolist or would-be monopolist. Good-quality money is a foundation of a liberal political order as well as prosperity. It goes along with better economic and social outcomes. What we mean by good-quality money will become clearer in the course of this book. Suffice to mention now that it should be reliable, easy to use, widely acceptable and be expected to maintain its value in the very long run. It should also go along with a responsive and a diverse array of competitive banking and other financial services.

Nowhere in the world can we observe such a money in operation. Official spokespersons insist that the public trust the current monetary system which, they say, safely looks after people's money and supports business activity. In our contemporary world (though we must now make exception for the pandemic inflation shock of 2021 followed by the European war shock of 2022), many people, at least in the major industrial economies, in their everyday financial decision-making act as if the value of money were broadly stable. Interest rates are low by modern historical comparison and people deemed creditworthy can obtain loans—for example, for house purchase, albeit at highly inflated property prices.

However, we shall argue that official reassurances are empty. Just to point to some obvious problems; the money system is laden with debt; financial crises recur; and nobody in the corridors of power knows how to prevent them short of at least partially nationalising the entire system while amassing armies of regulators and compliance officers. Further, we shall argue that social ills seemingly unconnected to the monetary system are to a large extent its unintended consequences. Capital investment has been weak in many countries for many years, as has productivity growth. Linked to this, middle-class incomes have stagnated or advanced so slightly as to be imperceptible in many nations for a generation of more. Looking ahead, millions are likely to lose their jobs in the next severe downturn with little prospect of finding new employment except at very low pay, as occurred in the last economic expansion. The financial system discriminates against small and medium-sized firms in the sense that they face higher costs in large part due to their more restricted access to competing suppliers of services (especially loans)—with regulatory and compliance hurdles an important factor here. (Yes, there is private equity, but that is a story for later in this volume!). At the same time, asset inflation has increased financial and wider economic fragility from a long-run perspective, while increasing inequality of wealth and in many countries inequality of incomes as well (See Glossary for a definition of asset inflation). We argue that asset inflation has critically strengthened the destructive forces of monopoly capitalism which both Adam Smith and Karl Marx warned in their own ways would imperil the liberal capitalist order.

While low-quality money has worsened many social ills, it is by no means their sole cause. Nor do we claim that high-quality money would be a panacea for them. Indeed, it is wrong to expect money, however "good", to solve political and economic problems, though it should make some of these less difficult in so far as it can raise the general level of prosperity compared to where this would be under inferior money regimes. Rather, we should view good money as a critical foundation block of the good society. We reject the notion that there is a trade-off whereby chipping at that foundation block or weakening it in any way can produce a better society. The erroneous belief that you can address so many social and economic problems by throwing money at them is itself one of the sources of the deterioration of the quality of money. Indeed, we take issue with the whole idea that an ideal condition described as "full employment" can be reached by use of active monetary policies. Such ideas can easily end up producing what we call "bad money". Indeed, that is what has happened. It is easy to understand why governments make such claims—it helps to get them elected—but we will show that these claims rest on continuous state propaganda and historical myth-making. It is often asserted, for example, that a plentiful supply of money ensured recovery from the Great Recession of 2007–2009 and lessened the economic pain of the corona virus pandemic. We argue that these assertions are false.

Although a good monetary regime would not guarantee progress towards a good society, it could and would contribute mightily to its possibility. Good money is a necessary but not a sufficient condition on its own of a good society. Without good money, there will not be a good society. But this requires more than good money. Beyond that statement of principle, as presented in subsequent chapters, we argue that good money would help to counter several key challenges facing liberal democracies. These include the legacy of the virus crisis and those unresolved problems left behind by the global financial crisis 12 years previously, such as a historically high and damaging level of state indebtedness, as well as new challenges including a backlash against globalisation. At the level of geopolitics, money is and will be an important front in how the US/the West deals with the menace of the expansionist Communist regime in China or more broadly of the Moscow-Beijing-Teheran—Pyongyang axis to global peace and a global order based on ideals of economic and political freedom. But to serve these key roles, money itself has to be desirable.

Look at it this way. By common consent, our economies suffer from at least five basic defects: an obsessive search for short-term returns, where this obsession is directly stimulated by bad money as we will explain; low levels of capital investment; high levels of entrenched social inequality; the capture of power over money by special interests (crony capitalism and more broadly monopoly capitalism); and excessive levels of indebtedness. As individuals and societies, many of us are borrowing far too much (although poor management, whether of firms, of public finances or indeed of our personal finances, is often a factor). We will show that each of these problems can be traced back, in full or in part, to "bad money". This is the common denominator underlying the symptoms of ill-health. A move to a good money would help remedy all of them and restore society to health. But it would demand great determination and indeed brilliance in the political arena which indeed we can observe at crucial turning points from bad back to good money in the laboratory of history. When conditions are in place, the role of ideas and indeed ideology is crucial in this process.

In this short guide, we explain the principles and main features of good money without resort to jargon. We present examples of good and bad monies. We illustrate what good money can do and make clear its limits. We must be on our guard. Many modern social ills are down to unrealistic and exaggerated beliefs about what the state can do with our money. It is wrong to raise false hopes. Yet most monies have become so rotten that we have to go back to first principles. We need to restate the case. And we intend to level with our readers. Any blueprint for a good money includes assertions or hypotheses which are as yet untested. A shift to a good money regime from a bad money regime involves experimentation with risks. For the game to be worth the candle, we have to convince you that the journey is worth embarking on. We believe it certainly is given the wretchedness of the monetary regime at present and given the prospects for success, even if this depends on multiple revisions of the original blueprint along the way and even if the destination appears far distant. So this is the Guide to Good Money.

A Work in Five Parts

Part I: The Present Scene describes how money currently circulates at national and international levels and the parts played by governments, central banks and regulators along with markets in spreading inflation and crises internationally. The final chapter in this part analyses what we call "the global menace of US monetary policies". It also examines important episodes when an individual country tried to make a stand and assert its independence. It suggests that the US and its allies have lost much by failing to learn the right lessons from such resistance.

Part II: The Essence of Good Money presents our (the joint authors') vision of what a good money regime would look like. It argues that certain key ingredients or elements should play crucial roles in such a regime—including "super-money", "convertibility into a real asset" and "a solid anchor". We demonstrate that these have indeed worked in practice when applied consistently.

Part III: The Grip of Bad Money reveals how far we are from having a good money regime; and how citizens are tricked into believing the present set-up to be normal and unavoidable. This involves a more detailed critique of the damage done by modern money, why resistance has been low and the costs to society high. The chapter headings speak for themselves: Asset Inflation and the Illusions of Prosperity; Exposing the State Theory of Money; A Short History of Modern Money; Symptoms and Consequences of Bad Money.

Part IV: Vested Interests, Politics and the Pandemic is about the political economy of money. It analyses the forces keeping a bad system in power, including cronyism and blatant corruption and how they played out to pervert public policy in the pandemic. Big Tech and other monopolists which have benefited from the zero cost of capital (courtesy of central banks) have used recent emergencies such as the global financial crisis of 2008 and the pandemic of 2020–2022 to strengthen their position. Meanwhile, elite groups including the mainstream media have been captured by a seemingly progressive agenda that actually serves to entrench bad money regimes even more deeply in our societies.

Part V: Reform, Idealism and Prosperity is all about implementation. Reform is possible despite these formidable obstacles. How can we instal a good money regime? The first chapter sets out a bold vision for the core of a reform—a really solid monetary anchor (See Glossary). Then, seizing the spectacles of the sceptical reader, we quiz ourselves on every aspect of our analysis and proposed reforms. Recognising that there is no short cut, the chapter "Pathways to Good Money" charts ways through the politics of reform. Thus equipped, we assess the prospects for reform globally, starting with the US, and then turning to the European Union, Switzerland, the United Kingdom and Japan (the wild card is China). In conclusion, as the path ahead runs uphill all the way to the top, we recognise that reformers will need large reserves of idealism and zeal. Yet, somehow or other, we believe that they will put money in its proper place as a pillar of a free, prosperous and equitable society.

Contents

Part I

The Present Scene

1

Modern Money—A Matter of Trust

How to Think About Money

We start by describing modern money, how it is supposed to work; how it is created and managed; what banks and other financial institutions do; and its main flaws.

One prominent feature is the large role of the state; nation states have their fingerprints all over modern money. Governments like creating money and scattering it around. As more and more citizens become dependent on this "generosity", they naturally look to governments to solve social and economic problems. If money is essentially a tool of the state, then governments should first create as much of it as is needed to solve such problems, and only then worry about possible side-effects such as inflation.

Is this the right way to think about money? Well, it's true that governments have always claimed the right to decide what counts as money. In their territories or states, they define the unit used—what counts as a dollar, a euro or a pound. They can and do enforce their definition of money; for example, they always require citizens to pay taxes in the official state money. State sovereignty and money are closely tied together. How can we, the citizens, defend ourselves and wage war if we cannot pay our soldiers and sailors? How can we do that if we do not control our money? Most states therefore issue their own currencies. But there is a limit to the state's ability to force people to use its money; for example, in the German hyperinflation of 1923 the US dollar became the main money for a time, whatever the law said. In general, states aim, therefore, to make their monies sufficiently attractive

B. Brown and R. Pringle, *A Guide to Good Money*, https://doi.org/10.1007/978-3-031-06041-0_1

that citizens will decide to hold them without exorbitant compulsion. They adopt various strategies towards achieving this level of "minimal attractiveness" while pursuing wider objectives including high levels of employment. Such strategies have had a mixed record of success, to say the least.

Plainly, this mixed performance raises questions that cannot be quickly dealt with by a few simple, common sense answers. There are other ways to think about money. Perhaps we can start by laying down a few basic requirements. To make money acceptable, it should be trusted by users. That means, the people and institutions that control how much is issued must be trusted not to issue too much or (less likely) too little of it. How (and how well) this works depends on what is called the "monetary regime" in place at a given place and time. Too little money can for some time starve an economy of the essential "oil" to keep it working well. Too much money will depress its value in terms of purchasing power—persistent inflation is the result of "too much money chasing too few goods". This is what happened in Germany in the early 1920s, in China and to a lesser extent Japan immediately after World War II, and in Venezuela, Zimbabwe and other countries recently; there were at least 100 such periods of "hyperinflation"—truly man-made disasters—in the twentieth century. Even in developed countries, there was a bad inflationary scare in the 1970s.

So the need to make money attractive by limiting its supply comes up against the pressure felt by governments to spend more money on various projects and social services, while keeping taxes low to make the current government popular and win elections. The politicians in power are naturally tempted to take the easy way out and get the money to spend on such projects by borrowing from the government's bank—the central bank. But this can have political costs also, most of all if high inflation is the result. During the "greatest peacetime inflation" of the mid/late 1960s and 1970s, for example, governments discovered that very high inflation rates were deeply unpopular.

In the event, governments responded by modifying the monetary regime. First came the experiment with monetarism (targeting the growth of the money supply), brief in the US and UK, much longer and starting earlier in Germany. Later came what we describe as the "2 per cent inflation standard" where governments delegated authority over money to central banks and granted them "independence" to set short-term interest rates in order to keep prices under control. That was the idea, at any rate.

Yet would this regime be robust enough to restrain governments while allowing sufficient credit and money creation to meet the needs of industry, commerce and consumers? What would happen in a crisis? There were no easy answers.

Evidently, it is difficult to keep the state out; but the guardians of money would have to earn our trust.

The Trust Deficit

As politicians are aware of the difficulty of earning trust and the ease with which, once earned, it may be lost, they may resort to various methods to shore up confidence in money.

One strategy is to link the local currency to a larger one with an established reputation for being reliable and trustworthy. Countries where for some reason trust is lacking (they may, for example, recently have emerged from a civil war, as in Bosnia in the 1990s) and some other, often small, countries are attracted by this option. They enhance trust by assuring citizens that they, the citizens, can convert their local currency at a fixed exchange rate into the currency of a country or area that already has a global reputation. Thus, many countries link their currencies to the US dollar, others to the euro. Such states sacrifice control over their money. The supply of local currency is determined by how much demand there is for it at the fixed rate with the US dollar or the euro. (The supply can even be produced automatically; the institution that issues the money has no discretion about how much it should issue.) The monetary policy and core interest rate are set by the US Federal Reserve or, in the case of currencies linked to the euro, the European Central Bank (ECB). Yet many people in such countries feel that the sacrifice of control over money is worthwhile. In effect, they "piggyback" on the credibility of another currency. That is quite a sensible option as long as the currency which is used as the pillar is itself stable—and expected to remain so. This has not always been true even of the US dollar or the euro. We return to this question later on (see Chapter 5).

States protect their national money from exposure to the competition of alternative monies. One powerful "natural" obstacle to competition is exchange rate volatility between the home currency and others. Exchange risk means that residents have an in-built reason to prefer domestic money; so domestic inflation has to rise above a certain threshold to justify diversification into alternative competitor national monies. Also, domestic banks enjoy privileges in conducting deposit and loan business in the local money. As a result, these banks can preserve market share against more efficient foreign banks. Such obstacles raise the costs of international trade and investment. Monetary protectionism can be as damaging as the more familiar strategy of protecting trade by, for example, rising tariffs against imports. Trust in a nation's money is the basis of its entire monetary and banking system. Yet, monetary protectionism means citizens in practice decide to use it to a considerable extent whether or not they trust it.

These adverse effects result from one basic idea—the idea that money is an object of the state, and thus a "resource" at the disposal of the government—together with the fact it is almost impossible to stop governments from putting their hands in the till (see Part Three, especially Chapters 6 and 7). So governments, fearing citizens will see through these deceits, invariably assure people that money is "safe" and in good hands. "We will not manipulate it" they say, in effect, "look, we have taken our hands off it!"

How the Roles and the Powers of Officialdom Have Grown

As already mentioned, central banks implement monetary policies within contours set in the political arena. In doing this, they enjoy a degree of protection from official interference in their day-to-day operations. Why does government (whether the executive or legislative branch or both) grant them this? Well, as we have just noted, government wants to reassure citizens that its power over money will not be abused. Let us look at this in a little detail. What is the background here?

Under the current monetary regimes, governments (or sometimes legislatures) give central banks and allied agencies several objectives. In most countries, these include an inflation target, an economic objective and financial regulation. Under the latter, they are charged not only with monitoring the soundness of individual banks (ensuring, for example, they meet minimum standards of capital) but also with reducing risk to the entire financial system and the costs of financial crises (institutional arrangements differ widely among countries and monetary areas). They and allied agencies are also charged with a variety of other key roles, including ensuring the soundness of the payment system and in many cases administration of anti-money laundering codes. They are granted far-reaching powers to reach these objectives. They are guided not by objective rules buttressed by public audits and the courts but by broad aims that are usually a matter for interpretation. They are given a large degree of discretion in how they carry out such responsibilities.

—Especially Since the Global Financial Crisis

The Global Financial Crisis (GFC) of 2007–8 and the pandemic crises of 2020–22 (ongoing at the time of writing) both resulted in further changes to central banks' aims and methods. Between the early or mid-1990s and 2007, they usually had one over-riding stated objective—to deliver their concept of price stability (sometimes alongside a second objective in some form such as "maximum employment"). During the first few years, many nations (including the US) did not put a precise number on what they meant by price stability. Gradually, however, the new regime emerged more fully as, in effect, an attempt to set up an international monetary standard of consumer prices rising at 2% a year. We analyse the effects of this policy below. Then, from the great recession that followed the GFC central banks turned to massive monetary stimulus because, they said, inflation was coming in below target. The result is clear. As the state's role increased further after the GFC, central banks claimed to empower the expansion. The state's policy response also involved commercial banks. With private demand for credit low, the central banks stepped in to create money through a vast expansion of their size and their weight in the financial system. Governments guaranteed to secure the survival of their most important banks when their entire banking systems were under dire threat of insolvency and bankruptcy. These banks received huge subsidies from the taxpayer.

This increased role for the state continues, though its degree, shape and form differ say between the US and Europe, especially given the still ailing condition of key parts of the European banking industry. In return for bailouts, the state naturally took a greater say in banks' lending to various economic sectors and in which companies were kept afloat. But lingering poor profitability (again, a European rather than US phenomenon) and intrusive regulation (designed to ensure they would never again require bailouts) reduced their attractiveness to investors and discouraged enterprise. As responsibility for ensuring the safety and soundness of banking passed out of the hands of bankers themselves to bureaucrats, so customers— though again more in Europe than in America—started to view bankers as box-tickers, functionaries working to the book of rules written by regulators.

Central Banks' Mandates and Confused Messages

It is a widespread view that democratic governments should maintain full employment and economic growth. Surely, then, money should be plentiful and it should be easy and cheap to borrow. Thus, governments, unconstrained in monetary matters by effective constitutions, have an in-built preference for low interest rates. But they don't want too much inflation either, knowing that episodes of high inflation can bring election defeat. So governments or legislatures juggle two aims. This is reflected in the legal framework they set for their agents, the central banks. For example, the so-called dual mandate of the Federal Reserve, enshrined in legislation of 1977, includes objectives for prices, interest rates and employment. Since the late 1990s, the Fed has gradually come to interpret its price mandate to mean perpetual 2% inflation and there has been no Congressional or legal challenge to this. The Bank of England sets monetary policy "to meet the 2% inflation target, and in a way that helps to sustain growth and employment". It uses two main monetary policy tools. First, it sets the interest rate that banks and building societies earn on deposits, or "reserves", placed with it—this is Bank Rate. Second, it buys government and corporate bonds, this is "asset purchases" or "quantitative easing". How does it pay for such purchases? Simply by creating money—it adds so many billions of pounds to the account of the bank or institution from which it bought the assets. But the link between such operations and the path of interest rates to the broader objectives of official policy is complex and sometimes indeterminate, even given use of high-powered econometric models specifying the statistical relationships that are believed to hold between various economic quantities; plus armies of economists.

Given the big part money plays in the economic system, you might assume that central banks should aim to control or influence the total amount of money in the economy. But they do not. Indeed, they see that as an obsolete notion—a relic from the "failed" monetarist experiment of the early 1980s in the case of the US. Often they seem to avoid talking about "money" as if it was a dirty word, a hangover from the dark years of "turmoil" between the collapse of the Bretton Woods "order" and the modern bright era of the 2% inflation standard. Indeed, they have done much to muddy the concept, so that money today is far from the crisp distinct asset which it was assumed to be in classical monetary theory. Central bankers now much prefer the adjective "monetary", as in "monetary policy". Search their reports on monetary policy—where they account for their actions to parliament—and ultimately to the public—and you will find that the word "money" appears infrequently, if at all.

For example, the basic guide by the Federal Reserve Board of Governors called *Monetary Policy: What Are Its Goals? How Does It Work?* mentions the word "monetary" 44 times but does not mention money itself (Board of Governors 2021). The UK Monetary Policy Committee never mentions "money" in its quarterly policy reports and pays little or no attention to the money supply. Indicators of the money supply are not used either as policy targets or as part of the mechanism by which policy affects the economy. The official line is that, although the stock or amount of money held by consumers and businesses may influence prices over time, the time lags involved between a policy measure and money and then from money to prices are so variable that it is useless as a policy tool. That's what central bankers tell us.

Yet policies—what they actually do—*involve creating more and more money.* Thus, top monetary policy-makers speak, write and take decisions about money in a totally confusing way. Their own accounts of their work and their economic assessments ignore it even as their political masters (and/or their view of the needs of the economy) make them conjure up more of it. On the one hand, money does not feature in central bankers' economic analysis. On the other hand, money creation, especially in its guise as Quantitative Easing, is their main policy weapon. More than that, creating money has become central bankers' default response to almost any problem (as former Bank of England governor Mervyn King recognises, see Chapter 2). In short, their theory bears only a sketchy relationship to their practice—and that's putting it politely.

Some Flaws of the Policy Regimes—

Already some of the main flaws of contemporary policy regimes are becoming apparent. We explore these in detail later but to mention just a few here:

Firstly, the regimes follow contemporary mainstream economics in having "no real, coherent, firmly based theory of inflation at all" (Goodhart 2021). Secondly, the regimes contain no mechanism for limiting the quantity of money.
Thirdly, a policy based on fixing interest rates has failed to attain its objectives and distorted market signals.

Fourthly, resort to blasts of "quantitative easing" (vast asset purchases financed by the creation of money) as the major instrument by which central banks have attempted to sustain growth and prevent recession was plainly a leap in the dark and an admission of the failure of the former policy regime. Frankly, it was always silly to pretend that it could be healthy for central banks to carry around such swollen balance sheets and to operate on such a large scale in markets with many clearly undesirable effects on normal market functions.

—Asset Inflation and Hidden Taxes

We analyse these in later chapters. But we should flag two aspects right away.

Firstly, *asset inflation* is an endemic feature of the regime (see Glossary for definition and explanation of our use of this term). The role of money in generating this can remain in part camouflaged, not coming into the glare of attention, when for extended periods there are powerful forces, such as rapid productivity growth, which on their own would tend to push prices of goods and services prices down—i.e. deflation. This occurred during the last half decade of the twentieth century and the first half decade of the twenty-first century. Several factors were at work during that period. These included downward pressure on prices of consumer goods resulting from the entry of China and other countries with huge pools of low-paid workers to the world economy; the development of the "gig economy"—where firms hire individuals for temporary jobs at low wage rates; the weakening of trades unions; and the widening of consumer choice through the global spread of the internet and online shopping, and large gains in productivity (which faded away in the second decade of the twenty-first century)—to name but a few. So until about 2010 central banks were fighting an underlying tendency for prices of goods and services to fall; as we shall see in this volume that fight continued in a different form after 2010. We should also note (to be discussed in subsequent chapters) that asset inflation in the context of the digitalisation revolution empowers monopoly capitalism, and there are other effects which combine to produce a kind of economic sclerosis (see Glossary). To sum up, ultra-low interest rates and other measures to pump up the monetary base create asset inflation without necessarily raising goods and prices services sufficiently to meet the central banks' official inflation targets.

Secondly, the monetary regime imposes taxes—some new, some old, some hidden, some obvious. Many people are aware that inflation shock exposes them to a form of tax—it means falls in the real value of government debts at the expense of anybody who holds money or government bonds (as almost of us do directly or indirectly). The availability of index-linked bonds offers citizens one way of protecting their savings to a limited extent from this form of expropriation. A second form of monetary taxation, named here monetary repression tax, has in recent years loomed larger than inflation tax (though in 2021, the second year of the pandemic, inflation tax made a big comeback, and also into 2022). Monetary repression tax arises because of the artificial low level of interest rates compared with the average level in real terms that would exist if central banks were not fighting a battle against the odds to raise inflation to the target rate. With such repressed markets, savers and all creditors suffer from unnaturally low levels of return or yield from their investments. This is also taxation without representation (see Chapter 6 and Glossary).

—Fomenting Injustices and Arbitrary Power

To be sure, many people may regard our present money regime as unobjectionable, even as normal. The system appears to work reasonably well most of the time for the day-to-day purposes that we all use it for. We know when and if we have to save up for a major purchase. We know about the investments we can make if we have some surplus savings and we know that some investments are safer than others and that we have to accept a risk of losing money if we want our savings to produce a high yield or interest rate—sometimes only bonds issued by rather dodgy firms or countries offer any kind of decent return. We expect that money is "safe" at the big banks. Most of us therefore assume that money is doing its job.

In fact, however, the money regime is closely connected to the obvious injustices of contemporary capitalism—the rise of monopoly power, stagnation in middle-class real incomes over the long-run, the growing disparities of wealth and oppressive taxation. The connecting links are cunningly hidden or denied. Powerful interests that benefit from the money regime have every incentive not to let the sun in. We aim to expose these hidden links. We have already pointed to some structural issues. Later, we shall show that money as a means of payment is also subject to much imperfection. We shall trace the causes back to credit and debit card oligopolies and regulations that suppress opportunities for cash or more recently digitalisation of existing fiat monies. We have touched on the banks' role as suppliers of money and of credit. Later, we shall show that banking has become very bad at performing that role—crucial to any thriving business.

The role of the state is pervasive and complex but often mischievous. Banks and other regulated entities now look to agents of the state not only for general rules and guidance but for specific approvals and permissions, including guidance on granting themselves bonuses. This behaviour is perhaps more striking in the UK and Europe amidst the advanced economies than in North America. The long arms and watchful eyes of the regulators reach into every nook and cranny of the financial edifice—at least of those parts of it that are regulated (which at present excludes, for example, the cryptocurrency space). At the same time, the governments' readiness to provide a safe harbour to banks in a storm now goes far beyond the traditional "lender of last resort" function. There are also broader constitutional angles to consider. The current regulatory regime gives appointed officials wide-ranging discretionary authority over companies and individuals (see "the regulation juggernaut" in the next chapter). This kind of delegated power is traditionally considered to be a danger to, and inconsistent with, liberty of the individual, as Hayek pointed out (1944).

Chapter Plan and a Warning

That wraps up our bird's eye view of the current policy regimes operating at national level by national governments and central banks. In the next chapter of this opening part of the book, we describe how this fits in with the global flows of money, and the rising part played by "shadow" banks such as mortgage lenders, money market funds, insurance companies, hedge funds, private equity funds and wholesale money markets that are now the dominant form of funding for these shadow banks. Later chapters fill out our account of the framework in which policy is made and explain why money and finance still have not been brought back to serve the real economy. Yet it is within our reach to install a much better regime—to have a better kind of money. Our aim is to help readers not only to make sense of the daily flow of news on TV, online and in the newspapers, but also to challenge what they are told.

Clearly, one warning is already in order. When it comes to money, citizens would be wise to treat the statements of policy-makers and the smooth rationalisations of too much of the media with a large dose of scepticism.

References

Board of Governors of the Federal Reserve System (2021) Monetary Policy: What Are Its Goals? How Does It Work?

Goodhart, CEA (2021) Interview. *Central Banking*, Vol. XXXII, No. 1, September 2021.

2

Globalisation Without Global Money

People need money to make payments internationally for the same purposes as they need it at home. They may, for example, wish to purchase a good or service from abroad, acquire a property or financial asset, such as an equity share or foreign bond, or send money to a relative. Companies likewise need money to make foreign investments—setting up a branch or subsidiary, or buying another company, for example. There is usually, however, a distinction between making payments to a person or company in a country that has a different currency than domestically. In this case, your domestic/home money may well not be readily accepted by the person or institution you are paying. Even if they agree, there will be costs—for example related to banks charging a fee to change it into their domestic money. And the conversion rate of one currency into the other is likely to fluctuate. This brings added uncertainty and risk into international trade and investment that are absent in transactions within a single currency area. Such uncertainty and risk raise the costs of doing business internationally. For example, an exporter selling goods that the foreign buyer will pay for in three months time can insure the risk of a change in the exchange rate but may need to pay a premium to somebody willing to take on that risk for him. Such insurance is readily available normally for up to one year at most.

These costs do not arise, or they remain only slight, if there is a distinct global money acceptable everywhere. Gold and silver used to serve this role but war and national economic policies ended this during the early decades of the twentieth century (we consider in a later chapter whether gold could

© The Author(s), under exclusive license to Springer Nature
Switzerland AG 2022
B. Brown and R. Pringle, *A Guide to Good Money*,
https://doi.org/10.1007/978-3-031-06041-0_2

stage a comeback but this is not on the cards at present). The development of the euro issued by the European Central Bank meant that payments between individuals and firms in different countries within the monetary union became like domestic payments. That benefit however involves each member country pooling monetary sovereignty—an exercise fraught with difficulty unless there is general popular consent in all member countries to the union's money being at least as good as the best national currencies it replaces. Monetary union in the European sense, as we shall see growingly influenced by bad money concepts, is not an idea that has spread. So traders and investors must at present use national currencies or the euro to make and receive payments across national borders or currency areas, with the attendant uncertainties and costs. This only makes sense, however, if the gains from national (or in the case of the euro, regional) control of money outweigh the additional costs for consumers and society when compared with a universal money. If governments use such control to benefit special interests rather than the community as a whole, this justification for independent currencies, whether at the national or regional level, falls away.

In practice, the uncertainty and costs of a system with multiple independent currencies and bilateral exchange rates are reduced by the emergence of currency zones. Many small and even some medium-size currencies in practice track one of the major currencies. Given a choice among currencies, international traders and investors naturally prefer one that is convenient, easy to use and offers easy access to a range of financial services and investment opportunities—in other words, a well-developed financial and legal infrastructure. But above all, it must inspire confidence in its relative stability in terms of purchasing power. These three "c's"—confidence, convenience and cost—go far to explain why certain national currencies are widely used internationally.

In the first great age of economic globalisation, in the nineteenth century, the pound sterling was the natural choice—it was the currency of Great Britain, the leading economic power until say, the 1880s. It would be wrong to describe the pound at that time as a "national money"; rather we should think of it as the national brand in a worldwide monetary system in which gold was the global core asset; the pound was the leading gold money among many monies tied to gold including those of the US, Germany, France and Japan; and the City of London offered all the accompanying services needed, including short-term money markets where any surplus funds could earn a return—even overnight. In the second great age of globalisation, from say, the 1990s to the 2010s, that dominant currency was the US dollar, the leading fiat money in a world of fiat monies. Unlike in the first great age of globalisation, there was no global monetary core to the leading monies. The euro came second, while sterling and other currencies such as the Japanese yen and Swiss franc played more limited roles in international transactions.

Globalised Money and Its Flaws

The money mechanism that has emerged in our world of national monies with no global base consists of a web of interactions among and between a set of institutions including the national issuers of currencies and private sector participants. These interactions take place primarily through markets, such as those in foreign exchange. Regulators and market conventions set the rules under which participants operate. Generally, money flows freely, though some countries, notably China, still restrict the freedom of residents to convert domestic money into foreign currencies. Furthermore, the application of sanctions can restrict the ability of those sanctioned (whether individuals or states) to access international markets (as in the sanctions applied to Russia and many named individuals after its invasion of Ukraine in February 2022). This mobility of capital has led to considerable interdependence between credit and asset market conditions in different countries. While global funds move across currency frontiers in milli-seconds, crossing frontiers means that exchange risk is incurred. Such funds can find homes in any number of international investments denominated in national currencies or the currency of a monetary union such as the euro. Indeed, differing rates of inflation among leading countries have been key factors driving capital flows especially participation in currency "carry trade" booms—where funds move out of low or negative interest earning monies into higher rate monies despite the exchange risk.

The flaws of the global mechanism are well known. Here are some of them. It has become a machine for transmitting shocks around the world. It is critically dependent on the national currency of one country—the US. It can raise international political tensions e.g. through currency wars. It facilitates destabilising swings in exchange rates and cycles of cross-border credit expansion and contraction. It has high maintenance costs and requires a standing army of regulators—see later this chapter.

At the same time, the mechanism works, warts and all. We have globalisation of money without a global money.

We discuss this mechanism or "set of arrangements"—call it what you will—in more detail later in this chapter and subsequent chapters; but first, we look back at how it developed.

How It Came About

Between the late 1940s and the 1960s, under the so-called Bretton Woods system, money circulated much more than it does today within national borders. Most nations imposed controls, either intermittently or on a permanent basis, over the freedom of residents to move money abroad. The entire system was linked, albeit very imperfectly, to gold. The US was obliged under the Agreement of 1944 (made between 44 allied nations that attended the summit at Bretton Woods, New Hampshire) to keep the dollar fixed to gold at $35 an ounce meaning the US Treasury stood ready to convert dollars presented to it by foreign official holders into gold at that rate. The currencies of other countries were fixed to the US dollar and could only be changed in exceptional circumstances and by international agreement. In principle the gold link and fixed exchange rates meant there was a force, backed by official commitments and agreements, inhibiting national central banks—even including the US Federal Reserve—from expanding their money supplies at will. This inhibiting force though could be lessened by exchange restrictions (in forms compliant with the Treaty) and by devaluations, albeit the latter had to be sanctioned by international agreement (at the IMF). And in the case of the US, there were only a few times when the Federal Reserve found itself constrained (during the Bretton Woods years) by gold flows in its setting of monetary policy; even then the influence was rather feeble (see Meltzer 2009).

Most people who thought about it agreed that the path of inflation and devaluation should be avoided. There was a broad acceptance among the "thinkers" and policy-makers of leading countries outside the US that excessive creation of money—or credit expansion as they tended to term it in those days—would threaten the fixed, agreed rates against the dollar, which was the lynchpin of the regime and often seen as sacrosanct. The US was committed to the system that it had taken the lead in creating, including its definition of dollar convertibility into gold, which had its origins in the Tripartite Agreement of 1936.

These beliefs became shakier and less prevalent in the environment of the 1960s especially in the US where the Kennedy and Johnson Administrations embraced economic "activism" and appointed advisors including economic officials versed in the latest version of Keynesian economics. Interestingly, Arthur Burns (who was not a Keynesian), chairman of the Fed from 1970 to 1978, had written a book in the 1950s bemoaning the fact that US inflation was running in the second half of that decade at around 2% per annum on average (Burns 1958). Yet as chairman nominated by President Nixon he injected the monetary stimulus which ultimately brought the already tottering edifice of Bretton Woods crashing down. Later he blamed irresistible political pressures on the Fed and the power of labour unions for its inability to tighten monetary policy (Burns 1979).

This "Bretton Woods" system had some achievements. Governments around the world could hold dollars confident that they had access to an alternative asset—gold—that was expected to maintain its value in the long term. World trade and investment expanded rapidly, albeit subject to the scourge of exchange restrictions which the system permitted especially during "balance of payments crises". The Bretton Woods System in its most active phase (1958–68/71) coincided with the economic miracles in Japan, Germany, France and Italy and with a sustained spurt in American living standards. President Nixon's decision in 1971 to break the residual link between the dollar and gold signalled that, politically, it had become too costly for the US to implement the extent of monetary deflation which by then would have been essential to maintaining the official gold value of the dollar even given the continuing prohibition on US citizens holding monetary gold.

An Age of Economic Growthmanship

The main feature of floating exchange rates in the 1970s was, however, not greater national control over money but the way governments abused their new freedom from the "fetters" of gold and fixed exchange rates. It was the age of growthmanship (Pringle 1979). A decade of high inflation in the US and the UK, France and Italy duly followed (West Germany and its monetary satellites being honourable exceptions)). Like Arthur Burns, many attributed inflation to a jump in oil prices engineered by the OPEC cartel, plus trades union pressures for higher wages and higher costs generally. But it was in reality due to governments' attempts to raise the rate of economic growth by ensuring a high pressure of monetary demand, i.e. over-expansionary fiscal and monetary policies.

In Part Three, we shall see how the "machinery of money" was getting out of control as other central banks (with some noble exceptions) followed the lead set by the Federal Reserve. We shall also describe how first in Japan, and then after the Global Financial Crisis, more generally, leading central banks themselves became large players in markets, engaging in massive purchases and sales of investments including all kinds of securities; and how such operations have had a bigger impact at times on global monetary conditions than "traditional" policy tools.

We just here note how, as market players, central banks's market operations can set in motion huge surges of global money or "liquidity" through globally interlinked markets.

"Lake Districts of Money"

We can visualise large "lakes" of money/liquidity in each of the main currency areas with currents, surges, channels and other connections of various kinds between them. These "lakes" are formed from the liquid wealth holdings of individuals and businesses in each currency area which are potentially available and ready to be deployed by their owner across a range of assets in different currencies, often in the pursuit of short-run speculative gains. Without a world central bank and in the absence of real coordination among existing central banks, nobody controls the flows of funds between these lakes. Plausibly we should be thankful for their absence. Yet we must confront the fact that the global monetary circuit—those great linked-up lakes—lack any mechanism to keep the machinery of money well under control. The first crisis of this increasingly global system came in the 1980s after numerous states, especially in Latin America, tapped these lakes for vast streams of credit. The money circuit became part of a system producing mega-sized credit bubbles. When they burst many developing countries entered a decade of lost growth, the start of a series of boom and bust cycles.

In principle, you might imagine that bank regulation could dampen or even prevent bubble formation. Yes, after the Global Financial Crisis governments and their regulatory authorities implemented programmes whose purpose was to strengthen banks. Some of those responsible for these programmes argue that measures such as required reserve and capital ratios are an effective brake on the formation of credit bubbles. But these measures are elastic; given persistent monetary stimulus in major central banks and related speculatively hot markets for equity and credit paper (especially high yield), many banks have no problem raising more capital. Moreover, credit creation occurred increasingly in unregulated entities.

With credit demand stimulated by low interest rates, much of it for the purpose of increasing leverage (borrowing to buy more assets), massive sums are involved. Dollar loans extended to companies, countries and other non-bank borrowers outside the US in 2020 totalled some $12 trillion (of which $4 trillion was to emerging markets). Euro credit to borrowers outside the euro area was some Euro 4.0 trillion ($3.5 trillion). Together this sum was not much less than the total money supply of the US (using a broad definition of money). In the decade prior to the financial crisis of 2008, banking already grew faster than world economic activity and trade and growth continued after that crisis, although the leading players changed. As European banks retrenched, the roles of non-European banks and non-bank financial institutions grew. Corporate debt financing shifted to capital markets, at least in advanced economies. The global assets of non-banks such as insurance and pension funds as well as unregulated financial institutions soared.

Now, flows between money lakes are led by shadow banks, sovereign wealth funds, a wide range of private asset managers and corporate foreign investment. Behind these stand central banks acting sometimes as injectors of money and credit, at other times as absorbers. Far from being mere overseers, these institutions are leading players in the international money game.

How Boom-Bust Waves Spread like Tsunamis

Any shock affecting the mood of market participants such as a plausible report that the Fed will tighten policy may readily affect flows of credit between and within the great lakes of liquidity. These in turn set up fluctuations in asset prices around the world, involving commodities such as agricultural goods, oil and natural gas as well as property, stocks and shares. These boom-bust swings have serious economic consequences. They often occur almost simultaneously across countries, gathering force like a tsunami as they race round the globe. Small countries in the front line of importing monetary conditions from abroad sometimes resort to the illiberal tool of exchange restrictions so as to dampen the movement of their national currency (its exchange rate); anyhow these are never water-tight and in practice policy-makers feel impelled to follow the monetary policies set in the main central banks. Common factors drive capital flows; bond and equity prices often rise or fall in tandem, seemingly irrespective of differing national circumstances.

Such are some of the gripes about financial globalisation—and there are many others. You may well feel that it has more costs than benefits. But read on.

"The Dollar Is Our Currency, but It's Your Problem"

When John Connally, US Treasury Secretary, made this remark in 1971, at the start of a new era, he highlighted what was to be a running sore. Use of the US dollar as global money bestows a big competitive advantage on the US financial industry, relative to foreign financial institutions. The US remains the global monetary hegemon—its policies have an outsized influence on all other countries, albeit in principle these can resist in various ways, as discussed in the next chapter. True, reliance on a single global currency has diminished slowly since 1971. Yet the US dollar continues to play a preponderant role in international trade and finance, with the euro playing second fiddle. Indeed one could say that the potential monetary hegemony of the US has increased since 1971, as expressed in terms of its scope to influence monetary conditions throughout the globe, though as we shall see this depends on foreign countries taking no defensive measures. How does this work in practice?

There are several indicators. As a means of exchange, the dollar is on one side of no less than 87% of foreign exchange market transactions, with an even higher share of forward and swap transactions. Its dominance in foreign exchange markets makes the dollar the sole intervention currency outside Europe and Japan—that is, it is the money used by central banks and governments when they want to influence the exchange rate of their currency in the markets—they use dollars to buy their own currency if they want to support it (strengthen its exchange rate). More than half of world trade is invoiced and settled in dollars, pointing to the greenback's pre-eminent role as a unit of account. At 61%, it maintains almost three times the share of the second place euro in the total foreign exchange reserves held by all countries. Its share in both official reserves and private portfolios is sustained by the scale of what can be termed the "dollar zone" of economies whose currencies move more closely with the dollar than with the euro. At half or more of world GDP, the dollar zone is far larger than the US economy, which is less than a quarter. This gives the US great influence on how money flows around the globe.

We should note that US government policy (and monetary policy is part of this albeit with some insulation) promotes domestic objectives such as full employment. It does not aim to help the world economy. In addition, it is shaped by governments' short-term horizons. That is a crucial difference from a hypothetic globalised economy in which a global money is dominant, as was the case in the first great globalisation (1870–1914). Look at the history of how successive US presidents have swayed the Federal Reserve to spur economic growth as they tried to win elections regardless of long-term cost—to America itself as well as the outside world. Suasion here can be more subtle than direct pressure—involving instead the interactions of the Fed Chair with Congress to which the Fed is answerable and the nomination power of the White House. The history includes notably the re-election campaigns of Nixon in 1972, the pre-campaign strategic planning of top Reagan official James Baker in advance of the 1988 election where then Vice President H. W. Bush was a candidate, the strategy of George W Bush towards re-election in 2004, as well as Donald Trump in advance of the 2020 election and we should also include challenging mid-term elections. In all these examples, the Fed was guided by the President via a process which involved important new appointments to its Board. A short-term horizon combined with a domestic focus is inconsistent with any type of international monetary order.

Currency Wars—Back to the 1930s?

During the second decade of the present century, the leading advanced economies maintained rates near zero or even below, in an effort to spur economic activity. Many other central banks chose to imitate their monetary stance by setting policy rates low. This was because they were worried about the danger of attracting "hot money". Such an inflow would have pushed up their exchange rates—making exporting less profitable and imports cheaper—and potentially push them into a payments deficit. This applied even to a large advanced economy such as Japan. But it often appeared to outside commentators—and to politicians in the core countries—as if such countries were artificially holding down their exchange rates. Governments have often been accused of "exchange rate manipulation". But in fact many of the offenders would claim that they had no choice: they say they were impelled in self-defence to engage in a currency war (see glossary). This involved matching each other's loose money policies so as to avoid a slump. Yes, in theory there was the possibility of defying loose money elsewhere and allowing the domestic currency to rise rapidly; in some circumstances, as we argue in the next chapter, this might have produced preferable economic outcomes but would have always encountered some forms of political pushback and required boldness. In short, the accusations of currency manipulation were often unfounded. But they poisoned international relations. Currency wars are a serious cost—not just economic but also geopolitically—of our era of globalisation based on national (or bloc as in the case of euro) monies rather than global money. (See Glossary for definition of currency war).

We have been here before. In the mid-twentieth century, governments used pervasive administrative controls over cross-border money flows. As already noted, for many years after World War II most currencies were not freely convertible into others—even to buy imports. Capital transactions were largely prohibited—people could not send money overseas without official permission. An English resident could not send money to buy a property in France for example. The reason? Most often it was government trying to get the advantages politically of greater monetary growth than consistent with the fixed exchange rate under a freely convertible currency regime. There was also chatter about governments fearing a return to the chaos of the interwar years (which according to some critics had been due to "uncontrolled capital flows"). Anyhow, at the time exchange restrictions could mean avoiding a tightening of monetary policy otherwise essential to maintaining a given peg or target for the exchange rate. But in order to achieve this, while giving some space in which they could adjust interest rates and tax policy to suit their political agenda for the domestic economy, they imposed controls.

The dominant view among economists in the 1940s—indeed, anyone in the corridors of power—was that the key economic problems in the 1930s could be attributed to destabilising flows of international money. They took their cue from an academic study by economist Ragnar Nurkse for the League of Nations (1944). They saw the interwar currency experience as a financial disaster. This, they said, was the main reason why the Great Depression lasted so long, ignoring alternative views as expressed for example by the economist Gottfried Haberler (1937) and others, who blamed exchange market interventions or unsound monetary policies for the troubles. This dominant mantra was used to justify the imposition of exchange restrictions and the decision to fix exchange rates at given rates to the US dollar in the Bretton Woods system, as already noted. This apparatus, in short, used controls to prevent governments from engaging in "competitive currency depreciation"—pushing your exchange rate down to gain a competitive advantage for your exporters and making imports more expensive.

Then there followed an interval during which the view gained ground that exchange rates between national (or bloc) monies, each with their independent regimes but unfettered by exchange controls, should be allowed to move freely in response to supply and demand. Indeed, governments in Europe and Japan acted to allow that in the 1980s. It suited the shift in political ideologies back to greater reliance on markets, privatisation of formerly state-owned companies and encouragement of enterprise. But now, 40 years later, the pendulum has swung again. Economic commentators fuss about how to curb "the excesses" of international money flows. Some economists are again urging a return to controls, most of all in the context of small economies potentially overwhelmed by *tsunamis* of capital inflows and outflows. The opponents of controls, however, see these as emanating from the dark past of Nazi doctrine (first implemented by Hjalmar Schacht when he was the German economics minister under Hitler in the 1930s). On this view, they are no substitutes for sound money doctrine and free markets. Yes, some might agree that global money would be the best solution in our highly globalised economies, but they see this as a pipe-dream. There is, anyhow, no sign of any clear political shift to the Left that would raise the threat of new controls. Indeed, is it plausible to believe that people in the West would accept such curbs on their freedom to move money around the world?

Accusations flying around, whether between currency diplomats or more broadly in markets, about the unleashing of currency wars (and the aggressor usually can present some plausible justifications) have damaging effects—all unhelpful to the evolution of a well-functioning global monetary order.

As if that were not enough, the first two decades of the twenty-first century revealed further deep-seated flaws in the global circulation of national monies as a second best arrangement when a global money does not exist.

Further Symptoms of Monetary Malaise

Symptoms of monetary ill-health included a war on privacy, central banks persistence with quantitative easing long after the initial crisis had passed, and the cryptocurrency bombshell.

Big Government—with the US and EU in the lead—launched an assault on legal rights to privacy in monetary affairs following the attacks on the World Trade Centre in New York (2001) and the pursuit of tax evasion as they confronted a serious degradation in the state of public finances in the wake of the Global Financial Crisis (2008). The first Obama Administration enacted the Foreign Account Tax Compliance Act, in effect potentially freezing foreign banks out of dollar transactions if they failed to report income and assets of US residents to the IRS. The EU followed with its signing up to an automatic exchange of tax information as drawn up by the OECD; Switzerland and Luxembourg this time under the threat of continuing huge legal penalties for their banks now joined in, as did a whole range of countries outside the EU including the offshore centres.

Meanwhile, the decline in social respect for money reached a new low when central bankers became persuaded of the need for massive doses of Quantitative Easing in response to any significant signs of looming crisis or serious economic downturn. As a former governor of the Bank of England, Mervyn King, has sarcastically remarked, the belief took hold "that monetary stimulus is an appropriate response to all economic problems" (King 2021).

The combination of suppression of privacy, asset inflation, deep weaknesses in public finances and the digital revolution all figured in the birth and rapid growth of cryptocurrencies through the second decade of the twenty-first century. Bitcoin and a few other cryptocurrencies appealed to a wide range of investors increasingly desirous to hold new substitutes for conventional fiat money. So the crypto monetary asset boom continued amidst signs (ominous in the eyes of sceptics) that the movement was becoming "mainstream". In terms of the analogy used at the start of this chapter, cryptocurrencies seemed to form a new and startlingly deep pool of liquidity of some $3 trillion (when Bitcoin was at a speculative high over $70,000 in Summer 2021, down to $20,000 by summer 2022) and were also encouraging the monetisation of a wide range of other assets using blockchain technology, as in the huge boom in non-fungible tokens, unique items of data stored on a blockchain. Early in 2022, the total market capitalization of crypto assets was 35% of the size of the US monetary base so that shocks in the crypto space evidently have the potential to seriously impact the global flow of funds—a potential which is now being explored in real time in the "crypto-winter" of summer 2022. (And we are not just talking here of measured capital flows—most of the inflows and outflows into crypto are unregistered in IMF balance of payments data!) We return to this fashionable topic, a symptom of growing distrust of money, later in this book, see especially Chapters 9 and 14.

The bigger questions in all of this are these: First, did the global clampdown on monetary privacy (and the "war on cash" that formed part of it) actually produce results in the war against terror which could justify it? Second, was this really a good time for even more tax enforcement given its potential wide negative consequences and the simultaneous growth of monetary taxation (mainly in form of monetary repression tax at this stage)? Third, was another gigantic shock forming which could one day cause substantial damage to the global financial system and economy? We examine these questions in more detail in later chapters—here we just draw our reader's attention to some highlights, especially regarding the "maintenance costs" of the system, the decline in a rules-based order and the ongoing hydra-headed regulation monster. The costs of these and the wider effects of the crisis depress economic growth, while fomenting further financial instability.

Our general view is that what we call "moderately bad" money regimes are responsible ultimately for the observed faults. They lead to multiple problems, including excessive lending and risk-taking with low levels of capital and liquidity leading to vast state bailouts, loss of freedom and responsibility growth in inequality and declining ethical standards.

We point to four further distinct evil effects: massive ongoing costs, the erosion of a rules-based order for money, an ever-growing apparatus of detailed regulations; and a dangerous muddling of responsibilities for oversight of the system.

Let's look at each in turn.

Large Maintenance Costs

The budgetary and off-budgetary costs of a big crisis have been compared to the costs of fighting a major war—though we must be careful to distinguish budgetary costs which are in the nature of transfers from one group in society to another and others which are squandered resources of labour and capital. Some people might argue that such costs, awesome as they may be (estimates of the costs of the GFC range as high as $5 trillion), are an unavoidable feature of a system that on balance produces good results (see also below on costs of regulation). That is a pessimistic and fatalistic view that we do not share. Rather, we argue, much could and should be done to improve and reform the system—basically to replace it with a better model. We discuss these policy issues in subsequent chapters. Here we focus on describing and analysing the system as it is, not as we would wish it to be.

The Erosion of a Rules-Based Order

Naturally, given the benefits that governments derive from "globalization without global money", they prop it up. In an emergency, they use taxpayers' money to bailout financial institutions that have grown so big and developed so many connections with the centres of political power that they cannot be allowed to fail. As such massive expenditure of tax money is rightly unpopular, leaders invariably promise that the banks will not be allowed to get away with it "next time", and that they will take action to reduce inequality and gross unfairness of the system—but do they reform it? Not really. Knowing the political unpopularity of such bailouts, however, states have also cooperated to strengthen the supervision and regulation of finance. This is to plaster over the cracks in the building.

Look at what has happened to the international institutions set up after World War II such as the General Agreements on Tariffs and Trade (GATT), later succeeded by the World Trade Organisation (WTO), World Bank and IMF. These bodies were originally designed to monitor and police an international order based on rules. But many of these rules have been torn up. The rule that a country must obtain the agreement of the IMF before changing its exchange rate allowed the international community to express a view on whether the proposed change was appropriate and necessary and recognised that a country's exchange rate was a matter of interest to trading partners, i.e. a legitimate matter of international concern—a change in a country's rate has a direct effect on its partners' prospects. The collapse of fixed exchange rates did not bring an end to powerful nations treating the international institutions as levers to pursue their national aims. In fact the leverage became even more powerful. We see this later in the volume with respect to the funding of the Yeltsin regime in Russia or the shoring up of European Monetary Union to avoid its collapse in 2012. Yes, officials of these institutions still try to be objective in the assistance they give. The IMF, for example, seeks to apply common rules and conditions to its assistance. But the major developed nations—notably the US now joined by Russia and China—make sure that nations important to them for foreign policy reasons obtain the support they seek.

The Regulation Juggernaut

Unsound monetary policy and inadequate capital lead to fears of bank failure and therefore costly runs and crises. To prevent this we require safety nets, but safety nets create moral hazard. To offset this we need regulation, but this in turn leads to evasion. We can get rid of all of this by fixing the "bad" monetary foundation. Instead, however, these crises are used as pretexts for world leaders to propose interventionist "reforms" to address "urgent" current issues arising precisely from financial crises that they have failed to prevent.

This international layer of regulatory requirements is laid on top of a patchwork of national and regional regulations over banking and finance. American banks spend at least $10,000 per annum for each employee just in complying with regulation—to which had to be added the huge costs of staffing and financing the myriad regulatory bodies themselves. The costs are estimated to have risen fourfold between 2010 and 2020. Not only are the measurable costs enormous but there are also the side-effects of this burden in stifling innovation in banking and directing enterprising people working in this field to unregulated areas such as real estate or the art market. All these damage the economy.[1] Credit needs to be directed to enterprises and sectors with the best commercial prospects. Good bankers and expert wealth managers more generally in credit markets are trained to discern these. Yet few do. This gap attracts little scrutiny let alone criticism from academics or journalists. Indeed, the usual message is to plead for even more rules.

An example can be drawn from the fashionable topic of so-called macro-prudential regulation. This is a fast-growing empire of regulators that is supposed to reduce risks of the system as a whole—such as indeed the risks of unsustainable booms and bubbles. But the same process can be seen at work as in micro-prudential regulation (i.e. regulations of individual banks and other financial institutions), that is, continual pressure to expand the field and intrusiveness of regulation and take responsibility away from the leadership of individual private sector market participants. For example, the search for yield in a low interest environment—indeed, steeply negative real rates—was always likely to produce systemic risks and fragilities.

The answer of some central bankers and economists was to call for even more "macro" regulation. As high capital adequacy regulations led to a decline in bank intermediation, dodgy money market funds and the desta-bilising impact of highly leveraged non-bank intermediaries all came to the fore. Addressing such risks, said one report, "requires broad-ranging macro-prudential policy responses beyond the scope of existing instruments, which are limited mainly to the banking sector". The macro-prudential toolkit, they said, should give regulators instruments that can be used to deal directly with risks related to structural changes in the financial system: "a move from traditional banking activities and related risks to non-bank financial interme-diation requires the development of macro-prudential policy beyond banking and of activity-based regulation". Instead of restoring responsibility to the management of financial institutions, the report, in effect, said government-appointed bureaucrats should: "The rise of indebtedness and leverage, the risks to market liquidity, the weaknesses in the EU banking, insurance and

---

[1] It has been shown, for example, that the so-called Basel III rules on capital standards introduced after the Global Financial Crisis led to a sharp fall in bank lending, relative to national output, to corporate customers and a "collapse" in UK bank lending to SMEs (Congdon 2021). If replicated in other countries, then banking re-regulation since 2008 resulted in lower and sub-optimal levels of financial intermediation.

pension fund sectors all pose risks to financial stability that the macro-prudential framework should recognise" (Fell et al. 2021). Note the deep ambiguity in the word "recognise".

This is typical of the pressures at work continually to expand the powers of regulators. Behind it is an attitude or approach that mistrusts the private sector.

Are official bodies properly accountable for the proper use of the extensive powers they have acquired? Accountability seems more formal than real. At the most basic level, while central banks are expected to meet inflation targets for consumer prices, there is no accountability on them for the damage inflicted by asset inflation caused by their monetary policies or the resulting financial instability. Instead, they and regulators are given new "toolkits" consisting of variable regulations to be imposed, on the whim of officials, on entire banking systems.

Muddled Responsibilities

A fundamental weakness exposed by this growing reliance on regulators to "keep us safe" is the way it muddies responsibility. Are bank management and shareholders ultimately responsible for bank safety and viability or are supervisors? And outside the banking area, are asset managers and pension fund managers appropriately responsible and legally exposed to challenge (including for damages) from those for which they ultimately perform their functions? In some high profile cases, the European Central bank has strongly criticised bank management and called for change in policies and structure yet these were simply rebuffed by management. Yet if official agencies have powers to order specific banks to behave in certain specific ways, then clearly the onus of responsibility moves to the regulators. In effect, bankers become public servants, carrying out orders though with an undefined degree of autonomy (rather like the way central banks were co-opted by the state).

Bank supervisors deny this dilemma exists or talk their way smoothly out of it but such reassurances fail to convince. The public watches with dismay as government is "forced" into further multi-billion euro bailouts because they are even more frightened to let banks fail than they are of the public anger at the unfairness of such gifts of public money to "bad bankers". Yet in a properly designed system, the management of commercial banks will in their own interests build defences not only against specific shocks but also wider systemic shocks at a social cost significantly less than that imposed by substituting the judgement of officials for those of bankers.

All this helps to explain why finance still does not focus on serving the real economy of jobs and production of goods and services. Incentives are skewed. Regulation protects state coffers at high real cost. Costs of the current globalized financial and goods markets without a global money are widely spread, while the benefits accrue to a minority. We show in later chapters how this all reflects much deeper forces than usually assumed. Ultimately, it reflects mistaken ideas about the nature of money itself (see Chapter 7). However, it's worth pointing out already that the current global regime of flexible exchange rates deprives us of the benefits and cost reduction that a common money would bring (in its key role as a unit of account and medium of payment). In other words, one should ask two questions. Firstly, are the costs of the system and of the regulatory apparatus that goes along with it more or less than the benefits citizens of countries gain from having a degree of freedom to set their own monetary policies? Secondly, do those supposed benefits of nominally independent monetary policies outweigh those of the alternative of a shared money with its reduction in uncertainty and lower costs of conducting international trade and investment?

As the costs of the present regime rise, the balance of advantage appears to shift in favour of a broader international move towards a shared money. However, for such a money to work well for society as a whole, it should be secured by a strong anchor—a device constraining the supply of money. This is a key element in our concept of an ideal money regime. The topic is explored in Part Two when we focus on "The Essence of Good Money". But first we look into the special "privileged" role of the US dollar and the global influence it gives to the US.

References

Burns, Arthur (1958) *Prosperity Without Inflation*; and (1979), *The Anguish of Central Banking*.

Congdon, Tim (2021) "How Have Changes in Regulation Affected Bank Credit Since the Great Recession?" Research Paper 9, Institute of International Monetary Research, September 2021.

Fell, J., Peltonen, T., Portes, R. (2021) "Lower for Longer—Macro-Prudential Policy Issues Arising from the Low Interest Rate Environment" VOXEU, June 2.

Haberler, Gottfried (1937) *Prosperity and Depression: A Theoretical Analysis of Cyclical Movements*.

King, Mervyn (2021) *Monetary Policy in a World of Radical Uncertainty*.

Meltzer, Allan (2009) *History of the Federal Reserve*, Vol. 2, Book 1, 1951–1986, University of Chicago.

Nurkse, Ragnar (1944) *International Currency Experience: Lessons of the Interwar Experience*.

Pringle, R (1979) *The Growth Merchants*. Centre for Policy Studies.

3

The Global Menace of US Monetary Policies

For most of the century of US monetary hegemony since World War I, the US has spread inflation. Sometimes, the key visible symptoms of such "made in America" inflation have been in asset markets; at other times, in goods and services markets—and sometimes in both. The two notable exceptions— the Great Monetary Contraction of 1929–1933 and the Volcker Monetarist Experiment of 1979–1984—do not detract from the validity of the general statement. Ultimately, the inflation exacted a heavy toll not only on economic prosperity globally but also on America's geopolitical position, weakening US allies, lowering US standing in the world and strengthening its enemies.

We will show that resistance abroad to the spread of US inflation has on occasion limited and even reversed these bad consequences. In one long episode of severe US inflation from the mid-1960s to the end-1970s, foreign resistance led by (then West) Germany was effective in containing its global costs and dangers. But there has been sadly little resistance outside of that period. In the now quarter century of US monetary policy under the so-called 2% inflation standard, there have been two long episodes (1996–2007, 2013 to present) where symptoms of persistent inflation have been evident globally in asset markets. Symptoms of inflation in goods and services markets, however, were either camouflaged by non-monetary disinflation (as in the first episode) or suppressed by economic sclerosis, itself stemming from unsound money (as in the second episode until the pandemic break-out of high inflation). It is too late for foreign resistance to form and improve outcomes economically and geopolitically with respect to this most recent

© The Author(s), under exclusive license to Springer Nature Switzerland AG 2022
B. Brown and R. Pringle, *A Guide to Good Money*,
https://doi.org/10.1007/978-3-031-06041-0_3

episode of bad money. Even so, it is not too late to put the case in both the US and abroad for a regime of good money to promote prosperity, freedom and peace. Politically, sound money advocates require allies if the case for it is to triumph and there is a natural fit in this respect with those working for peace on the basis of maintaining strong defences.

How US Inflation spreads—And How It Can Be Resisted

In this chapter, we have three main aims: first, to explain how US monetary policies spread inflation abroad and its effects; secondly, to describe and analyse the main episodes of resistance and why they have been so rare; and thirdly to highlight the costs of the policies adopted—including the impact on the geopolitical balance. We also address the questions: what might have happened if the US had pursued sound money? Or if other countries or the eurozone had had well-anchored currencies?

Consider the case where a foreign country X is in the dollar zone, and its currency tied tightly to the US dollar; its central bank will then be, in effect, a satellite of the Federal Reserve. Inflation will generally closely follow that in the United States (though there are circumstances when they may differ over quite a long period, they are not germane to our argument at this point).

The least direct spread is where the foreign country Y's currency is freely floating and where the monetary system in Y has a potentially solid domestic anchor (see Glossary). A good anchor will prevent the "machinery of money" getting out of control, as evidenced by the emergence of inflation. In this context a good anchor would mean that monetary conditions in that country or area would have maximum scope to be set independently of the US (the concept of the anchor plays a key role in our analysis, see Chapter 5). While a floating currency will not protect a country from the effects of future losses of global prosperity that result from US inflationary policies, it is an important possible barrier to imported inflation, in both the form of asset inflation and goods inflation. (We say "possible barrier" because it would only become an actual barrier if the central bank used the floating exchange rate to pursue an independent monetary policy from the US.)

A good money regime in Y would, for example, spare investors there from feeling that they have to join in a desperate search for yield; interest rates would remain above zero and real returns on money could be considerable, especially during the period of initial local currency appreciation when the US Fed starts down the path of a new *monetary inflation*, (See Glossary).

Domestic investors in country Y will not be prompted to engage in irrational strategies nor will they easily accept dubious speculative narratives—both key characteristics of the asset inflation (see Glossary) process. Yes, when they venture into global markets they will encounter the same often crazy high prices in local currency terms; but they will be buying these assets at cheap prices in terms of Y's currency because it will have appreciated so much—likely far overshooting plausibly long-run assessments of its value—and so they will expect that their currency will tend to depreciate over the long-run. Hence, investors resident in country Y can look forward to higher returns including exchange rate gains than their foreign counterparts.[1]

Investors in countries with good money regimes would be more likely (than those under unsound regimes) to resist the temptation to invest in those assets traded in the global market-place where dubious "get-rich-quick" narratives push prices up. As such investors will not experience real "income famine" on their domestic monetary assets, they have less reason to kid themselves into believing these stories. Many domestic assets will stand aside from the global speculative fever as resident investors will receive significantly positive real yields on safe investments in the domestic money while foreign investors would be disinclined to borrow Y's currency (given its normal positive long-term real rates) to ramp up purchases of assets in country Y.

Yes, domestic assets which share characteristics with those at the epicentre of the global speculative mania may still get caught up in the frenzy. But the residential real estate market in "defiant" sound money country Y is likely to be mainly outside that category (An exception here could be the emergence of luxury international real estate wherever it is as a hot global asset class). Hence, "defiance" will hold down the price of homes. They will not join in the crazy price rises seen in many foreign centres. With less distortions of asset prices generally in the domestic market there should be less mal-investment.

Defiance of US monetary policy could have further benefits. If the domestic money (the currency of Y) became popular internationally, foreigners would boost their holdings, attracted by the soundness of its monetary regime at a time of increased US monetary inflation. The financial centre

---

[1] It is possible to construct models of destabilizing speculation in the currency of country Y driven by a process in which global monetary inflation stimulates irrational expectations that currency Y will continue rising because it has risen in the recent past. Significantly, though, these models based on momentum trading are usually flawed in that that they assume also such irrational expectations on the part of residents of country Y when there is no domestic monetary force prompting them in that direction: without being plagued by such irrationality Y residents would seize on the opportunity to sell their domestic currency at peak valuations. The exception, where such models might have validity, is the very special case where the domestic currency is tiny so that domestic investor expectations are totally swamped in exchange rate pricing by manic foreign speculation. Some writers have quoted the Iceland bubble of the early 2000s in this regard (see Aliber and Zoega 2011).

of country Y would gain by having a money which is in demand internationally. As its role develops, local firms would be able to raise loans in a much broadened credit market denominated in the domestic money—and thereby likely more competitive and cheaper than otherwise.

Official Destabilisation Policies

Let us explain in a little more practical detail how monetary policies of central banks with key international currencies often make life more difficult for other countries. The effects can be divided into direct and indirect. Take the direct effects first.

In the case of the dollar, globally a huge amount of dollars are borrowed—for example, in the form of bank loans or longer-term bonds—by companies and governments outside the United States. Because they are denominated in US dollars, US Federal Reserve interest rate policies are transmitted directly to these borrowers and thus to other economies. As the cost of the dollars to banks that borrow them rises, so they have to pass on that to companies/governments that in turn borrow from them. The impact depends on the characteristics of the instrument in which the borrowing has been made.

For instance, in the case of bank loans, changes in US short-term policy rates pass through within weeks. Over half of dollar loans to borrowers outside the United States and euro area takes the form of bank loans. Offshore dollar credit grows fastest in those countries where it is cheap relative to local funding, as is the case in many developing economies. Thus lower US rates often lead to a big rise in borrowing by companies in developing economies—more than they can easily service when conditions change. The United States is like a liner ploughing through the ocean—smaller boats get tossed around in its wake.

The same mechanism applies, even if on a smaller scale, to the direct effects of the monetary policies of the ECB on monetary conditions around the world—especially for countries that peg their currencies to the euro or have close trading relationships with the economies of eurozone countries. When the ECB conducts large-scale purchases of euro denominated bonds, pushing down long-term interest rates, borrowers outside the euro area naturally take advantage of the opportunity to increase their euro borrowings—usually by bond issues. This is one reason for the rapid growth in various quantitative measures of "global liquidity", which measures the ease of financing in global financial markets. Cycles in the flows of these credit and changing policies in the main financial centres naturally have global repercussions.

So much for the direct effect of central bank policies. But monetary regimes also interact indirectly, through central bank responses to each other's policies. When setting monetary policy, central banks always keep an eye on that of the Federal Reserve or ECB. This behaviour is sometimes explicitly noted, as in the cases of the Central Bank of Norway and the Swiss National Bank with reference to ECB policy, but is widespread and indeed easily explicable. One reason is that highly volatile exchange rates can cause disturbances in countries' domestic economies. Exchange rate flexibility is often considered desirable but is not effective in insulating the domestic economy totally from external developments and their unwanted side-effects.

These are felt whether the local currency falls or rises in value against foreign currencies. Exchange rate *appreciation* of the local currency makes firms with debts denominated in foreign currency to look better—to have more capital and be more creditworthy—than they really are. This increases the availability of credit, including credit from international markets. This may unleash a further inflow of short-term capital, which can push local currencies far out of line with any objective view of their true value. On the other hand, a fall in the value of the domestic currency (i.e. depreciation) can trigger bankruptcies among firms with foreign currency debt since it now costs much more in terms of local currencies to pay interest and repay principal.

Why Has Resistance Been Rare?

Lack of foreign resistance to US monetary inflation in the past quarter century can be explained in part by the nature of asset inflation itself. The damage from joining in asset inflation is long-run; while the benefits for some—including enjoyment of rising values of owner-occupied homes and investments—come in the short-run and even medium term. Non-resistance also has the benefit, as we shall see, of the export sector and import-competing sector being spared from pain. In aggregate, such a calculus of gains and losses make a compelling case for political leaders whose horizon stretches only to the next election to offer no resistance.

Asset inflation has political attractions to powerful groups in society. These groups exert outsized influence on the policy-making process whether explicitly or via crony channels—including as illustration the political influence of private equity firms and the monopolists, most blatantly Big Tech but reaching far beyond that. Asset inflation not only swells pools of liquidity but also drives speculative capital into any enterprise that promises monopoly profits. The cheap cost of capital enables well-positioned firms to crush their competitors (by pre-emptive buy-up or other forms of predatory action). This unholy alliance of asset inflation and monopoly capital is not just a US phenomenon.

Warnings of the eventual consequences (less prosperity due to widespread mal-investment coupled with potential crashes) count for little; nobody ever won an election by acting the part of a Cassandra, whose accurate predictions of catastrophe are doomed never to be believed. Moreover, as discussed in other chapters, these warnings are based on economic theories which run counter to the dominant ideology of policy-making establishments globally.

By contrast, where monetary inflation takes the form of a sharp rise in consumer prices, popular discontent will readily arise, causing a different constellation of forces in the political arena. These can galvanise resistance to the import of US monetary inflation. Even so, would-be rebels face a big obstacle, whatever form the inflation threat takes. This is the pain already referred to above that could be suffered by export industries and more gener-ally the tradable goods industries in the resisting country. This is because of the implications for the value of the local currency. Defence against the import of either consumer or asset price inflation will typically make the local currency appreciate against the dollar, cutting profit margins in those sectors. The gain to consumers from lower prices of imported goods is diffused widely and thus "invisible" while the pain is focused on a few sectors. These are often politically powerful—and any difficulties they face in adjusting are easily dramatised in the media.

Currency appreciation is less of a political or economic problem where the country determined to resist imported inflation is cushioned against exchange rate change shocks—for example, where its exports are highly distinct with no close competition. Where the country contemplating defensive action is large or acting jointly with other countries, the effective exchange rate change resulting from defensive action and its economic impact will be less than otherwise. Other factors are at work, however. As the financial industry tends to be a net gainer from asset inflation, countries (e.g. the UK) where it is large and powerful may be less willing to defy imported US monetary infla-tion, although they might gain long term from the international popularity of a still sound domestic money and the new business this might attract. In fact, there could be some clash between different sectors within the finan-cial industry; private equity, real estate and securities business typically profit from asset inflation while the potential advantages of a good money which gains ground as an international money tend to accrue only in the longer term.

Geopolitical considerations come into play too. International money is a source of power. The international growth of the Deutsche mark was a factor undermining Soviet domination of Eastern Europe. The DM became a principal medium of savings throughout the East European countries, fuelling the growth of grey and black markets there. Within Western Europe, the hard DM with its solid anchoring independent of the US became a foreign currency anchor for neighbouring monies. That was how Germany assumed monetary hegemony in Europe (see below).

How US and Its Allies Lose, While Their Enemies Gain

US monetary policies have weakened the West and hurt the US itself.

US goods and services inflation averaged about 2.5–3.0% per annum in the 100 years to 2020. This 100 year period included the Great Depression and other periods of falling prices. There were, therefore, obviously long bouts of severe monetary inflation. Sometimes, these did not include consumer price inflation as officially measured but showed up as asset inflation culminating in financial crashes (with all the implications such crashes have for the amount of mal-investment and sharp business cycle fluctuations etc.).

Such a sustained average inflation rate over the long-run also involved the extended periodic levying of inflation and monetary repression taxes on US residents with their corollary incentive to bigger government spending while making conditions harder than they needed to be for individuals making long-term savings decisions (For a definition of these taxes, see Glossary). Individuals' natural efforts to avoid these taxes push up prices on alternative assets not directly subject to the tax and produce a whole set of illusions and uncertainties regarding whether these assets in fact offer an escape; there will be related distortions in the signalling of asset market prices. The typical failure of tax regimes to take inflation into account also means that even a relatively low rate of inflation goes along with huge distortions in real terms— very heavy taxation on the real interest income from debt assets and in some cases very high taxation on the real content of capital gains. The incentives to reduce holdings of money below what they would be in a sound money regime means a reduction in welfare.

The US authorities invariably promised what they called "price stability"; in the past quarter century, they have meant by that holding consumer price inflation on average to 2% per annum average but there was no solid basis for the belief that they could stabilise the inflation rate in the long-run. The government's interest, from the viewpoint of maximising monetary inflation tax revenues, is to convince the populace that prices will remain stable and then suddenly raise them. We are not saying here that every big levying of inflation tax was planned in advance by a Machiavellian American ruling elite. Rather, the elites supported a monetary regime knowing full well its flaws, because fortuitously if these became realised there would be clear advantages from their viewpoint—whether personal enrichment, vast monetary taxation for Big Government to which they had a crony relationship, and so on. In the main, though, they may well not have expected these flaws to emerge any time soon. Beyond such tainted calculation, this uncertainty about the future inflation tax was a further disincentive to optimal holdings of money and people's natural impulse to hedge against this danger caused a loss of prosperity over the long-run compared to the sound money alternative. Behavioural finance theory offers plausible accounts showing how individuals, when faced with the prospect of certain loss, often take on ultimately bad bets (see Kahneman 2011). They pretend that the bad bet is actually good by readily swallowing dubious narratives in the meantime as to why they will win the wager. Moreover, lurches of inflation usually trigger periodic spells of sharply tighter monetary policy and recession.

In sum, US inflationary monetary policy has bad outcomes first and foremost for the US itself; these bear on its allies not just to the extent that they import the inflation or its globally spread side-effects but also include the impact of such policy in shrinking the potential economic and geopolitical weight of the United States. The enemies of the West have been made more confident by the effects of bad money in the US; economic turmoil, corruption and cronyism, the growth of monopoly power (including the Big Tech monopolists) in the US and Europe are good news for dictatorial regimes along the Moscow-Teheran-Beijing-Pyong Yang axis.

Consider the Counterfactual

Counterfactually, how would these enemies have fared in a world where the US hegemon had had sound money? That soundness would have been based on a strong anchor in some form. Most of the Western world would under those circumstances have joined the dollar zone. There would have been no point in experimenting with currency and monetary independence and its risks (exchange rate volatility, the difficult and sometimes perilous search for a rock-solid domestic anchor) if indeed there were no inflation danger from the US. In this world, there would have been no talk of a reserve role for the

Chinese currency, or China's inclusion in the SDR (this would have had no customers). One could imagine that inside both China and Russia the business and personal sentiment under such conditions would have favoured also tying their currencies to the dollar in fully convertible form rather than accept a very inferior domestic alternative. Domestic pressure could have grown for full currency convertibility, weakening the power of the dictatorship.

German Defiance

In our historical survey (Chapter 8), we tell the story of the great US inflation of the mid-1960s to the end-1970s (see also Brown 2017), the brief monetarist interlude and then its sequel in the second half of the 1980s. We then show how good money options came to be rejected. We should, however, mention here that (then West) Germany had already proved that it was possible to break free of the US inflationary model.

True, Germany had more scope to launch such a defence than smaller economies like say, Korea. Germany benefited not only from the high reputation of the quality of its exports and (notably after re-unification in 1990) its large size but also because—even before the euro in 1999—neighbouring countries' currencies closely tracked Germany's. Even so, we should not ignore the influence of German export industries in the political process, especially via the centre-right parties. As we have mentioned, an obstacle in the way of any country mounting a fight against US monetary inflation is the power of the export industry. Exporters always fear the effect on their export sales and profits of an appreciation of the domestic currency on the foreign exchange market—which means that any overseas sales they make are worth less than before when converted into domestic currency. This power may come through funding links to one of the main political parties (one thinks here of the LDP in Japan and its funding base in big export corporations; or the funding support for the CDU in Germany). But for many years the German government supported the lead of its central bank and resisted such political pressures.

Fast Forward to the Present

No US ally seriously resists following the inflationary example symbolised by the Fed's 2% inflation standard. Their domestic political situations do not fuel any resistance. Correspondingly, no US ally makes the case in Washington about its effects in undermining the Western alliances and strengthening its enemies. The European Monetary Union does not follow sound money principles; hopes that the euro would be the new European Deutsche mark have been dashed. The ECB contravenes the principles of good money. Although lip-service was paid in the first few years to the so-called second pillar of money supply "monitoring ranges", this had little significance in terms of policy setting.

How did this happen? Even before the ECB opened its doors, it had in effect signed up to the 2% inflation standard, copying the US despite the fact that the information technology revolution and the spurt in globalisation were already powering non-monetary disinflationary forces.[2] When, in the wake of the 2001 mini-recession and the subsequent phase of weak economic recovery the Federal Reserve went into monetary overdrive, the ECB followed suit. Its French president Claude Trichet, alarmed by the strength of the euro, in effect submitted to the Fed's lead. As described in Chapter 8, the result of this further injection of monetary inflation on top of that starting with the euro's launch was a credit bubble and bust that meant the end of any prospect that the euro would be the European version of the Deutsche mark.

The loss of prosperity in Europe resulting from the euro debt and banking crashes of 2008–2012/2013 was compounded by the cost of salvaging operations. These included massive transfers via the ECB into weak banks and sovereigns, in effect gravy trains from the frugal members in the North to the South. We should contemplate how much more prosperous Germany—and indeed the whole euro area—would be today if the huge export of savings from that country into delinquent borrowers had gone into productive use. Although German public finances look stronger than others in the union, this impression is deceptive; vast contingent liabilities are not properly accounted for while ongoing transfers out of Germany are presented as essential for European solidarity.

The illusions fed by the asset inflation process—including in the last decade rampant real estate speculation in many parts of Germany—have kept resentment within bounds (see also Chapter 6). Discontent has not been powerful enough to shake the euro establishment. Yet, the bad effects have been extensive. To the East, the weakening of Europe and Germany by this euro-debacle has been a plus for Russian President Putin as he gained domestic support from the evidence of dissatisfaction and populist resentment in the EU. The reality of an ailing Western Europe with a rotten money at its core surely emboldened Russian foreign policy. In turn, the

---

[2] In 1997, Greenspan was moving in favor of the 2% inflation standard but he balked at adopting it formally, never wanting to express an actual target.

weariness with debts and the burdens of the EMU have made it more difficult politically for Germany to honour its NATO commitments and raise its level of defence spending accordingly, although this may change following the Russian invasion of Ukraine.

What Might Have Happened in Europe-

By contrast, suppose a hard money union in Western Europe had come into being, fostered by a good money regime in the US (Brown and Simonnot 2020). A prosperous Germany amidst a thriving West European union could have undermined the Putin regime. The beacon of success and prosperity of Europe at its core might have pulled Britain back from embarking on a doubled-down course of monetary inflation through the past quarter century together with boarding the train to Brexit, with Russia a cheerleader for any journey towards EU disintegration. In turn, if a break-out of high CPI inflation in the US had come in the context of a successful good money regime in Europe, the political clamour for monetary reform would surely have been louder.

Moreover, the full consequences of Europe's decision to renounce a solid anchor have yet to show themselves. If and when asset market deflation emerges and the bubbles burst in various asset markets, economic and social trauma with seriously adverse consequences both in terms of domestic and geopolitical tranquillity could follow. Wealth and income depletion stretching across all layers of the socio-economic fabric, falling living standards amidst the discovery of much mal-investment, higher burden of taxation across all categories (from explicit taxation on income and sales to monetary taxation in the form of monetary repression tax and inflation tax) would all take their toll. No doubt the losses and traumas will extend to Russia and China, including the latter's long-running bubble economy. But the regimes there will be able to blame setbacks on the corrupt and unstable West, tighten state control, and pursue repression.

—And in Japan?

Outside Europe, Japan's capitulations to America's inflationary policy (recently under the guise of "Abe economics", earlier in response to "the Nixon shock" of 1971 and the "Plaza shock" of 1986) have enfeebled Japan's economy, the world's fourth largest as estimated on the basis of market prices and market exchange rates. They have sapped its political will. Suppose instead that Japan had continued in the more independent path pioneered by the Bank of Japan under Masaaki Shirakawa from 2008 to 2013. Yes, the yen would have been super-strong and wages in yen would surely have fallen in export industries. Japan would have suffered the pain accompanying a transition to sound money. But it would have avoided full exposure to asset price deflation in the future which is likely to leave an impoverished and resentful Japanese population in its wake. Big Government would have been reined back. Japanese savings, instead of ploughing into government paper and an ever bigger panoply of bubble-type assets, would have gone into more worthwhile activities, including investments outside Japan (as discussed earlier).

With a well-anchored currency, Japan could have served as a good money exemplar for the rest of East and South-East Asia. The yen could have become a principal form of monetary saving throughout the region as investors valued its role in their portfolios. Yes, it would have fluctuated against the dollar, raising exchange risk and risking the ire of Japanese exporters; but prices in the average shopping basket in various Asian economies would not have been as volatile given the weight there of Japanese goods and services. Further, given the importance of Japanese trade for the region, some other Asian countries would have tracked Japanese monetary policy (possibly increasing the extent to which the yen was represented in composite indices for the purpose of currency pegging). A good yen could even have become an important form of monetary saving in China, included in grey and black markets, among a population distrustful of the local financially repressed system.

The possible benefits might have been considerable. Might such developments have persuaded China to pursue a more peaceful path in its relations with Japan (e.g. over Senkaku Islands)? Might they also have advanced plans for yuan convertibility? Might competition from a hard yen money have curbed the scope for financial repression imposed by the Chinese Communist Party? The stakes were high—including the possibility of social and political liberalisation on the mainland of China. Tokyo might even have found a new international role as a financial centre for Chinese savers and borrowers. In turn, Tokyo's challenge to Hong Kong and Shanghai might have encouraged domestic pressures towards liberalisation in China. (See Chapter 8 for more on the historical background to Japan's policy.)

Of course, nobody can know exactly what course events would have taken. But we have no doubt that a principled stand in defence of good money by Tokyo would have had far-reaching effects. America's persistence with soft money policies and the supine acceptance of them by its principal allies have cost the Western alliance dearly.

References

Aliber R.Z. and Zoega, Gylfie (eds.) (2011) *Preludes to the Iceland Financial Crisis.* Basingstoke, UK, pp. 241–275.

Brown, Brendan and Simonnot, Philippe (2020) *Europe's Century of Crises Under Dollar Hegemony* (Palgrave).

Brown (2017) Goods Inflation, Asset Inflation, and the Greatest Peacetime Inflation in the US. *Atlantic Economic Journal*, Vol. 45, November, pp. 420–442

Kahneman, Daniel (2011) "Thinking, Fast and Slow".

Sinn, Hans Werner and Wettermann, Frank (2001) "The Deutsche mark in Eastern Europe: Black Money and the Euro. On the Size of the Effect". IFO Institute for Economic Research, 2, no. 3 (February).

Part II

The Essence of Good Money

Introduction

In this part of the book, we set out the principles on which a good money regime should be based. In Chapter 4, we discuss the distinction between what is good money for the individual and what is good for society and explain why there is no conflict between them. A good money will be supported by broad and stable demand among individuals and institutions such as banks for its core group of assets. The supply of this core group of assets will set a clear path for the expected evolution of prices over the long run. These enjoy "super-money qualities"—a new term which we develop in this volume and which refers to a set of qualities which amount to "extreme moneyness" in ways which we will describe.

In Chapter 5, we discuss how to provide money with safeguards against government or sectional interests "taking over the controls". The main safeguard is that money should be secured by a credible anchor with strong popular support. We discuss anchors suitable for the kinds of so-called "fiat" (government) money that are in universal use today. We also trace how "real" (i.e. commodity-based) anchors emerged and how they worked in practice. We postpone discussion of the leading candidates for the role of "solid anchor" in a reformed monetary regime to Part V.

4

What We Mean by "Good Money"

We can think of the essence of good money at two levels.

First, from the viewpoint of the individual; and
Second, the viewpoint of society as a whole.

Although these perspectives are very different, it turns out that for money to be good for society it should be good for the individual. Indeed, the better money is at an individual level the better it is at the level of society. If a money is bad widely for individuals, then it will fail for society.

Good money is an essential condition for market capitalism to deliver its potential benefits to society. Under a good money regime the "machinery of money" works well and critically does not become, in the phrase of J.S. Mill, a "monkey wrench" in the machinery of the economy (see Friedman 2005). Mill, a formative philosopher in "classical liberalism", (see Raico 2006) regarded money of "stable value" as an indispensable foundation block of liberty. (We return to Mill's views later, see especially in Chapter 7.) However, the case for good money should appeal to people across a wide spectrum of political and philosophical viewpoints.

© The Author(s), under exclusive license to Springer Nature
Switzerland AG 2022
B. Brown and R. Pringle, *A Guide to Good Money*,
https://doi.org/10.1007/978-3-031-06041-0_4

Good Money at the Level of the Individual

To assess the quality of a money, we need a composite view of how well it fulfils its four essential functions (see below). Some economists give pride of place to one of these functions. Indeed, fierce battles have been fought on this question (see for example Selgin 2021; Ingham 2004). Our view is that money has to be a widely accepted medium of payment but that the other functions are what make money *desirable*. A money that is used only as a means of payment is indeed a bad money. To be sure, individual perceptions of the "goodness" of something will not be identical, whether we are talking of "good money" or the "beauty of the tree". Yet there are features that emerge in every characterisation of a good money; as Plato argued, all beautiful things, such as a tree, however different they may appear, seem to have something in common.

A money that fluctuates violently in purchasing power over short-run periods would not be a good medium of exchange, for example. People want to be able to plan their earning and spending of money over time in a useful way—impossible if they cannot count on money keeping relatively stable real value. The importance of any one function in the overall quality of money varies, however, whether for an individual through time or across the population as a whole at any given time.

Money as a Medium of Exchange

A money is a good *medium of exchange* from the viewpoint of any individual if it satisfies a range of transaction requirements to his or her satisfaction. These vary from person to person.

Some people prefer using a payments medium which involves only the payer and payee—no third party. Cash (bank notes and coins) is the leading example; today some also include crypto tokens in the sense that the payments process involving these takes place via a distributive ledger blockchain with no middleman who knows the identity of the customer and may intrude. Some fret about using payments cards with their problems (including exposure to fraud and the nuisances of the security departments of the card companies who periodically intervene, transaction mistakes, and high, if well-camouflaged costs). Some prefer to make payment in a form that legally represents "final payment" of a transaction (the exact moment when funds transferred become the legal property of the transferee). Some, maybe not a large percentage of population but perhaps appreciable in terms of total demand, like large denomination banknotes so as not to have full wallets or because they also appreciate these as a store of value without storage or other maintenance including reporting costs—so they can be dual purpose (for transactions and store of value).

Some free market economists believe that the central bank monopoly of cash issuance should be abolished and opened up to the private sector. This would provide incentives to issuers to build the qualities of medium of exchange that different people prefer into their products, whether with respect to, say, sight deposits, banknotes or digital coins. Given public demand for safety, these notes or digital coins could be issued by stand-alone vehicles and in open competitive conditions. Such forms of currency would be backed by "the most money-like form of money"—whether that is a government *fiat money asset* or a core *real asset, such as a commodity* into which the given money is convertible. Some observers expect digital money to be especially useful for international payments, where costs are often high. Others are enthusiastic about the prospect of central banks joining this evolutionary process as producers of digital cash—so-called central bank digital currency; economists who favour competition in the supply of money forms would evidently prefer this also to apply to the progress of digitalization.

Consider next the function of money as a *store of value*.

Whose Store of Value?

Another key aspect of a good money is that holders expect it to retain its value over the long-run. Over the short-run, while they do not expect big swings in purchasing power, nor do they expect complete purchasing power stability. They realise that under good money regimes, there is a natural rhythm of goods and services prices upwards and downwards dependent on such factors as the pace of productivity growth, technological change, globalisation, the course of the business cycle and temporary shortages or gluts of resources perhaps amidst supply disruptions (see Brown 2017). Attempts to suppress this natural rhythm, as we shall see, induce episodes of what we describe as asset inflation, which is more than just a spell of rising asset prices but rather a type of monetary disease which carries a heightened vulnerability to financial crisis and ultimately economic and social trauma.

The larger the number of people and businesses using a money as a store of value and for payments, the better from the point of view of its convenience to individuals. The broader its use across the world, the less variability there should be in its purchasing power over short or even medium-term periods due to fluctuations in the exchange rate between it and other monies. This is true whether we are considering exchange rates between monies which have at their base concentrated geographical use (for example national fiat monies) or otherwise. Broad use should arise out of long experience and market use as good money.

The Loan Standard

Turning to the third function of money—as *standard of deferred payment*, or as denominator of loan contracts—in this role too good money should have an assured future value. Although, as already explained, this cannot be a guarantee, and would hold true only on average over the long-term future, at a minimum the money should not be subject to huge uncertainty as to future purchasing power. Money must be a widely accepted way to value a debt if goods and services are to be acquired now and paid for in the future. In the absence of such a function, alternative arrangements would have substantial costs, especially for longer-term contracts. For example, borrowers and lenders may agree to rolling over short-maturity contracts at variable interest rates; or in the case of long-term rental contracts, the lessee and lessor might need to negotiate complex and costly rent review clauses rather than enter into a long-term, fixed-rent contract. A good money in its function as denominator of loan agreements is required if the market for these is to be free and efficient.

By contrast, in contemporary money regimes, the market in these loan agreements is subject to intensive government intervention aimed at manipulating key benchmark interest rates. A money where such intervention occurs is liable to lose attraction as lenders become exposed to sudden changes in official policy in addition to various forms of monetary taxation (see Chapter 6 for details). Ultimately, rates quoted in such a rigged loan market lose the capacity to provide vital information that is crucial to the operation of the economy. This is another example of the dual proposition that bad money at the level of the individual (poor application as loan denominator) translates into bad money at the level of society, and the converse is also true in this case.

The Numeraire Function

Users benefit when they do not have to incur the costs of changing their currency into another money in order to make a transaction. Such costs pile up if the money is not widely used to post prices or for quotation purposes; i.e. when it has to be converted first into the currency quoted in such pricing. Where a given currency is widely used for quotation purposes, in effect as the "money of account" or *numeraire* (goods and services having prices quoted in this currency), then the incidence of exchange costs is low.

Again, competition can play a useful role. If the users of a given money find that certain sellers quote prices to them (in that money) which are keener than others due to their business strategies for minimising exchange costs, then they would gravitate towards those sellers. Certainly, in some retail arenas, exchange costs are so small relative to other costs that sellers do not find themselves under pressure to quote prices in several currencies. Customers are won by competition in non-currency issues. In other areas, though, competitive pressures in effect force sellers to adopt several quotation currencies. A widespread use of alternative monies as numeraire may help to broaden the effective choice for individuals as they assess their qualities in performing the other functions (for example medium of exchange, store of value) while reducing the value of any one money as a unit of account. In turn, enhanced competition between monies should encourage issuers to focus on ways to bolster the qualities appreciated by individuals.

Businesses typically choose one currency in which to make their calculations. They fix their usual selling price in this "base" currency, with prices quoted in alternative currencies derived from that using the current exchange rate. Competition together with efficient management of their foreign currency operations—including the ability to offset payments and receipts in foreign currencies where these are different from their base currency without effecting exchange transactions—make sellers quote prices in these currencies based on mid-point exchange rates with no implicit fee added. That is the basis of a currency's use as numeraire. By the same token, businesses shift away from that favoured currency if it becomes highly unstable. Rather than changing prices several times a day or week or month as quoted in the usual domestic money, it might be less costly and more efficient to use an international money as numeraire and the local currency price be derived at any point in time from that and the fluctuating exchange rate. That is the underlying basis for the widespread use of the US dollar as an invoicing and settlement currency by businesses around the world.

The more people use a currency as a unit in which to quote prices and make payments, the more valuable that currency will be to its users. That explains why a currency, once it achieves a dominant position, is very hard to dislodge. This gives the issuers of such currencies the capacity to abuse their position—e.g. by issuing too much money, or by using it as a foreign policy weapon. Issuers know that people do not change their habits easily even if the quality of a particular money deteriorates. So is there a tension here between the benefits of competition on the one hand and the possible gains from a body (typically the state) mandating the "national" currency unit? Read on!

Good Money for Society

Having reviewed the meaning of good money from the viewpoint of the individual, let's shift attention back to good money in the context of society.

Many contemporary economists believe that the machinery of the economy can suffer a serious breakdown even under a money regime that provides money which is good at an individual level. In such a case, they argue that the "authorities" should take over the controls of the machinery of money; even if this lowered the quality of money at the level of the individual (making it less good, for example, as a store of value or denominator of long-term contracts), it would be justified on broad social grounds. Individuals in effect would sacrifice the availability of good money at their personal level for the greater good of society.

An illustration of this argument for sacrificing good money at the level of the individual comes from the historical experience of the Great Depression of the 1930s (see Bernanke 2004). We fill out our response to this charge in subsequent chapters (in particular Chapter 8). In sum, these "crises of capitalism"—whether the Great Depression of the early and mid-1930s or the global financial crisis and its aftermath of 2008–2018—were in reality preceded by and attributable to prior episodes of asset inflation and booms encouraged by governments. In both episodes, bad money corrupted the operation of markets. Some economists have advanced other cases of alleged trade-offs or conflict between good money at the level of the individual at the level of society. We examine these in subsequent chapters (notably Chapter 5).

Our conclusion is clear: in a well-designed monetary system, there will be no conflict between what is good money for the individual and money that is good for society. Indeed we go further: the better is money at the level of the individual, the better it is at the level of society.

Enter Super-Money

To demonstrate how this connection works, we retrieve a concept of money from its recent neglect by mainstream monetary economists. This is *high-powered* money *or base money* (the terms are equivalent). On its own this is a statistical category—under a fiat money system its constituents include banknotes and coins in circulation and reserve deposits held by commercial banks at the central bank. The supply of such base money in a fiat money regime is in principle fully under the control of the central bank. We argue that the economic importance of high-powered money derives not only from this controllability but also from its potential to overlap to a considerable degree a group of core assets which have *super qualities as money*. These cause demand for this group in aggregate and thereby for high-powered money to be broad, strong and stable.[1]

Let's backtrack first in an effort to get these important points across to our readers, including illustrations.

High-powered money is traditionally presented by economists as the base of an inverted money "pyramid". As already mentioned, in the case of fiat money, this bottom layer consists of banknotes and coin in circulation among the public and reserves that commercial banks hold at the central bank or clearing house. The layer above that includes sight (or current account) deposits while those further up include savings and time deposits, certificates of deposits and other kinds of near-money. Traditionally, growth of the high-powered money layer at the bottom is seen as driving the growth of the broader money aggregates in the upper layers in a fairly predictable fashion; a rise in base or high-powered money allows banks to increase their lending and deposits by a multiple of the increase. That is not the route we follow here. Rather, our grounds for resuscitating this concept lie in our contention that in the case of good money the bottom (smallest) layer of the inverted pyramid largely overlaps with what we describe as *"super-money"*. *This is* the core of a good money system. The components of high-powered money should have super-money qualities.

The challenge is to design a monetary system where the super-money qualities of the core will flourish. Bottom line: the flourishing of super-money qualities in the core of the monetary system, meaning that money is excellent from the viewpoint of the individual, is the basis of money being good for society. Stable, broad and strong underlying demand for high-powered

---

[1] We shall see in Chapter 12 what is meant by "controllability" in the context of non-fiat monetary systems (for example those based on real assets or commodities).

money together with the controllability of its supply is the basis of a money that sustains its value over the long-run.

Why Super-Money Is so Important

When the assets at the core of the system perform their functions as money so well that there emerges a wide, strong and stable demand for them, they earn the title/description of super-money; i.e. they are assets *strongly desired* as money (Yuran 2014; Pringle 2020). These super-money qualities are not found in broader forms of money such as savings deposits, money market securities, mutual funds and other time deposits. Such assets typically pay interest; assets with super-money qualities do not need to. These qualities are the essence of *moneyness*.

Super-money qualities can be viewed from two angles—from outside and from inside. The first is related to how the monetary assets which have these qualities behave as money, and in particular the power they have in aggregate to influence prices. The second explores why and how they develop such power.

How should the monetary core behave as money? Demand for it will be robust, meaning that the amount people want is desensitised to— but not totally insensitive to—changes in interest rates. As illustration, consider one component of core money with potential super-money qualities—banknotes—in an environment with no inflation. These banknotes, available in several denominations from small to large, are an important form of payment. Suppose they are also an excellent store of value as well as medium of exchange with particular qualities unmatched by any alternatives (simplicity of use, no hassle, easy to transfer without instructing third parties etc., ownership does not require registration or legal/reporting requirements, but rather the convenience of being purely bearer in form). In such conditions, even if interest rates on other assets, such as time bank deposits or short-maturity government bonds and bills, were to rise, then the holders of these banknotes would not slash their holdings for the sake of an additional quite small interest income; any change would be measured and likely gradual. People holding such money can be viewed as "buying" it in giving up the income they would have obtained by investing it in an interest-bearing security, savings account or time deposit. Similarly, if interest rates on near-money assets (beyond the monetary core) were to fall, holders would not rush to cash these.

Crucially, imbalances between the supply and demand for high-powered money, where this largely overlaps monetary assets which have super-money qualities, give rise to important real economic effects. For example, where individuals and businesses find themselves with an excess of such money (i.e. more than they normally hold in relation to their income and assets), they will tend to increase their demand for goods and services in consequence, so as to shed the excess. And the fall in interest rates as spurred by the excess will further encourage spending, increasing demand and thus spreading monetary inflation through the economy, lowering the value of money. The opposite process would take place where the supply of high-powered money falls short of underlying demand.[2]

If there were no particular/super quality in high-powered money components then people would switch out of (or into) these and into interest-bearing forms of money (CDs, time deposits, etc.) given any incentive to do so. Yes, there might be a residual demand for high-powered money forms, but a small rise in interest rates would cause individuals to make big proportionate reductions in their holdings. So if, for any reason, the supply of high-powered money were to rise sharply above underlying demand for it, this would in such conditions have little impact on the wider economic scene; individuals/businesses would not be stimulated to increase their spending on goods and services. They would simply rearrange their portfolios of monetary assets. High-powered money supply and demand would become as irrelevant to the behaviour of the economy as a whole as the supply and demand for apples.

Thus, where high-powered money has special/super-money qualities, an increase or reduction in the supply will over time have a significant economic impact. Individuals, finding they have too much (or too little) of this consumer good (money) in relation to their income will use some of the excess to buy other goods—driving up their price; or, in the case of a shortage, they will refrain from their usual purchases, as they will have too little money in relation to their income or normal holdings (Most people have a fairly clear, or customary, idea of the amount of cash they need to keep readily available to spend and meet expected invoices; this varies of course in line with an individual's level of income and wealth or assets). Through this process, as people adjust their holding of money to a desired level, the value of money will change so as to restore a balance between supply and demand. In the

---

[2] In this volume we do not treat money as neutral, in the sense that increases in its supply would ultimately work their way through the system and only in the end influence the overall level of prices while leaving real variables unchanged. Instead, we suggest that how money enters the system has crucial real economic affect. These include the distortions, including malinvestment, which form part of the asset inflation process (See Glossary for definitions of terms).

case of an excess supply of money, the value of money in terms of goods and services will over time fall. This is the essence of the process often described as "too much money spent chasing too few goods". When, on the other hand, there is a shortage, the value of money will over time rise. This shows the importance of constraining the money supply appropriately.

But that description of the essence of good money still does not fully capture the nature of money, especially its strange power for good or ill. Here we have to take a closer look at the machinery and what drives it.

The Components of a Good Money System

A good money system is two-faced—from one angle, it provides us as individuals with a tool, as money in our pocket or at the bank, to help us make our way through daily life; on the other, it is an impersonal structure standing outside us. It runs on rules that we respect as unbreakable. Children learn that as they grow up. It has an authority of its own. Indeed, money is at its strongest when it acts as a constructive discipline, acting impersonally in our society. Then it has power—power that we have as a society given it.

The construction of a good money system built on and at the same time constraining the power of super-money is a cooperative, creative endeavour that may take years to build. As we explain in more detail later, governments can provide suitable conditions for it to grow; they cannot bring it about just by waving a magic wand. For example, cash as a super-money store of value gains in esteem with the level of confidence people have in the particular money sustaining its purchasing power over the very long-run.

No-one knows for sure, of course, how much potential demand there is for each core money asset—extended in our illustrations here to include forms such as safe sight deposits and digital dollar coins as well as banknotes. Demand for these will rise as and when their super-money qualities shine brighter. Take the example of banknotes. The sceptics on banknote demand say there is no going back; online shopping is set to win ever larger amounts of retail business and cash cannot be used here; modern generations just have no appetite for carrying large amounts of money around. By contrast, banknote optimists expect to see the role of banknotes growing in importance and helping thereby to strengthen the core to the monetary system. They point to a range of factors. A break-up of the Big Tech monopolies and credit card monopolies could revolutionise the payments process. No longer would it be the cash customers who effectively pay for everyone else; instead they would enjoy keener prices. Nor is there any sign of use of bank notes dying out. The global market is growing at about 3% annually. For the US $2.2 tn of banknotes are in global circulation, double 10 years ago, and now around 10% of US GDP. In the UK, £70 billion pounds worth of notes are in circulation, also double the amount ten years previously (though a much smaller rise in real, inflation-adjusted, terms) and equivalent to about £1,000 per person; in addition to the cash in wallets, in shop tills, in banks and ATM machines, people hold banknotes as savings, while large sums are also held overseas and in the shadow economy.

Just as banknotes are one component of high-powered money which could have considerably strengthened super-money qualities, the same could apply to digital forms of fiat money and with hypothetical safe sight deposits. Suppose for example a US dollar means of payment were available in the form of digital coins (in fact alpha-numeric codes, as presently used in stablecoins), issued by banks and other financial institutions. Suppose competition to satisfy the public demand for a safe asset led each such institution to back its digital coin with cash (where the backing was subject to inspection). Each issuer could belong to a jointly established clearing house which would help individuals using these to make payment (in that individuals who preferred to hold a Bank A coin to a Bank B coin, if presented with B coin can easily exchange, if preferred via coin brokers who specialise in facilitating this). Historically this is how banknotes issued by a range of banks in each US state became excellent means of payment under the free banking era in the US during the 30 years or more before the Civil War (see Fessenden, Helen, 2018). Again, the critic/cynic may question the potential demand for these digital coins, as for large banknotes. That is why in this volume we present our ideas for constructing good money as proposals to be judged in the light of possible future circumstances rather than as recommendations for all time. Our readers are invited to be the judges.

But core money assets may include more than banknotes, bank reserves and safe stablecoins. Another asset with potential super-money qualities would be safe sight (current account) deposits differentiated by having high backing in cash (legally dedicated to the deposits). In a competitive banking system the super-money qualities of such safe depsoits would be much in demand. Important props to perceived security of deposits found in non-competitive systems—whether monopoly power (in the case of large banks) or extensive state interventions—would not be present.

At present, the various broad monetary aggregates, whether M2 (as for US) or M3 (as for eurozone) are more a reflection of the behaviour or the expected path of the economy than a driving force. Quantitative Easing, involving massive central bank purchases of assets paid for by printing money, expose money's hollow core. Later, when we trace the decline of good money (see Chapter 8) we show how demand for money became unstable when national governments started using it blatantly for their own political ends, e.g. cutting interest rates to maximise short-term goals of employment and growth, especially before elections. When the public complained about the resulting high inflation, governments promised consumer price stability—assuming that was what citizens wanted—but that promise was delivered in a flawed form, meaning that it led to wounding episodes of asset inflation and crises. Some residual super-power features of money faded along the way. And so we arrive at the present juncture where money exercises no discipline over governments, the banks or the financial system.

When the Banks Need Super-Money

Let's delve a little further into the demand for super-money. We have described why individuals need and value it. But another element in demand for monetary base/high-powered money comes from the banks. Being profit-making enterprises, banks want to use as much of their assets as possible in ways that produce a return—either by lending them to clients or by investing them in interest-bearing bonds and other securities. But they also need a reserve of ready cash in case customers want more of it—or other banks fail to renew their own inter-bank lines. Banks therefore have to manage their holdings of cash at the clearing house for inter-bank payments or the central bank. (Here we are discussing classical monetary system where reserves pay no interest.) If bankers believe that there is a very low probability that they will be rescued in a crisis, whether by the lender of last resort, or the office of too big to fail, or by the deposit insurance office, they will make sure they can meet demand for cash whether by customers or by other banks. So they will maintain reserves at the central bank or clearing house that are instantly available at all times. They derive super-money-like services from these reserves in that they could play a crucial role in saving them from destruction during a financial storm. For a small prospective change in interest income (as in context of small rate rise) they are not going to make a big adjustment of their cash positions. Their demand for cash is desensitized to a considerable degree (but not altogether) to changes in interest rates on account of these super-money qualities which they value highly.

   If cash and other constituents of high-powered money (as conventionally defined) are in fact hardly distinct in their qualities from other elements in the broader money supply, then indeed small changes in interest rates would restore balance in the money markets even when the initial imbalance was large. Banks which started the day believing that they held large excess reserves could find by lunchtime that a small fall in rates had eliminated these (as their opportunity cost in terms of foregone interest earnings on alternative assets such as short-maturity bonds or bills had shrunk). It is quite different though when the cash and other components of high-powered money have special qualities meriting the term "super-money", as we have seen earlier in the example of large denomination banknotes. Then a tiny fall in rates would not alter the perception of the bank that its reserves were excessive. Their efforts to reduce these would force the whole structure of rates down, and in such ways affect the wider economy.

Money's Wider Role

The evolution of a good money is a creative, cooperative endeavour. A key stage is reached when the public understand that to get full value out of the money system we, members of the public, should respect its rules. We do so in the belief that, while some individuals will flourish and prosper more than others, the benefits to society and in the long-run to us as individuals of good money outweigh the costs. Our analysis reveals how superficial is the understanding of money shown by those who simply claim that we, the public, should "trust" the official guardians of money. It is not a matter of trust or lack of it.

Let's illustrate the role and importance of "community assent" to the building of good money. Suppose that indeed a good money regime has been in place for many years and earned popular respect and indeed endearment. Then suppose a president or prime minister decides that the best strategy for winning the next general election is to administer an almighty monetary stimulus to bring about an economic boom. To put this policy into effect, the constitutional and other rules in a good money system would have to be suspended (in some degree) but the significance of this act might be blurred for some time, especially if the president/prime minister took the opportunity of an empty seat (or emptied seat!) to install a monetary bureaucrat close to their own thinking on best monetary policy at this stage to run the central bank. Could the president succeed? Would he/she even persevere with the original planned stimulus? The answers in a good money regime which is firmly secured in popular assent would be "no". At the level of electoral calculation, a wide range of voters would turn against the president and his party for spoiling their monetary regime. In parliament (or congress) a majority of members would vote against the proposed monetary action. And the courts, realising the popular groundswell of opinion, would have the confidence to uphold the constitution. This factor of community assent lends essential moral authority to a good money regime.

The basic point is this: money is not to be viewed as something that governments create for our benefit; nor can "bad money" be made into "good money" by merely attaching to it some technical device. Money is a social construct the value of which is maintained by demand from us, members of the public and which "we" allow governments to use on certain conditions. This way of looking at money ties in with our claim that good money and effective defences against monopoly—together with the provision of a select range of public goods such as law and order by the state, as already mentioned—are necessary conditions for market capitalism to thrive.

That would not be so if money were powerless to influence prices. One can observe the proper role of money in action when, if individuals feel they have excess super-money, they spend some of this—for instance, on durable goods and buildings—rather than buying finance bills or the equivalent. Similarly, when businesses feel they have excess money balances they spend some of it on investment. And that process changes key prices and the whole level of average goods and services' prices as the effects ripple out. Another foundation of good money is that all parties who use it, including states, companies, charities and individuals, and whatever their nationality may be, however distant any of us may be from the centre of power, whether that distance be geographical, or measured in terms of wealth, social status or corporate size, will have complete confidence that those at the centre will not derive any advantage, nor be able to manipulate it for their benefit i.e. that it will be in this sense neutral. It thus encourages decentralisation. It is "impersonal".

Don't Fret Over Volatile Short-Term Rates

In a good money regime as described, where control over the machinery of money is exercised via constraints on the supply of high-powered money given a strong, broad and stable underlying demand for this (as fitting the super-money qualities of its components), we should expect that short-term interest rates will be highly volatile day-to-day.

Fluctuations in short-term rates are natural and normal. They do not get in the way of the long-term interest rate markets adjusting to balance the supply of, and demand for, loan capital based on the decentralised decisions of millions of savers and capital spenders.[3] By contrast, under money systems where central banks peg short-term rates, their intentions regarding the future level of this peg become a focal point for speculation in long-term rate markets about the intentions of the authorities. In consequence, the markets where long-term interest rates are determined become unstable and unable to fulfil their proper role of guiding resources into most productive uses.

Far better to have market rates freely floating in the money markets if indeed the suitable conditions apply on the demand side for high-powered money which consists mainly of what we call super-money. In the case of fiat money, the supply of high-powered money can be controlled by the monetary authority; indeed, it consists of liabilities of the central bank (cash and bank reserves at the central bank). And as we shall see in Chapter 5, the supply of high-powered money can also be made subject to outside constraints to ensure its growth is low within narrow bands. By contrast, such constraints cannot be devised for the supply of broad money.

Sustained purchasing power over the long-run is a quality sought by individuals both with respect to high-powered or super-money and money in its broader forms. High confidence in this actually being delivered will further strengthen the super qualities in the assets which make up the high-powered money aggregate. In these conditions, these assets will be super-money and enjoy a broad and stable demand which, as we have mentioned, is an essential condition for good money. (The regrettable "withering away" of super-money and the related growing insignificance of high-powered money as a focus of controlling the machinery of money are discussed later in this book.)

We have seen that the properties which would broaden and sharpen demand for high-powered money are those which foster the emergence of super-money qualities for its components. Under the present system, however, the implicit or explicit state provided backstops for bank deposits mean only weak potential demand for a "safe" category of deposits—i.e. deposits that banks back with high-powered money (for example cash). If these props were to be removed during the journey to good money, banks would need to hold in large and stable quantities forms of money (including cash and reserves at the central bank) that provide instant and

---

[3] The long-term rate so determined in aggregate by individuals and businesses all with their particular information sets will indicate an equilibrium where what economists call "the marginal rate of time preference" for individuals (the amount by which they value the benefit of immediate consumption relative to postponed consumption) equals the marginal rate of return on capital. Economists among our readers will recognize that equality as the ideal condition for resource allocation through time, leading to higher productivity and prosperity (see Hirshleifer 1970).

universal liquidity. Removing the props will disrupt some comfort zones; but we should consider the benefits of good money and how these depend on super-money qualities.

Absence of super-money qualities at the core of money carries major disadvantages and risks. In particular, an inflationary process leading to a serious fall in the value of money can get under way unnoticed. This is because no-one can confidently judge whether a spurt of money growth reflects a shift in demand into money from other assets caused by, say, a war scare, or whether it indicates excess money supply which will lower the value of money. In such conditions, public debate about inflation focuses on the behaviour of consumer price indices, which are often unreliable indicators of monetary inflation. Warning signs in excess money growth will be dismissed or excused as "temporary", or as "needed to get the economy moving" or sidelined as only "possible speculative bubbles which will resolve themselves". There is no readily identifiable smoking gun. By contrast, where money has a core with super-money qualities, it should be possible to make at least a provisional diagnosis of monetary inflation before its symptoms emerge in stark form. This is possible by monitoring the growth in high-powered money supply and assessing for example whether any sustained acceleration is well in excess of where one estimates demand to be based on its normal relation to key variables such as real incomes.

"Price Stability"—An Empty Slogan?

Pulling together various aspects of good money at the level of society discussed in this chapter, the main aim should be to prevent money turning into a "monkey wrench" in the economy. Consistent with this, most people would feel comfortable with a money that fulfilled a promise broadly to sustain its real value on average over the long-run. As for the central bankers' favourite term, "price stability", beware! Prices doubling every generation is now—officially—the essence of "price stability". This is an Orwellian use of the term, a kind of "Newspeak" re-definition of language that would be laughed out of court at any time before the mid-twentieth century. As Orwell taught, abuse of language can corrupt thought—he had in mind its abuse by totalitarian regimes—and this is a case in point.

If we want to use the term "price stability" at all, we should give it sufficient content without over-specifying it. Thus, it could refer to a state where the public expects that, when prices rise far above their historical average, they will over a long period return to this long-term mean or average level (conversely when prices fall far below average, they will be expected to regain that average over time).

Other Paths for Prices

There are however other possibilities. Some economists claim that a good money at the level of society as a whole would be characterised by gradually rising prices. Some say that historically prosperity and economic growth were often associated with a broad-based rise in prices and that price rise serves to boost corporate profits, perhaps because labour is fooled into accepting lower real wages, and in turn higher profits mean higher investment. As long as creditors and wage earners suffered from such "money illusion", inflation favoured borrowers and new wealth creators at the cost of creditors and "old money". Keynes (1930) mischievously proclaimed that periods of inflation were often eras of cultural achievement. A more potent argument for advocating creeping inflation in recent decades has been that it provides a "safety margin" above the level at which much-dreaded deflation sets in.

This discussion assumes that policy is in the hands of a committee and that they will have sufficient time to lower interest rates to avert such a risk if they aim normally at a significant level of inflation. This remains an influential argument behind the 2% inflation standard. Yet experience suggests it provides little if any of the "insurance" expected of it. It is also subject to "target inflation creep". The evidence in our view shows that prices should be expected under a good money regime to sometimes rise persistently and sometimes fall with no expectation of a sustained loss of purchasing power over the long-run.

In addition to the options of, first, long-term stability (or more precisely reversion to a mean level), and, secondly, a gradually rising path for prices, a third option would be to let prices gradually fall with the growth of the productive power of the economy; i.e. a gently rising real value of money. This was supported by Milton Friedman, the intellectual father of monetarism in the 1970s and 1980s.[4] One of our purposes here is to resurrect this objective as a legitimate topic of debate (See Selgin 1997 and Chapters 5 and 12). At its most basic, a gradual rise in the value of money would give every citizen through their money a stake in and participation in the rewards

---

[4] Friedman's advocacy of gradually falling prices in the long-run (see Friedman 1969) was for the case of a fiat money regime; here the marginal cost of producing banknotes and other components of high-powered money is zero; so it would be suboptimal for individuals, banks and businesses to economize on holding these due to a significantly positive nominal rate of interest; if prices are on a long downward trend then these nominal rates would be lower than otherwise).

of economic advance. It would give security to lenders and investors, thus potentially making them feel more comfortable with assuming the risks of long-gestation investment projects (whether as equity or debt holders); and for the ordinary citizen, it would take some of the worry out of money.

But enough of this debate for the moment. In the next chapter, we move from a description and analysis of the principles of good money and desirable paths for prices to focus on the question: how in practice can these features of good money be secured for the benefit of all citizens?

References

Bernanke, B. (2004) *Essays on the Great Depression*. Princeton University Press.

Bernanke, B. and Mishkin, F. (1997) "Inflation Targeting: A New Framework for Monetary Policy" NBER Working Paper 5893 (January 1997).

Brown, Brendan (2017) *The Case Against 2 Per Cent Inflation* (Palgrave).

Fisher Stanley (1977) Long-Term Contracts, Rational Expectations and the Optimal Money Supply. *Journal of Political Economy*.

Friedman. (2005). *The Optimum Quantity of Money*. Transaction Publishers.

Friedman, M. (1963) *A Monetary History of the United States*.

Friedman, M. (1969) *The Optimum Quantity of Money*. Transaction Publishers.

Hirshleifer, Jack (1970) *Investment Interest and Capital*. Prentice-Hall.

Keynes, J.M. (1930) *A Treatise on Money*.

Levy, Haim (2011) *The Capital-Asset Pricing Model in the Twenty First Century*. Cambridge University Press.

Pringle, Robert (2020) *The Power of Money: How Ideas About Money Shaped the Modern World*.

Raico, Ralph (2006) "What Is Classical Liberalism" Mises Institute

Sayers, R.S. (1967) *Modern Banking*. Oxford University Press.

Selgin, George (1997) Less than Zero Hobart Paper 132, Institute for Economic Affairs.

Yuran, Noam (2014) What Money Wants: An Economy of Desire Paperback. 30 March.

5

Why Good Money Has a Solid Anchor

Is there a wonder-mechanism which can foster the qualities of a good money as set out in the previous chapter? The short answer is yes there is—a "solid anchor" for the monetary system. We have already referred to this concept several times in previous chapters; we now should describe it in more detail (and the reader should also refer to the Glossary).

Our aims in this chapter are threefold: first, to describe what constitutes a solid anchor and why it matters; secondly, to show how the role of anchor developed historically; and thirdly to discuss and assess whether anchors which operate by tying down the supply of modern (fiat) money can be sufficiently solid.

A word of explanation about the terms we use may be useful. What do we mean by using the nautical term "anchor"? What do we want a (monetary) anchor to do?

Just as a ship's anchor secures the vessel to the sea bed to prevent it being moved out of position by wind or currents, so a monetary anchor is a device that constrains the supply of money in a way that prevents the emergence of monetary inflation (see glossary) and the damage it does to society, including the enjoyment of prosperity and freedom.

B. Brown and R. Pringle, *A Guide to Good Money*, https://doi.org/10.1007/978-3-031-06041-0_5

What Constitutes a Solid Anchor?

An anchor in a solid form provides safety to the machinery of money by sustaining the purchasing power of money while protecting the signalling function of interest rates. Constraining the supply of money is crucial to the operation of a solid anchor. This constraint is, however, not sufficient. The demand for money must also be broad and stable, at least as regards its core components (which make up high-powered money); as we saw in the previous chapter that broadness and stability depend on those core components having super-money qualities. We can understand why these attributes of the demand for money are so important to solid anchoring by looking at the history of monetarism (see Chapter 8). This failed as a guide to practical policy in the 1980s according to its critics because the demand for money became so unstable—or equivalent because the so-called "velocity of money" was so volatile and unpredictable (see White, 2013). The answer to this criticism is clear: fundamental reforms are necessary to the monetary system to bolster the super-money qualities of its core components.

Here we return briefly to the debate in the previous chapter about the desirable path for prices. "Sustaining purchasing power" is a term which is both obvious but also nuanced in meaning. The details are arguable and indeed we might say ideally chosen by the users of money: consumers would doubtless opt for the money which promises to be a good store of value in the sense they most appreciate; entrepreneurial investors might like one that provides a safe haven for part of their wealth against the risk of an unexpected rise or fall of the stock market, so they can focus analysis on the real, underlying prospects for the project. Equally, some might prefer a good store of value to be defined in terms of a basket of consumer goods; others might prefer a basket which contains both consumer goods and particular capital goods (and housing is a hybrid between the two); some might like a basket to include mainly business assets (or more broadly the stock of business capital in its various forms).

We have mentioned also (at the end of the last chapter) the possible option of a gradually rising value of money (fall in money prices). We return to it here as our preferences as regards the path of prices will influence our choice of an anchor. How many would like money especially in its non-interest bearing forms (as for those components of high-powered money with super-money qualities) to realise cumulative gains in purchasing power over the long-run? This would come about for example if productivity growth were fully reflected in falling prices. The great early twentieth-century British economist, D.H. Robertson discussed this latter type of money as a moral monetary standard (see Robertson, 1922). It would favour those whose money incomes are relatively fixed, by law or custom and, who are "not as a rule the most self-assertive members of the community." Perhaps he had in mind pensioners living on small annuities. (Note that Robertson was writing before the age of powerful public sector unions; and at a time when geographical and social immobility made for a relatively inflexible labour market). Is it not desirable, he asked, that they should receive automatically a share in the fruits of progress through falling prices? And why, Robertson asks, should wage earners not secure "a share of any booty that is going" without having to demand wage increases?

Milton Friedman in his optimum quantity of money essay (see Friedman, 1969) also advocated a gradual fall in the price level (see argument as summarised in footnote in previous chapter). Well, the reader may wonder, would that not be great? Why shouldn't money always be gaining in value? Have we all been missing something? Perhaps we have, but there could be problems with this. The issue is that if money is made out to be riskless (as it can be under a good standard), then a substantially positive real rate of return available on cash could be problematic in a low-growth economy.[1]

Why It Matters

Let us take one step back. In any monetary system, anchored or not anchored, the supply of money is critical to the path of prices (except in the special dysfunctional case where money has lost all its special qualities). If the supply (expressed as a stock) of money is running persistently and far ahead of the underlying demand for money (within the budget constraints of income and wealth) prices will rise (though if the natural rhythm of prices is strongly downwards at the time, this rise might be camouflaged—see glossary entry for "natural rhythm of prices" and "goods inflation"). Individuals and businesses finding themselves with money in excess of their desired holdings increase their spending, and so prices of goods and services come under upward pressure. Asset inflation (see glossary) emerges as price signals in capital markets become corrupted. We should be cautious about simplifying here; the Austrian economists tell us (see Salerno, 2010) that the ways

---

[1] An illustration: if individuals could pile up cash whose real rate of return is substantially positive, their propensity to undertake risky investments at the feeble rates of return available or to consume might be so weak as to mean permanent recession. Yes a big fall of prices in the present coupled with expectations of higher prices in the future could stimulate spending, but in the context of a money reputed to gain substantially in real value over the long-run such expectations might not form. Note this reservation does not apply to a novel type of money—equity money—to be discussed in Chapter 12.

in which excess money "enters the system" are multifarious and affect the channels which lead to the particular observed outcomes. But the basic mechanism and processes at work are well established; too much money chasing too few goods is at the root of inflation. Supply shocks—whether a group of oil producer nations cutting production or people withdrawing en masse from employment due to disease fear—cannot cause sustained price inflation (though high prices could persist for some time until the natural rhythm of prices changes direction). Sustained price inflation requires a growth in the money supply running ahead of underlying demand for money (see glossary on monetary inflation). Note, however, that anchoring, even at its best (the most solid), does not imply a straitjacket on prices of goods and services, though we should not experience the violent or persistent and large moves of prices on average which we get in an unanchored or badly anchored monetary system.

Advocates of good money should not have a hang-up about stable prices (see glossary on "natural rhythm of prices"). But a solid anchor, a condition of good money, means that fluctuations in the value of money are bounded. (We should note here that there is no price index that satisfactorily summarises the "value of money"). An anchor that steers money supply over the very long-run so that the purchasing power of the money "returns to the mean" would be a very good anchor. There are several reasons for this. First, this is what many/most "consumers" of money would choose as a desirable quality; second, alternatives could distort a crucial market-determined signal in the global economy—real interest rates; third, confidence in a long-run expected constancy of purchasing power helps the process by which market forces pull the economy out of recession. It does this by lowering prices relative to their level expected in the long-run. This encourages consumers to spend money, before prices rise, thus raising demand.

How an Anchor Secures Money

There are two basic ways in which money may be anchored securely.

EITHER by a pledge (promise) that a unit of the money is convertible (i.e. exchangeable) on demand into a fixed amount of a real asset (or a claim on this same amount) which is fundamentally scarce; this is the traditional way. OR, in the case of inconvertible or fiat money, by a firm control over the supply of high-powered money, whose components are well-differentiated by superior "moneyness" from other elements in more broadly defined measures of the money supply. The architects of the fiat regime should strive in their designs to encourage the development of "super money" qualities as discussed in the previous chapter to attract a strong, broad and stable demand for high-powered money.

These two ways of anchoring money have key elements in common. In the first way, alongside a convertibility pledge, the supply of high-powered (or "base") money is constrained in a responsive manner as described by the physical supply conditions of the real commodity. Where there is no such responsive external constraint imposed by nature, constitutional rules determine how and when the monetary authority should accelerate or decelerate the growth of high-powered money, but always within overall limits.

Convertibility to a Real Asset or Fixed Money Supply?

This real asset or commodity will have a dual use; it will be demanded both as money (a means of payment, store of value and unit of account) and as a consumption or investment good or asset. That has an important implication; non-monetary demand for the real asset or commodity to which the given money is tied plays a crucial role in the anchoring process.

Why not just make life simple and anchor money by keeping its nominal supply fixed? We, the authors, have spent much time discussing this question. And some great sound money theorists have strongly advocated this on the grounds that it is easier for people to understand and thus likely to win popular support (see Salerno (2010). Under such an anchor, money would gain value as output rose. However there are advantages in an anchor that allows some flexibility in the money supply to respond to changes in the real demand for money,

Let us explain more fully these ideas about flexibility in money supply and prices reverting to a mean; we beg our reader's permission to delve into some points which are not bedtime reading.

Benefits of a Solid Anchor

A solid anchor brings many benefits both at the level of the individual and of society as a whole. It fosters trust in a money as a long-term store of value. This is necessary if entrepreneurs, investors and ordinary savers are to make sober-rational estimates of future returns and risks from capital investments and compare alternatives including present consumption instead of saving to consume in the future. By that token, it ties money to the real world of work and enterprise. As discussed in Chapter 4, money must be widely accepted in payment for goods and services, and should also serve as a numeraire or measure of value that sellers of goods and services use to post prices on their sales lists and to express sums of money lent or borrowed. These are the classic functions of money (economists disagree on which function is primary but in fact they are bundled together, each supporting the others).

A well-anchored monetary system is trans-generational. It encourages members of a society to see themselves as belonging to a community across space and time. Typically, this anchor acts as a base on which private financial institutions including banks can build competitively a structure of wider money and credit featuring a variety of instruments including at the most basic current bank deposits, time deposits, certificates of deposits. A solid anchor will also be robust against attempts by the government or special interest groups to subvert it.

In a market economy with a well-anchored money and competitive markets, prices function reliably as signals which guide households and businesses whether on the side of demand or supply to produce outcomes which are efficient in the allocation of scare resources and satisfaction of consumer preferences. In goods and services markets, a persistent downswing or upswing in prices on average should take place only when such trends reflect real, non-monetary factors including as illustration big swings in the rate of technical progress, globalisation or productivity, or resource shortage or abundance, or business cycle fluctuations. Also a solid anchor will correct for a big cumulative jump of prices in the past that was a result of inadvertent monetary inflation. Even the most solid anchor is not perfect and it may have allowed money supply to run well ahead of demand for some time, but then it makes a correction for the error. (If we had had anything like a solid anchor in place in 2022, the inflation "error" experienced by several developed countries in 2021–2022 would have been followed by a period of substantial price declines as the solid anchor set off forces to reverse the monetary expansion and work towards prices returning to their long-run average—see Chapter 11 for more on policy in the pandemic). In asset markets, price signals will guide savings and investment decisions, including allocation of capital among various uses, on the basis of rational calculation. They will not be impaired by distortions caused by factors such as a "hunt for yield" (a characteristic of many contemporary investment fashions) but will reflect to a greater extent the considered judgement of investors based on the information available.

How Anchors Emerged Historically

No anchor is perfect, but some are less imperfect than others. Simplifying, traditional anchors took generally the form of a commodity standard or a foreign currency standard. In this section, we describe how the oldest forms of money were anchored, then proceed to more modern examples.

Gold and silver are the oldest forms of coined money. The first coins were made of electrum—a naturally occurring alloy of gold and silver—in Lydia, around 600 BC. But it was the Athenians who in the following centuries turned metal coinage into a universal standard by defining the monetary unit as a fixed and precise quantity of metal—4.3 g of silver. Soon every Greek city state started minting its own coins but the Athenian currency dominated trade. This model was followed by the Romans—the development of Roman coinage was a key to the extensive system of financial links across the Roman Empire—which in turn set the pattern for subsequent Western, Islamic and Indian coinage. The Romans relied on silver: Caligula threw silver coins from the Basilica into the multitude. China, pre-1934, had a silver standard, as did India prior to the conversion to gold at the end of the nineteenth century, and Japan prior to Meiji restoration in 1868. (see Brown, 2002) Many German states were on a silver standard pre-1871. In the US, bimetallism (where both gold and silver coins were legal tender) only came to an end with the US coinage act of 1873.

No Golden Guarantee

To delve into history a little deeper, gold and silver money was not fool-proof against monetary inflation. Later Roman emperors started to debase the coinage—using such debasement in effect as a tax. By decreasing the amount of silver in the coinage, they were able to make more coins with the same face value. This meant they could spend more; by the late third century, a Roman standard coin only contained about 5% silver. People were reluctant to accept such debased coins. Gradually the monetary economy, and the complex trading system that it had facilitated, unravelled; taxes were commuted into payments in kind, thus contributing to the dissolution of the Empire and the transition to the land-based economy of feudalism, featuring vast, largely self-sufficient, estates. Communities were held together by personal pledges of service and, for most, this meant an end to freedom of movement.

Monarchs throughout history have debased the coinage. One well-known example was the so-called Great Debasement started by King Henry VIII of England in the mid-sixteenth century. This saw the amount of precious metal in gold and silver coins drastically reduced and in some cases replaced entirely with cheaper base metals such as copper. This shocked contemporaries. Although debasement had been common throughout much of mediaeval Europe, especially in France, English monarchs had generally upheld the purity of the sterling coinage. From the ninth century to the late thirteenth-century silver pennies were the only coins in circulation in England. In the mid-fourteenth century, a regular coinage of gold was introduced and the gold sovereign was launched in 1489 under King Henry VII. Throughout this period, counterfeiting coinage was a crime against the state and was punishable by death.

We can think also of the sustained rise in prices amidst the inflow of gold and silver to Europe from Latin America during the sixteenth and seventeenth century; alongside there was the famous Dutch asset inflation of the 1630s (tulip bulbs, shares in the Dutch East India company, and Amsterdam real estate), in which the Bank of Amsterdam was a pioneer in fractional reserve banking (see Garber, 1989). Thus, gold and silver anchors have not always prevented monetary inflation. For example, in the US, an unstable banking system, providing various forms of implicit guarantees to depositors, became an important engine of monetary inflation (evident mainly in asset inflation) at various points in the nineteenth century. However, as the US was at the time only a price taker rather than a price-setter in the global economy, and as its exchange rate was fixed when on gold against other currencies including the pound sterling, even banking instability could not propel the US economy into sustained goods and services inflation.

The Classic Anchors in Practice

The main monetary media of exchange used before the era of inconvertible paper currencies arrived in the twentieth century had two great inter-linked advantages. They were desired for their own sake and they were naturally scarce. They kept their real value over the long term. For around 2,500 years up to 1914, these were either coins made of precious metals or bank deposits and banknotes convertible on demand into coins (There were also mostly short-lived experience with unbacked paper money as in China and during the French Revolution) As we have noted, the growth of fractional reserve banking fostered a cumulative growth in supply of money (in broad form) far exceeding the metallic monetary base; this was driven in part by rapid growth in demand for credit, which in turn was satisfied in considerable part by the credit creation of the banks. The demand for money (broad form) in real terms rose in line with rising aggregate wealth and incomes during the industrial revolution. Hence the gold anchor did in general exercise restraint within the context of a growing monetary system, though there were sub-periods in which a monetary inflation got under way for some time, mostly in asset markets.

Yes, there was an Achilles heel in the form of banking instability. Banks told customers their deposits were "always" convertible on demand and most customers chose to believe this most of the time. In fully rational mode, though, customers would have understood that "always" could not mean what it appeared to. That would have required safe deposits to be 100 per cent cash backed. Such a class of money was not available, because bankers made money by lending most deposits out again and so it was best for them if somehow all deposits could be marketed to clients as safe. But having a good credit, a good "name", and the ability to distinguish good names from bad were highly valued assets and skills, buttressing trust in money.

Subject to such considerations, the system was flexible. This allowed a vast expansion of credit money to be built on that narrow gold base. Demand for high-powered money, mostly in the form of gold (especially gold coin), did increase, albeit that the element deriving from bankers could be less stable. The instability of demand for (and variations in the real value of) gold could mean that the gold anchor did not prevent spells of goods and particularly asset inflation (or deflation). This was how an anchor securing the whole structure of credit money emerged as a key element in the machinery of money.

Given a solid anchor, bankers and other entrepreneurs can be left free (subject to a legal code which includes effective anti-trust provisions) to develop various monetary instruments; these can be market determined. The bugbear is potential instability in the demand for high-powered money (whether in the form of reserves in the clearing house or under a gold regime physical holdings of metal) by the banks and the variable illusion-making of fractional reserve banking. The critique of economists in the Austrian School is that banks as protected by various regulatory regimes have been able to sell deposits with a dubious claim of always being convertible into cash. Fractional reserve banking evolved into a system where governments became largely responsible for under-writing that claim, meaning that bank deposits with such government support (notably "too big to fail" guarantees and deposit insurance) became hardly distinguishable from high-powered money, especially once this became fiat only. Hence an important element in core money in a real sense lost its distinctive characteristics, meaning that anchoring became ever more problematic, a subject to which we return. Most examples of virulent inflation historically and all episodes of hyperinflation have occurred under fiat money regimes.

Although history has plenty of examples of monetary debasement, before the twentieth century there was no concept of "monetary policy"—i.e. the active manipulation of money by governments to serve communal (or their own) interests. Yes, under the gold standard some central banks did raise and lower short-term interest rates but the main purpose of such operations was to maintain at all times the convertibility pledge; and this system could work without anybody pulling the strings of official interest rates etc.—indeed the US had no central bank throughout the 40 years or more of the classic international gold standard. People found creative ways of making a given stock of money go a long way—mainly by borrowing and lending it to each other—because they were confident that the system with its in-built control mechanisms would ensure its value in the long term. Long-term loans were common.

This money acquired moral authority. As a result, people and whole nations adapted their behaviour to the sometimes demanding requirements of the standard. Given sufficient wage and price flexibility, economies were well set to be self-stabilising. In practice, there were episodes of financial instability and related severe business cycle fluctuations to which later critics of the gold standard have drawn attention. In large part, these were, however, due to the "confidence tricks" and "illusion-making" of fractional reserve banking as growingly protected by regulations. (See further analysis in Chapters 6 and 8).

Anchors for Fiat Money—Foreign Currency Anchors

We now turn to the use of foreign currency as an anchor. We saw this for example in the Weimar Republic after 1924, when the Reichsmark—called initially the Rentenmark—was fixed to the US dollar. This came after the great German hyperinflation in 1923 and was intended to bolster confidence in the new currency. The dollar, however, was at the time fully convertible into gold including gold coin, with the US still on a full gold standard. We saw a type of foreign currency anchor at work again during the Bretton

Woods System (1945–1971), when other currencies were fixed to the US dollar, albeit that the US currency had some residual convertibility into gold bullion (only for non-US citizens and from 68–71 only for foreign governments).

Under wholly fiat money regimes, foreign currency is again found as anchor. Historically we can think of the Deutsche mark's use as anchor within Europe during the 1970s and 1980s most of all with respect to the Dutch guilder and Austrian schilling. The success of this turned on the DM's own anchoring—in this case by quantitative control of Germany's high-powered money supply.

The use of purely fiat money, itself with no firm anchor, as anchor for another money, raises big issues. It is better than no anchor at all in some circumstances—e.g. for countries without any feasible domestic anchor. Yet the anchor to the satellite money will lack solidity. Yes, there is a convertibility pledge (satellite money into the larger one effectively on demand). But the anchor to the satellite is in effect an extension anchor to that of the larger money, meaning that swings in the satellite's purchasing power over time could be wide. An alternative form of foreign currency anchor has been implemented by various small monies (see in particular Hanke (2018) is the setting up of a currency board which ensures that the high-powered money in the given small currency is 100 per cent backed by the foreign currency into which it is convertible virtually 1:1. These boards have worked comparatively well for sustained periods in many countries which lack the institutional capacity and market development to maintain an independent monetary regime. However, they involve a concentration of foreign exchange wealth in the hands of government or its agencies—difficult to countenance for corrupt regimes or when there is a threat that one such regime might come into power. In Hong Kong, where the dollar reserves held by the currency board were effectively taken over by China in 1997, these reserves are still legally intact—but we all know that China could change the system and take the dollars into its own reserves.

There are other ways to give citizens of the small country some of the advantages available to a major currency—for example, dollarization. The process by which a country formally or informally recognises use of a leading currency—notably the US dollar but also the euro—as a medium of exchange usually occurs when the local currency loses its functions often as a result of hyperinflation (as in the case of Zimbabwe in 2008–2019) but can also be a deliberate policy choice, in which case it is often termed "full dollarization". This is where the foreign currency and/or a clone is used for all financial transactions. Panama is a leading example. This has some advantages over a currency board; the credibility of the arrangement is strengthened by the market's awareness that it is very difficult to reverse dollarisation. As the risk of currency devaluation is eliminated, dollarised economies can borrow at lower interest rates. (although the default risk remains as does political risk in various forms including enforced de-dollarization with the launch of a new national currency). A government adopting full dollarisation gives up the revenue from seigniorage (issuing notes and coin) whereas a currency board country does not, although in some cases the country issuing the base money will be willing to share the gain in its seigniorage revenues, as in the arrangements between South Africa and three other states that use the rand (Lesotho, Namibia and Swaziland).

If the dollar (or euro) itself were well-anchored, dollarisation (euroisation) would be a good solution to the apparently insoluble dilemmas facing many countries as they attempt to operate independent monetary policies. Dollarization could enjoy considerable popularity among households and businesses which perhaps because of their small financial size lack access to the international dollar money and credit markets. Governments however in these countries would lose not just the conventional seigniorage obtainable from their own currency issue but also the forms of monetary taxation discussed in this volume.

Anchoring Money by Constitutional Rules

Is it possible to devise at least a semi-solid anchor for fiat money by constitutional rules to limit growth in the supply of high-powered money?

Nobel prize winner James Buchanan, the founder of constitutional economics, certainly thought so. He favoured "a supplementary constitutional amendment that would direct the Federal Reserve Board to increase the monetary base at a rate roughly equivalent to the rate of growth in real output in the national economy". (Buchanan and Wagner, 1977). No revision in the growth rate of high-powered money may be made without near-unanimous consensus. Buchanan strongly believed, as he put it, that "good games depend on good rules more than they depend on good players". So long as the decision-making horizon of policy-makers, including central bankers, is short, they will choose easy money. What must change is the incentive structure. With longer-term horizons, the rule acquires authority that will override the discretionary judgement of the official authority: "The foreknowledge that the rule will be followed can modify behaviour in such a manner as to make the rule, over an expected sequence of events, more desirable than the authority" (Buchanan, 1999).

True, to succeed such a rule requires a demanding set of conditions. For example, the constituents of this money should meet the standard of "super money". People would want to hold nearly as much super-money even if interest rates on liquid investments were to rise. High-powered money is made up of cash, bank notes and bank balances at the clearing house or central bank. So the monetary authority would be obliged under the rule to set the growth of this high-powered money at a certain specified rate.

Such a regime would also require a break from the trend towards tighter regulation of finance; when the state assumes risks previously borne by the private sector, i.e. mainly by the parties directly involved, then it can also unintentionally weaken/undercut other pillars of the economy, including the role of money itself. Even assuming such a proposal garnered sufficient support to be tried—doubtless after another monetary catastrophe—there would be strong pressure to break or bend constitutional rules limiting money growth. How to protect sound money from governments hell-bent on winning elections even at the cost of sowing the seeds of future monetary disorder? How would the monetary authority estimate demand for the high-powered money to keep prices stable?

Further, the regime would need to operate within a political context where the deregulation could in fact occur (White, 2014). It could be especially difficult for smaller economies to estimate the demand for high-powered or super-money. Following our remarks on dollarisation above, the best strategy could be for those countries that do not wish to dollarise to peg their currencies under currency board rules to currencies which had made a constitutionally binding monetary rule with political systems that would make it credibly sustainable. As Hanke (2018) states, "The sole function of a currency board is to exchange the domestic currency it issues for an anchor currency at a fixed rate. Consequently, the quantity of domestic currency in circulation is determined solely by market forces, namely the demand for domestic currency". True, linking a currency to an existing fiat currency such as the dollar or euro risks importing instability from the anchor currency itself.

BASIC PRINCIPLES

In this chapter, we have analysed the principles on which a mechanism that reliably constrains the supply of money can and should be designed. Historically, the role of anchor developed from the age-old use of precious metals as money. We have examined whether other forms of anchor intended to tie down the supply of modern (fiat) money can be sufficiently solid.

We do not rule out the possibility of a constitutional framework providing an adequate degree of monetary control to constitute a viable anchor for fiat money. How these principles may be put into practice in the modern world is considered in Part Five.

While there is no such thing as a perfect anchor valid for all times and places, a solid anchor built on the above principles would go a long way towards realising the ideal of a good money regime. With a solid anchor in place, it would become obvious that there is no incompatibility between a money that serves the interests of the individual and that which promotes the good of society including generalised prosperity. They go hand in glove. This would be a money that answers to Adam Smith's vision that the twin drivers of prosperity are moral capital and enlightened self-interest.

References

Brown. (2002). The Yo-Yo Yen. Palgrave.

Buchanan, James (co-author Richard Wagner). (1977). Democracy in Deficit.

Buchanan James. (1999). The Logical Foundations of Constitutional Liberty.

Friedman, M. (1969). The Optimum Quantity of Money.

Garber, Peter. (1989). Tulipmania Journal of Political Economy, Vol. 97, No. 2, June, pp. 535–560.

Hanke. (2018). The Menace of Central Banks: Iran and Turkey Front and Center. *Forbes*, September 18, 2018.

Robertson D.H. (1922). Money.

Salerno, Joe. (2010). Money Sound and Unsound Mises.

White, W. (2013). "Is Monetary Policy a Science? The Interaction of Theory and Practice Over the Last 50 Years." Federal Reserve Bank of Dallas Globalization and Monetary Policy Institute Working Paper no. 155.

White, W. (2014). "The Prudential Regulation of Financial Institutions: Why Regulatory Response to the Crisis might not prove sufficient." OECD Economic Department Working Paper No. 1108, OECD Publishing, Paris.

Part III

The Grip of Bad Money

Introduction

Over four chapters, Part III presents our detailed indictment of the monetary mechanism of Western democracies. We show:

- How the damage that bad money does can long remain hidden;
- How it serves the interests of private equity barons and monopolists;
- How it creates illusions of wealth among house-buyers, in equity markets and some economists ("the business cycle is dead") while allowing the government to pick our pockets (all in Chapter 6);
- How it is based on a quite recent, false theory of money (Chapter 7);
- The bad effects of this concept as it unfolded through modern history (Chapter 8);
- The damaging effects of bad money ranging from mega boom-bust cycles to Bitcoin and dotty ideas such as Modern Monetary Theory summed up in a few short pages (Chapter 9).

6

Asset Inflation and Illusions of Prosperity

Bad money can create powerful illusions of prosperity.

These illusions stem in part from the fact that the damage done by monetary inflation often remains long hidden from general view. For example, business investment decisions made on the basis of asset prices distorted by monetary inflation are likely to take a cumulative toll on society's economic well-being but this may not be apparent during the hum and bustle of its boom phase. Asset inflation is fertile ground for the growth of hot speculative narratives which under non-inflationary conditions would have encountered considerable scepticism in the market-place (See Glossary). The telling and retelling of these narratives while the excitement lasts can create a society-wide sense of economic progress. Behavioural finance theorist Robert Shiller describes how such narratives form and spread, though unfortunately he does not link this to observations about monetary conditions (see Shiller [2019] and Brown [2019]).

In fact, the lack of sober-rational resistance leads to an over-pricing of income streams in these speculative areas of activity; scarce capital gets misallocated there. As illustration, if real estate markets become hot, construction activity is likely to grab a bigger share of new investment than would occur under non-inflationary conditions; so investment in other enterprise activity gets squeezed out or households forego present consumption to a greater extent than if fewer people had put on rose-coloured spectacles. Pent-up forces with their source in bad money can trigger an economic and financial eruption described as a "great crash and great recession" (of which there have

© The Author(s), under exclusive license to Springer Nature
Switzerland AG 2022
B. Brown and R. Pringle, *A Guide to Good Money*,
https://doi.org/10.1007/978-3-031-06041-0_6

been six or seven in the last 120 years of US history). Before such an event occurs, however, economic data may suggest at least an "OK" performance. Some sections of the population may prosper. Other people will expect to be shielded from adverse consequences of the coming catastrophe through their political clout or crony relationship with decision-makers. Illusions of prosperity can persist for so long that the philosophers among us might even question whether illusion has become reality and reality illusory!

Occasionally, monetary inflation does coincide with a productivity spurt, as for the US in the 1920s, the late 1950s and early 1960s or during the ten years to the mid-2000s. A Great Crash and Great Recession do not wipe out the real technological progress which occurs during that miracle period or put into idleness all the accumulation of capital stock. The boom-time incomes are not clawed back retrospectively. But still we can say that the monetary inflation leaves individuals on average substantially worse off (taking account of the adversity during the recession and the revealed squandering of resources in the boom period) than if the miracle period had occurred under a regime of good money. Deception is the name of the game. Under bad money, one person's fortune is much more often another's misfortune (as against just part of an expanding cake) than is the case under good money and competitive market capitalism. The misfortunes, though they may be severe in aggregate, are in the main thinly spread—and may be disguised, for many, by the veneer of rising stock and real estate markets while these last.

How the Deceptions Form

Let us look at the processes involved in monetary inflation and its deceptions of prosperity in more detail. Long, persistent and sometimes virulent episodes of monetary inflation fuel "irrational" forces in markets (See Glossary) Sometimes these irrational forces are prominent in real estate and commodities amidst much story telling about how these hedge against inflation and much else. Sometimes they are evident principally at the "frontier of technological opportunity" where there is much excitement about prospective high returns especially when many monetary assets are falling in real value. Hot speculative temperatures handicap the proper operation of markets; fun for some but meaning nonetheless some widespread impairment of investors' mental processes. Investors are driven by fear of a loss on monetary assets and "safe" bonds into taking on bad bets; these are bets that, in reality, rationally appraised, have an "actuarial outcome" (including a small chance of gain) worse than the prospective loss. (The origin of this idea and supporting empirical tests can be found in Kahneman (2012), albeit that this work makes no reference to monetary conditions). Investors, however, don't like to admit to themselves that the bet is bad so they become unduly receptive to stories which turn this into a good bet so long as they drop their normal scepticism.

At the level of the individual, an incitement to such behaviour can be what psychologists describe as "feedback loops"; investors may have enjoyed runs of good investment performance for years—even a decade or more—and they extrapolate this experience into the future without assessing rationally the risks. At the level of society, though, asset market price signals distorted in this way by speculative fever, lead to cumulative economic loss. The reader will find examples of this throughout this book, with episodes including railroad mania in the mid-late nineteenth century, the massive building boom in Weimar Germany in the 1920s, and recently over-globalisation of supply chains (where components are sourced from numerous countries without due consideration of possible disruption risks), and perhaps also, now, over-investment in digitalisation.

In an environment of asset inflation, people often pin ill-founded hopes on the permanent power of monetary bureaucrats to manipulate interest rates and to make skilful use of other policies to improve economic outcomes. The market may, for example, expect central banks to keep the risk of a market collapse at bay by being ever ready to deliver massive doses of stimulus. There is much that resembles here the fable of the Emperor's New Clothes. Some investors readily drop their guard against the promises and deceptions of financial engineers who camouflage leverage and make other changes in capital structure to enhance apparent overall profit returns. Even without such intervention, high equity and real estate values make leverage ratios, as calculated using market values, appear to be at flatteringly low levels. (For example, consider a corporation which has 500 dollar debt and 500 dollar equity outstanding as estimated on the basis of "rational-sober" valuation; a doubling of the equity to 1000 in a hot market would reduce the debt as a proportion of total market value to 33%). The risky debt suddenly seems less risky. Portfolio investors find they have more space for holding such paper (risky debt) while keeping its overall proportion in their portfolio within a normal range. Similarly, higher debts at manipulated low interest rates also boost reported corporate earnings which in turn—thanks to high price-earnings multiples—can boost equity market performance if monetary inflation is sapping rationality. Investors, when in rational mode, as we shall see below, would not apply such high price/earnings multiples to the expected earnings boost from leveraging up.

The Anxious Walker Down Wall Street

All of this can produce asset price booms that have no basis in underlying economic prosperity and that in the longer-term impoverish society. Eventually, asset inflation goes into reverse, and many illusions of wealth and prosperity collapse. The reversal may be triggered by a decline of profits and/or an emerging downturn in the business cycle perhaps amidst rising credit defaults and fading narratives; or there might be a tightening of monetary conditions. Before that point is reached, however, many investors view the continuing high rewards for bearing equity risk as evidence of their investment skills—or the wisdom of those efficient market theorists who assert that the best prescription to success is to hold a diversified portfolio of risk-assets dominated by equities. Sit back, enjoy the "random walk down Wall Street" and earn the premium that history leads us to expect from equities. (Malkiel, 2019). We are definitely not saying here that during long periods of asset inflation individuals should abstain from investment in so-called risk-assets including equities. Rather it is a question of perspective, we should realise where our gains are coming from and how everything is on a less solid footing than under a good money regime where there is no such disease. This less solid footing is not grounds for abstinence but frustration about how the walk down Wall Street could have been more enjoyable and relaxing. Another big point is that the walker while profiting as an individual would have been happy to know that his investment served to promote the general good—by contrast with today. Self-interest should always be checked by "sympathy", the keyword in the *Theory of Moral Sentiments*, which Adam Smith wrote before turning to economics. In his view, the moral order and purposive self-interest are the twin drivers of general prosperity and "affluence".

Investors in their random walk down Wall Street in times of great monetary plague are not on the same path as investors during a period of strongly rising prosperity under a regime of good money. In the latter case returns to equity come out of a pot of rising prosperity for society as a whole. That would be the case in a vibrant economic age when income per head is rising 3 to 4% per annum based on rapid productivity advances. In such a context, yes, equities could yield their 4 to 6 per cent risk premium year after year on average at a normal level of leverage and those gains could be real and lasting. Then rising share prices would reflect real economic progress. Under conditions of monetary inflation, by contrast, where the gains in economic prosperity, if apparent, might include many dubious elements including huge cumulative mal-investment and camouflaged leverage, a rational investor will walk with anxiety even though he might continue to walk (See chapter 8 for an analysis of historical boom-bust episodes).

This anxious walker might console himself or herself with the cynical thought that, although his or her gains are not coming from lasting growth in aggregate prosperity for society, they are based on "solid" income transfers to him or her from other members of society. The advance of monopoly capitalism under unsound money gives credence to such assumptions. Narratives about potential long-run monopoly profits appeal especially to investors starved of interest incomes by low interest rates. The equity price of any enterprise where its gaining of monopoly power is remotely plausible may soar; and in turn their abnormally low cost of equity capital enables such enterprises to engage in predatory actions, whether in the form of delivering services and products in the present at artificially low or negative profit so as to bankrupt competitors, or takeovers to knock out competition and block possible competition from new entrants.

Growing monopoly profits are often the basis for high expectations regarding earnings in the favoured sectors—and these come not from generalised gains in prosperity, not from the "wealth of nations" that interested Adam Smith but from the "misfortune of others". This kind of thing makes people angry and turns the public against markets and competitive capitalism.

Private Equity Loves a Crony

Our age of digitalisation has provided further scope for monopoly power due to such elements as "network effects", "winner take all" and a weak anti-monopoly legal code. Correspondingly speculative narratives about future monopoly profits find remarkably receptive audiences. Monopoly power has increased in many other fields besides Big Tech. "Star firms" (Autor, 2020) build moats around their business models, preventing early adoption by possible new entrants. Crony capitalism, itself favoured by monetary inflation as we shall see in Chapter 10, contributes significantly to the ability of monopolists to build moats to protect their castles of privilege (Munk, 2013).

Of course, monopoly capitalism has always been a threat to the proper functioning of markets, as known to economists/philosophers from Adam Smith onwards. Crony capitalism did not start with private equity! But this age-old phenomenon has received a big new lease of life, for two main reasons. Firstly, private equity thrives on the diet of asset inflation as it buoys the price of risky debt; investors' search for yield provides fertile ground for financial engineering while high expectations about gains from equity investment favour speculation that the private equity firms can indeed take firms private, leverage them up to the hilt, and subsequently re-launch them on the stock market at much higher prices. Secondly, private equity tends to expand by taking over companies in areas of the economy where the relationship of business to government (local, state or federal) is crucial to winning business and profits (hotels, retail, service-providers for health systems). No coincidence that the US private equity industry includes among its top echelons so many ex-Treasury Secretaries, top Fed officials, and ex-cabinet ministers. The traffic also goes in the opposite direction, with private equity barons becoming Treasury Secretaries and Fed Chiefs. The gains to investors in private equity might prove to be ephemeral and much of them will be siphoned off by the founding partners. Admittedly, taxation and regulations of private equity might eventually be tightened especially if culprits are needed in the post-bubble era. Nonetheless, much of the income accumulated by insiders over many years might stick and survive the eventual tumult; and of course the high earnings from crony contracts with public sector entities will already have been pocketed. (We examine cronyism further, as part of the forces that keep a bad system going, in Chapter 10).

Monetary Repression—Escape from an Invisible Tax?[1]

More broadly, a further channel through which monetary inflation can create illusions of wealth is taxation—specifically, the illusion that there is an escape from monetary taxation Monetary inflation is likely to go along with two inter-related forms of monetary taxation—a monetary repression tax (MRT) and inflation taxation (IT). These taxes are not legislated or approved explicitly by any parliament and are not expressly a legal liability of any individual or corporation (See Glossary for definitions).

One way for investors to attempt to avoid the impact of these taxes is to go into assets that seem to benefit from, or to be at least relatively immune to, a bad money regime. These include many business enterprises, real estate, gold and hard fiat money (if this exists). Bonds that pay the riskless rate of return plus a credit premium—where the latter is not itself subject to direct levy of inflation tax or monetary repression tax—may also be attractive. Hence a tax haven premium will develop in such assets. Investors will pay above normal prices in order to escape from the ravages of IT and MRT on government bonds and money. Indeed, the gradual emergence of this tax premium can

---

[1] This and the following two sections are somewhat technical. The general reader may wish to move to the section entitled "The business cycle is dead."

be an important component of the observed rise in many asset prices. This in turn produces the impression of a rising trend, exciting the momentum players already in the grip of asset inflation (and also the finance professors and their disciples who claim validation of their models of excess returns from passive investment in equities even when overall prosperity is growing sluggishly if at all).

On the subject of taxation, another aspect of wealth illusion is that, at the level of the individual, people do not take account in the present of future taxation to pay for ballooning government outlays. Yes, in principle equity prices or real estate prices might be lowered today by an explosion of public debt which means higher taxes will be levied on income from these assets in the far future; but all of this may be seen as so distant—and perhaps concentrated on certain wealth holders whose well-being is not so crucial to overall economic or market conditions—that it is unlikely to have much effect on present asset prices.

Individuals may not feel worse off now on account of taxes which are likely to be raised in the future and that may not impact present asset prices even though in principle markets can discount the far-off future. Nevertheless, many will sense intuitively that somehow the "small saver" is to be milked now. And yes, monetary repression tax may be already at high levels. But if this is going along with apparent wealth gains and most investors don't see that this means less yield in the future, then there is no apparent (subjective) tax burden. Under the conditions of asset inflation, many individuals do not feel poorer today because of the chances that luck will run out and the MRT in the future will fail to be made up by continuing stock market or other asset gains.

In any case, there may be a realistic expectation that the taxation to service the debt will fall on generations which are not yet voting or even born. It is a well-known issue of public finance that today's prime working age generation can shift taxation on to future generation and enjoy benefits now; and much thought has gone into how to limit this "abuse". A good money regime would make such exercises more difficult. In the case of a commodity or real asset money large fiscal deficits unmatched by legislated commitments to levy taxes further ahead could trigger a flight from paper forms of money into the anchor commodity. This flight would tend to bring about a sharp rise in money market rates as the supply of high-powered money dwindled, causing potentially serious financial stress—all of which could force the government to change course.

Government debt run up as facilitated by MRT and IT (and soft money more generally) has no counterpart in voluntary servicing of this out of future income streams as is the case with the private issuance of debt; there the borrower intends to meet interest and repayment obligations either out of extra income accruing from investment made or out of a cut back in future level of consumption. The future servicing of government debt, by contrast, depends on compulsion in the form of tax levies. Yet the holders of the additional government debt regard it as a solid component of their wealth. For any given individual, the holding of government debt is a form of wealth; but amassed across society as a whole, these individual holdings of wealth add up to much less if anything at all. Monetary taxation is an important factor in resolving this dichotomy.

Monetary inflation, the enabler of monetary taxation, is an engine of illusion full of consequence at a political level. For example, in the US President Trump always cheered a rising stock market—and praised Fed officials who would, he hoped, deliver policies which could achieve that. Prime Minister Abe in Japan made similar political use of a rising stock market. No matter that this rising stock market wealth might have little to do with genuine economic prosperity. Such politicians reckon that present measured wealth win elections not estimates of prosperity (or loss of it) many years to come. In any case, it is quite plausible that the president or prime minister comes to believe that their policies of ostensible tax reductions and deregulation have in fact brought long-term prosperity.

When Reality Shatters Illusions

When prosperity, as viewed by individuals through the lens of their wealth accumulation, diverges widely from prosperity at the level of society as a whole, there are forces that will eventually bring convergence between the two. One might be sudden asset deflation. Another would be an outbreak of high goods and services inflation, shattering the illusion that huge accumulations of government debt are a real lasting component of wealth. A third (unlikely but not inconceivable) would be an economic miracle which suddenly delivered real prosperity sufficient to catch up with inflated asset values and so validate them. Finally, the public might become aware of the true burden of monetary taxation in whatever form—and resist it. Inflation tax is more obvious than the monetary repression tax, in part because it is levied suddenly and in large amounts (think of the inflation tax in 2021–2022 during the pandemic, or in earlier episodes of war). Yet people can subsequently become suddenly aware of MRT when there is no longer the illusion of being able to avoid it by basking in the sun of seemingly ever-rising asset prices.

The Stimulus Illusion and the Super-Long Cycle

But wait a moment. Let us look again at the illusion that governments can painlessly dose economies with repeated "fiscal and monetary stimulus" without serious side-effects. We can subdivide this illusion into its components. One is that central banks can endlessly manipulate interest rates, short and long, at will. Another is that a structural savings surplus—explained by shortage of investment opportunities, demographics and the nature of present technological change—means that the "neutral rate of interest" (the level of rates on average consistent with low inflation and full employment according to the central bank's super econometric model) is in any case near zero (supposedly). A corresponding illusion is that governments should raise finance for vast public sector projects and so gear up economic growth. On this view, there is no hangover to consider from running up government debt, especially given its negative real cost, and the fact that it is matched (in this example) by public projects of positive present value.

Illusions of illusions—or delusion? The alternative thesis presented in this volume is that rates are held low by the abuses of a bad money regime. Governments and legislatures have embraced monetary policies that promise to hold down the cost of public borrowing. A decade or more of powerful non-monetary forces applying downward pressure on prices, goods and services (as from the mid-1990s to the mid/ 2000s), followed by a decade of economic sclerosis (see glossary), meant that until the pandemic inflation shock of 2021–2022 inflation as measured by the CPI did not emit warnings of monetary inflation.

In reality, our bad money regime has undermined investment opportunity and corroded the springs of competitive capitalism. It has created a climate of extreme uncertainty about the long-run (fear of asset market crashes) and encouraged investors to pursue high returns in the short-term based for example on financial engineering and dubious narratives while harbouring profound excitement (and corresponding willingness to pay high prices) about potential profits from the advance of monopoly capitalism.

The corruption of market signals by the contagious spread of dubious narratives has led to widespread mal-investment (see glossary) which means ultimately loss of economic prosperity. The growth of monopoly power, as fostered by asset inflation, contributes to the appearance of savings surplus.

The so-called zero-rate bound problem (the difficulty of reducing market interest rates below zero) mentioned regularly by the bad money policy-makers is not a misfortune they confront but a self-made serious side-effect of persistent monetary inflation (see "economic sclerosis" in glossary). Asset inflation can long continue under those circumstances, especially if wild narratives find fertile ground.

The illusionists further mislead us when they claim that the cost of government borrowing is zero or negative and that this is the rate which should be used in assessing the present value of public sector projects. In reality, the cost of public borrowing is the actual interest rate plus the monetary repression tax (MRT); that is the opportunity cost such as would pertain in normal conditions with monetary stability. It is false to justify public spending by citing an interest rate and an apparent shortage of investment opportunities when both are the results of bad policy, not a "state of nature". The true cost of public projects apparently made viable by "bad money" prices would include the overall cost of the monetary inflation which accompanied this including all the misdirected investment to boot. But by the time people wake up to this, the illusionists have moved on.

"The Business Cycle is Dead"

The bad money illusionists have yet another big trick up their sleeves. This is, crudely, the idea that "the business cycle is dead". Under bad money regimes, governments seek to thwart any incipient business cycle downturn by pre-emptive stimulatory action. One such action is the so-called Greenspan put—the sharp easing of monetary policy in response to any stock-market fall or stalling of asset inflation; the aim is not just to sustain the asset inflation until perhaps an economic miracle comes along or more pragmatically until Election Day but also to prevent a business cycle downturn emerging.[2] The first and most important of these took place in October 1987, when the Fed's reflationary action (taken to protect the economy) was interpreted as implying this institution would always act to counter a sharp downturn in stock markets—and that underpinned the great asset boom that continued until the financial crisis of 2008 and then resumed afer it. It may seem that these pre-emptive actions are successful several times over—and there is often a big element of luck involved, especially as regards the development of market psychology. Greenspan's successes in 1997 and 1998, during the

---

[2] This had its origin in the Strong put of 1927 to be described in Chapter 8.

great asset inflation, in administering reflationary action just in time (first the Asian debt crisis then the Russian crisis) won him nickname of Maestro. The 2008 collapse happened after the chair of the Fed had moved on to his successor Ben Bernanke (although it came soon enough after Greenspan's term finished—in early 2006—that he could not escape some of the blame for the Global Financial Crisis).

Famous economists who should know better have become enticed by the "cycle is dead" narrative. The list starts with Irving Fisher, fooled by the Benjamin Strong "reflation" of 1927, Samuelson by the mid-60s reflation of the Martin Fed and the accompanying Keynesian "stimuli", and the "Great Moderation theorists" of the 1995–2006 decade who celebrated the "success" of the 2 per cent inflation standard and the apparent magic wand of the Greenspan Fed. (See Brown and Simonnot [2020]). Politicians have notoriously sung the same tune. Gordon Brown, British Chancellor of the Exchequer for 10 years to 2007, repeatedly claimed that the new policy-making structure he had put in place with independence for the central bank would end the old business cycle and promised that (in his last budget as chancellor) "we will never return to the old boom and bust" only a few months before one of the biggest "busts" ever. They all failed to see that a series of pre-emptive expansions end up with a much worse outcome considered over the long-run than having allowed modest business cycle downturns to take place over time as would occur under a good money regime allowing proper scope for the market forces. Such artificially prolonged expansions magnify the cumulative mal-investment through the long years involved (the cost of prolonged monetary inflation). They often end up producing a break-out of high goods and services inflation, although it is also possible for them to end directly in a big recession and asset deflation without high inflation first".

Even now, an economic depression deep enough to threaten the political order could in fact be coming down the road, with anger at rising inequality intensified by the pain of recession.

The Bricks-And-Mortar Fantasy

Let's move finally to one of the biggest illusions of all under bad money—residential real estate wealth.

Robert Shiller has noted that, in the US, residential real estate prices in real terms on average (allowing for depreciation and obsolescence) were broadly stable over the very long-run right up to the early 1990s. (See Shiller, 2013)

This changed from the mid-1990s onwards—with the first big nationwide real estate boom 1997–2007 and then a second powerful rise in the asset inflation of 2012/2013 onwards with a noted crescendo during the pandemic. In Europe, Germany's real estate boom came late (though we should note the climb in real estate prices in the late 1980s), skipping the first decade of the twenty-first century, perhaps due to the long history of hard money there (through the 1970s and 80s). But after 2010 it emerged with a vengeance from the soft money regime of the ECB. What was going on here?

In an environment of a large monetary repression tax and potential large inflation tax in the future (actual in 2021–2022) there are, indeed, new apparent attractions to buying one's own residential space. This is not subject to MRT or IT directly. And especially if real interest rates are negative, housing becomes attractive as the biggest (in value terms) consumer durable with the slowest pace of in-built depreciation. Why not buy this today, rather than deferring purchase far into the future (and paying rent in the interim)? There are obvious attractions under conditions of negative real rates and high inflation uncertainty for people as consumers of residential space to lock in future residential rents (imputed in the case of the homebuyer) rather than be subject to considerable upward risk. The rise in real estate prices triggered by such buying then becomes part of the momentum of market trends, as in equity markets. A host of narratives about why real estate prices should rise from here become readily accepted and pedalled in the media.

Related to all this is the mortgage phenomenon. Individuals who borrow to buy their home become *collectors* of monetary repression tax and inflation tax for themselves. They become *common beneficiaries with the government* from monetary inflation in this respect. However, they should beware. The prices of homes come to have a premium which reflects some of the future MRT and possible inflation tax to be collected over time. (In principle a limiting factor with respect to this premium should be the possibility of collecting MRT or inflation tax on other assets, for example, equity in enterprises which have considerable net borrowing outstanding, but we ignore this theoretical possibility for our present purpose). Thus, cash buyers of homes may find they are paying a premium for an advantage they do not in fact collect. But they are still likely to be content in many cases by gaining apparent exemption from inflation and monetary repression tax (less real than apparent if houses prices form a large premium to reflect this advantage). They can also look forward to large capital gains if any of the various stories about the housing market come true.

Given all these potential benefits, can a family borrow too much? Ultimately, if a family's holding of all assets considered together, including the home, is financed by heavy debt, that implies an elevated level of risk. Individuals can mitigate this by concentrating their asset holdings in what they consider as low risk equities and real estate (though there is no magic formula—they may be right or wrong on this). Many people may have a mortgage on their home and hold a portfolio of equities in companies some of which are leveraged but they may still have sufficient holdings of safe assets to reduce risk substantially. Their decision to have a mortgage is just part of a more general calculation as to how much to be invested in risk-assets as against safe assets. A high rate of monetary taxation logically drives them towards being prepared to pay a higher price for risk-assets exempted from MRT and inflation tax, housing included.

Note that a high rate of monetary taxation may induce individuals to raise leverage either by having more net debt outstanding relative to their holdings of pure equity and real estate risk or by reducing their net long position in safe bonds (netting out the borrowings of corporations in which they hold equity). But in aggregate how can everyone do this—if one group of people wants to increase their debt outstanding relative to assets, another group has to be moving in the opposite direction, surely? Here comes the illusion of illusions! If monetary inflation is indeed driving up the valuation of assets across a wide spectrum then it is possible for some individuals on the one hand to believe they are reducing the ratio of lending in their overall portfolio (where this is valued at market prices) while actually raising this in absolute terms; and simultaneously some individuals who previously had no borrowing outstanding can now introduce leverage into their portfolios. Moreover, some individuals (and institutions) would regard their build-up of risky-lending as in part proofed against monetary taxation in that the credit risk premium element in returns is free from this.

As in much of practical finance, these calculations based on theoretical analysis only go so far. Many individuals focus in error on each asset component separately including housing and the potential for gains there from leverage, when they should be looking at the overall risk of their portfolio as a whole. Others are just not involved directly in equity investment and housing is the dominant portfolio component.

As regards real estate itself, two aspects are critical in assessing whether it is proof against monetary taxation and indeed whether it provides scope to share in the revenues—the timing of sales/purchases and the supply of land. There comes a point where the premium on housing to reflect the tax advantages (avoidance of MRT and IT, possible collection of both) becomes so large that for newcomers there is no advantage to be gained. The outcome varies across zones depending crucially on whether the supply of land is fixed or elastic with respect to price rises. If we are in a zone where at the margin there is plenty of new land available, then the result of widespread buying to collect tax advantages will be to increase the supply of housing rather than its price. There could be greater residential space availability (including constructions on top of the land) here as a result of the monetary inflation. Correspondingly there could be some fall in near-term residential rents—an ostensible advantage to consumers (albeit at the level of society as a whole costly if the fall reflects overallocation of capital and labour to the creation of residential space).

By contrast, at the other extreme, where space is highly inelastic with respect to price, monetary inflation under the conditions described induces large price gains. There may, however, be some elasticity of supply of residential space over time due to structures being built higher. (Some would say, admittedly, space provided through elevation and multi-dwelling construction is inferior to the space in a self-contained home, so there may still be a considerable effective price rise). The higher prices induced by the flight from MRT and IT may not go along with increases in rents—that depends on how much home owners in their flight crowd out home renters.

The capital gains on residential space enjoyed by individuals or families in areas where supply is inelastic form part of the illusion of wealth under monetary inflation. The capital gains partly reflect the premium against implicit taxes whose emergence is captured by owners who bought at the right time. But even for them, in so far as they are occupying the space themselves, the gain is not a source of prosperity—unless the individuals or families are intending to downsize their living space requirements in the future (and then in the total picture there will be a loss for the person who is upsizing on the alternative side of the deal). Investors in real estate who are collecting rent, rather than occupying the property themselves, feel better off if they were in at the start, but going forward they often find that the rental income as a percentage of capital outlay declines. In that sense, they are worse off.

Infectious Myths

Speculative stories and myths about real estate are infectious. A headline story about "booming US residential real estate", for example, may turn out to be true only of some regions or some types of property; or news about a boom driven by foreign buyers may turn out to be based on retelling the same anecdotal stories about a flow of purchases which is tiny compared to the outstanding stock. It is a myth that buoyant house prices signal general prosperity. Perhaps the biggest myth of all is that owning property offers protection against monetary taxation. As we have tried to explain, this is not necessarily true—it all depends. There are capital gains taxes, purchase taxes (equivalent to turnover taxes), as well as local and state estate taxes and inheritance taxes—any rational tax hedge calculation should take all of these into account, not just monetary repression and inflation tax avoidance. In fact, real estate can be a tax trap; it cannot be hidden or otherwise shrunk when it comes to inspections by the tax assessor.

The total stock of US housing in 2020 was worth in excess of $36 trillion, say 170 per cent of GDP ($21 trillion), compared to total value of publicly traded US equities of around $50 trillion and total value of US commercial real estate of around $18 trillion (90 per cent of US GDP). By comparison the global stock of above ground gold of around $10 trillion is under 50 per cent of US GDP. By value as much as two thirds of this housing stock is owner-occupied. Asset inflation creates extra illusions of wealth on owner-occupied housing compared to those on other assets including equities.

One general point: as discussed above, much of the value of real estate reflects land scarcity in certain highly desirable areas. Ownership of property in such areas enables residents to avoid the costs associated with urban concentration while gaining the benefits. For example, residential ownership in the city centre may spare the owner from the costs and inconvenience of commuting while bringing within reach the benefits of cultural and education activities plus top medical care. If these benefits could be enjoyed without huge concentrations of population, then the relevant land values would fall. So high real estate values are not in themselves symptomatic of high prosperity; rather they could reflect mainly the scope for reducing for the individual the unpleasant aspects (included crowded conditions) of urbanisation. At present, many individuals find that the benefits of huge urban agglomerations are not offset by the costs, especially if they are in residential space where these are low. If there were ways in which these benefits could be enjoyed without so much cost (through more advanced technology, perhaps), this would be an improvement of the human condition, and real estate values would fall.

Next, as argued above, if real estate prices rise due to land scarcity—whether induced by broad real economic factors or changed pattern of regional/local demand—then the "in at the start" home owner is not as well off as a simple capital gains calculation suggests. If the owner decides to go on occupying the same space and for a long time ahead, then he or she will pay cumulatively much more imputed rent than previously; those payments of imputed rent should be offset against capital gains in determining whether he or she is better off in consequence of the land shortage.

Yet there is little pushback against bad money policies despite their potential (and often actual) highly negative implications for several broad categories of space users whether as home owners or home renters. Perhaps experience is just so varied and the population impacted in such differing ways and to such varying degrees that no unified outcry is heard. Home owners with large mortgages may consider that they are net beneficiaries in terms of collecting monetary repression tax and inflation tax themselves. Although the calculation is dubious in the case of land-restricted supplies (as we have shown above) large mortgage holders would not, however, welcome a decline in MRT or IT as then they would lose the benefits of their high leverage at the same time as capital values could fall. That is how households with large outstanding mortgages or other debts in relation to their assets become allies of government in the provision of bad money.

Take-Aways

1. Bad money facilitates asset price booms that have no basis in underlying economic prosperity—and indeed in the longer-term impoverish society, but benefit many parties including officials.
2. One important and largely neglected component of state finance comes from losses imposed on residents under conditions of monetary inflation. This is down to the levying of monetary taxation (inflation tax and monetary repression tax). The government is the net collector of these taxes.
3. Within the private sector entities and individuals pay and collect monetary taxation to or from each other. This is a zero-sum game; some are gainers, others are losers. Individuals who are net borrowers and net holders of real assets enjoy wealth gains which have nothing to do with general prosperity; individuals who are net lenders (and this includes a silent majority of small savers) are losers.
4. The rise in wealth produced via a rising premium price on assets that seem to escape monetary taxation is fundamentally illusory; yes, the long-time holders make gains, as the tax premium increases—but by the same token the prospective rate of return on such assets falls. The stream of future income is based on a higher price—and that premium itself could narrow from its hyper-elevated level. In fact, it is possible that the stream of income falls: a build-up of physical capital is stimulated by the lowered

cost of equity capital (taking account of the tax premium) and so its return at the margin falls.

5. In an age of monetary inflation there is deep and pervasive uncertainty about the long-run outlook for money, prices, output and employment. This results from the corruption of market (price and interest rate) signals, a strengthening of monopoly power (which restricts investment and impedes entry of new entrepreneurs into a market), and investors chasing momentum strategies based on financial engineering. Investors often eschew putting money into economic activities and opportunities requiring long gestation before achieving their full potential given huge monetary uncertainties and the danger that asset inflation might turn to asset deflation in the meantime.

6. Owning residential real estate is not a sure-fire way of evading these taxes. Rising real estate values create powerful illusions of prosperity that may endure for a long time but do not necessarily indicate that society is better off.

7. The levying of these hidden taxes depends on the power of officials to manipulate interest rates.

References

Brown, Brendan and Simonnot, Philippe. (2020). Europe's Century of Crises Under US dollar hegemony. Palgrave.

Brown, Brendan. (2019). Review: Narrative Economics: How Stories Go Viral and Drive Major Economic Events. The Quarterly Journal of Austrian Economics Vol.22 November, pp. 620–627.

David Autor, David Dorn, Laurence Kar, Christine Patterson, John van Reenan. (2020). Quarterly Journal of Economics (February).

Kahneman, Daniel. "Thinking Fast and Slow." 2012.

Malkiel, Bernard. (2019). A Random Walk Down Wall Street.

Munk, Bernard. "Disorganized Crimes." Palgrave 2013.

Shiller, Robert. (2013). Finance and the Good Society, Princeton University Press.

Shiller, Robert. (2019). Narrative Economics: How Stories Go Viral and Drive Major Economic Events. Princeton University Press.

7

Exposing the State Concept of Money

The Story and Argument in Brief

Running through monetary history and inescapably entwined in current debates are two great and incompatible concepts of money—the classical versus the state. In this chapter, we show how these concepts emerged, how they struggled for dominance and how the state school won. Today, the state school sets the intellectual framework in which monetary affairs are discussed and monetary policy made. It underlies the current monetary regime. It makes the regime appear legitimate, even natural. But that's an illusion. The classical school had deeper insight into the nature and functions of money. If our economies and societies are to be redeemed from their parlous condition, we have to expose the flaws in the dominant theory of money.

The Dominant State Theory

This usual story asserts that money gains value from the say-so of the state that issues it; "fiat", used to denote any money that is not backed by a commodity or real asset, derives from the Latin, "let it be". It is an order. On this view, money is like defence, law, police and education—a responsibility of the state. To provide money is a duty of the state and can only be delegated within narrow limits—as in delegation of some powers to the central bank. On this view, only a medium of payment sanctioned by the state is money. During the nineteenth-century gold standard, gold was money. But

© The Author(s), under exclusive license to Springer Nature
Switzerland AG 2022
B. Brown and R. Pringle, *A Guide to Good Money*,
https://doi.org/10.1007/978-3-031-06041-0_7

even then, the state defined the monetary unit—for example, the pound—as so much weight of gold. In some countries, including in particular the US and Prussia, the state demonetised silver en route to awarding gold prime place as money (see McMaken, 2022). According to advocates of the state theory, bank deposits created by banks in the course of their business were not money until the state recognised them as such. Such recognition took the form of the state accepting payment of taxes or fees in these and of course the state helped to "monetise" bank deposits by providing lender of last resort facilities. Liabilities of other non-bank financial institutions are not money. Again the state theorists maintain that privately issued "monies" such as cryptocurrencies are not money unless and until sanctioned as money officially. Gold is not money because it is not recognised as such by the state.

The first economist to lay out this theory was the German Friederick Knapp, with his book "The state theory of money" (1905). Money is a creature of the state, whose role is to uphold the law, decide what it will accept to discharge debts against itself and enforce its will on its citizens. Knapp compares money to tickets, stamps and tokens, which also have no intrinsic value but derive their meaning and value from the law. He concludes that political action of the State is the source of money's meaning. This notion was not completely new. Indeed, it may be found even in Adam Smith (1776, 256). On Money, he writes: "A prince who should enact that a certain proportion of his taxes should be paid in a paper money of a certain kind might thereby give a certain value to this paper money, even though the term of its final discharge and redemption should depend altogether upon the will of the prince." Knapp points out that the state "is not, in fact, bound by its laws, which it only maintains for its subjects: from time to time it of itself creates new rights and obligations to meet the facts administratively, and perhaps afterwards changes the law to make it correspond" (Knapp, 1905, UK edition 1924, 106–7). So in the end, the administration pays out a certain money and accepts it for payments to itself—whatever the law says! This is the power of the state, overriding every private interest that is not represented inside it. The emergence of a currency is hence due to the activity and interests of the state. This approach dominated monetary thinking and practice in the twentieth century. As Keynes remarked: "We are all Knappians now". The logic of the theory is still working itself out in the twenty-first century. This chapter and the next tell the story.

The application of this theory gives the state sweeping powers over money and thus over society. Its apologists say this flexibility is essential to let central state institutions adjust the supply of money to society's needs. We will show however that the state theory of money easily leads to a regime of bad money.

Admittedly, it need not do so. The advent of a bad money regime can be postponed and its arrival will be camouflaged. Central banks aim to uphold people's trust, as described in Chapter 1. When bad money takes hold, it is, however, very hard to dislodge. This is because it gets embedded in society and people's habits. It accustoms people to seek short-term returns, enhances the temptation for companies to build up excessive debt and feeds asset bubbles. These are tell-tale symptoms of the malady. Gradually, money starts to shed its functions; it becomes a poor store of value, and as the disease progresses merchants begin to quote prices in other currencies. In its last stage, it serves merely as a medium of payment. It loses those attributes that make it desirable. And yet any money, however bad its quality, is better than none.

The Dormant Classical Theory

The classical theory may be almost forgotten today but it has a superior intellectual pedigree. It goes back to Aristotle and was championed by thinkers such as John Locke, the philosopher who laid the intellectual foundations of political liberalism, and economists such as David Ricardo, JS Mill, WS Jevons, von Mises, FAHayek, Milton Friedman and Karl Brunner. According to classical theory, money gains value from forces or powers operating independently of the state—typically by the use of a precious metal, with intrinsic value in the market, as money. Although states latch onto money in their own interests (by putting the head of the monarch on coins, for example), money is described as emerging naturally from long periods of social interaction. Such thinkers understood that money facilitates a vast expansion of commerce. It is viewed as belonging to the community. States as well as individuals are subject to it as an impartial, objective standard. Thus, the only way for societies to get the most value out of money is first for citizens voluntarily to submit to this standard (in the sense of treating it with such respect as to regard it as guiding action to serve communal interests). Of course, given its universal desirability and acceptability, it can be abused by powerful governments and interest groups. But this concept provides a more secure basis for thinking about money and a more natural foundation on which to build a good monetary regime than to view it as the creature of state law.

John Locke gave a classic exposition and elaboration at the end of the seventeenth century: money should be a natural extension of a man's property rights and civil liberties. It needed protection from state interference. If money was merely an attribute of the rights of the monarchy, the sovereign power, then the individual would live "merely at the mercy of the Prince". Locke, like Aristotle 2,000 years earlier, was aware that money was a social convention—an invention that had been adopted through social custom. He did not need to wait for modern sociologists to tell him that it could act as a divisive agent; indeed, he was ambivalent about the morality of the new commercial, money-obsessed, society he saw growing up around him. But given the overriding need to constrain the arbitrary power of the government, money should be treated *as if it were* part of nature. The idea that a coin could retain its value despite losing 20% of its silver content just because the state stamped it with the same nominal value was an abomination. It would be like lengthening a foot by dividing it into 15 parts instead of 12 and calling them all "inches". Thus, it was essential that a pound was regarded as consisting of a certain weight in precious metal (silver in his day): "the quantity of silver established under the several denominations . . . should not be altered till there was an absolute necessity shown of such a change, which I think can never be" (Locke 1695), and that once the standard metallic alloy of coins has been settled, it "should be inviolably and immutably kept to perpetuity" (Locke 1691). Only such a standard would put it beyond the reach of meddling politicians and even of the sovereign. Whether it was a "myth" or not, only universal respect for money as an inviolable standard could preserve men's property. It would be immoral and deeply subversive of social order if the government were allowed to declare that the pound had been devalued—all creditors would immediately lose money through no fault of their own. Debtors would gain as they would not have to repay the original sum in real money. But this is exactly what had been happening in England at the time with mass clipping and melting down of silver coins. In his turn, 100 or so years after Locke, David Ricardo insisted on the need for "an object in nature" to which the monetary standard itself could be referred. Equally, JS Mill thought that the value of money was determined independently of its use as money.

America's Foundational Money

Such were the ideas about money that were realised in the founding acts of the US. The first President, Washington, ordered that the value of the standard should be "invariable and universal". James Madison, fourth president and another founding father, declared paper money to be "unconstitutional" because a depreciating currency "affects the rights of property as much as taking away equal value in land". Thomas Jefferson, third president and main author of The Declaration of Independence, wrote in 1784: "If we determine that a dollar shall be our unit, we must then say with some precision what a dollar is". Jefferson equally insisted that money should provide a dependable and unchanging standard. Alexander Hamilton, who would be the first US Treasury Secretary, declared that "to emit an unfunded paper as the sign of value ought not to constitute a formal part of the Constitution, not ever hereafter to be employed, being, in its nature, pregnant with abuses...." No surprise then that the authority over money granted to Congress by the US Constitution of 1788 is strictly limited. The authority given under Article 1, Section 8, "to coin money, regulate the value thereof, and of foreign coin, and fix the standards of weights and measures" means precisely specifying its metal content. This was accomplished by the Coinage Act passed by Congress on 2 April 1792. This legislation laid out in detail the specification of America's coins. Each dollar should contain 371.25 grains of pure silver and a coin equal to ten dollars (or units) was to be struck out of 247.50 grains of pure gold. Any debasement by officers of the Mint shall be punishable by death. This is very clear that the Founders had a rigid interpretation of the limited money powers granted to government by the Constitution.

In short, US money was intended to provide a standard of value as dependable and constant as the official weights and measures it would likewise adopt. Individual states were forbidden from making "anything but gold and silver coin" as tender in payment of debts" (See Shelton 2011). As a matter of historical record, these constitutional guardrails did not eventually prevent the ascendancy of the statist theory of money in the US. First, there was the issuing of paper money (greenbacks) unbacked by gold or silver during the Civil War and its aftermath; when this was challenged before the Supreme Court, with President Lincoln's Treasury Secretary Chase by then duly promoted to Chief Justice, it ruled in favour of the government's actions. Later, when the New Deal's executive orders and related legislation nationalising gold and abrogating gold clauses came under legal challenge, the Supreme Court ruled 5–4 in favour of these actions.

Mill on the Dangers of Bad Money

Nobody put it better than the Victorian champion of liberalism, JS Mill. He emphasised the dangers of depreciation: "There is no way in which a general and permanent rise of prices, or in other words, depreciation of money, can benefit anybody, except at the expense of somebody else" (this and subsequent quotations are from Mill, 1848).

While an issue of notes is clearly a gain to the issuers, all holders of currency lose, by the depreciation of its value, the exact equivalent of what the issuer gains. A tax is virtually levied on them for his benefit. Some people might say that gains are also made by the producers and dealers who, by means of the increased issue of notes, are accommodated with loans. However, this was "not an additional gain, but a portion of that which is reaped by the issuer at the expense of all possessors of money". Mill points out the general corruption this process causes. Besides the benefit reaped by the issuers, or by others through them, at the expense of the public generally, there is another unjust gain obtained by a larger class, namely by those who have debts fixed in terms of money:

"All such persons are freed, by a depreciation of the currency, from a portion of the burden of their debts or other engagements: in other words, part of the property of their creditors is gratuitously transferred to them. On a superficial view it may be imagined that this is an advantage to industry; since the productive classes are great borrowers, and generally owe larger debts to the unproductive (if we include among the latter all persons not actually in business) than the unproductive classes owe to them; especially if the national debt be included". And this, says Mill sarcastically, might be regarded as an advantage, "if integrity and good faith were of no importance to the world, and to industry and commerce in particular". Not many people however, would assert that the currency ought to be depreciated "on the simple ground of its being desirable to rob the national creditor and private creditors of a part of what is in their bond". With an inconvertible currency, there is no check on the increase (if permitted by law). The issuers may add to it indefinitely, lowering its value and raising prices in proportion; they may, in other words, depreciate the currency without limit. Such a power, in whomsoever vested, is "an intolerable evil":

> All variations in the value of the circulating medium are mischievous: they disturb existing contracts and expectations, and the liability to such changes renders every pecuniary engagement of long date entirely precarious. The person who buys for himself, or gives to another, an annuity of £100 does not know whether it will be equivalent to £200 or to £50 a few years hence. Great as this evil would be if it depended only on accident, it is still greater when placed at the arbitrary disposal of an individual or a body of individuals....

Mill remarks that the issuers may have, and in the case of a government paper, always have, a direct interest in lowering the value of the currency, because it is the medium in which their own debts are computed. This is why society needs the precious metals:

To secure the value of the currency from being altered by design, and as little as possible liable to fluctuation from accident, the articles least liable of all known commodities to vary in their value, the precious metals, have been made in all civilized countries the standard of value for the circulating medium; and no paper currency ought to exist of which the value cannot be made to conform to theirs.

But a still stronger consideration, says Mill, is the importance of adhering to a simple principle, intelligible even to the less-educated. Everybody can understand convertibility; everyone sees that what can be at any moment exchanged in the market for five pounds is actually worth five pounds. There are therefore many reasons in favour of a convertible, in preference to even the best regulated inconvertible currency. Above all, "The temptation to over-issue, in certain financial emergencies, is so strong, that nothing is admissible which can tend, in however slight a degree, to weaken the barriers that restrain it".

Mill anticipates the plausible arguments that would be advanced in favour of discretionary policy:

Although no doctrine in political economy rests on more obvious grounds than the mischief of a paper currency not maintained at the same value with a metallic, either by convertibility, or by some principle of limitation equivalent to it; and although, accordingly, this doctrine has, though not till after the discussions of many years, been tolerably effectually drummed into the public mind; yet dissentients are still numerous, and projectors every now and then start up, with plans for curing all the economical evils of society by means of an unlimited issue of inconvertible paper.

He recognises that there is, in truth, a "great charm" in the idea of monetary manipulation:

To be able to pay off the national debt, defray the expenses of government without taxation, and in fine, to make the fortunes of the whole community, is a brilliant prospect, when once a man is capable of believing that printing a few characters on bits of paper will do it. The philosopher's stone could not be expected to do more.

As such projects, however often they are exposed as shams, always resurface, it is always desirable to expose the fallacies by which the schemers attempt to impose such currencies on the public.

What is the State's Proper Role?

True, to re-attach an actual fiat money to a material anchor, such as gold, would be an act of state. It cannot now be represented as a natural accompaniment of an existing "primordial" state of affairs. At a stretch, the move could be presented as a return to system in tune with a primordial state of affairs after a very long and chaotic interlude. Alternatively, we could imagine the emergence of a private monetary use of gold acting as the stepping stone to gold money again becoming prominent at the level of society as a whole. As outlined elsewhere in this volume (see Chapters 4, 12 and 14), banks and other financial institutions could market gold deposits in some cases (the most secure) backed 100% by gold with balances settled between them in a gold clearing house; the same institutions could also market digital gold backed 100% by gold. In practice, however, for this to happen, the state would have to remove the regulations, taxes and restrictions which inhibit this happening at present.

Yes, the state has a vital role in securing the foundations of a free society, including maintaining the rule of law, the enforcement of contracts, the definition of property rights and anti-monopoly policies. These are prior conditions for private sector markets to flourish and necessary towards building social harmony among citizens. We do not advocate a "free-for-all" version of libertarianism. Also, social and monetary order in which individuals enjoy freedom under the law, like civilisation itself, are fragile plants. They need support of social norms of tolerance, sympathy and benevolence, i.e. people of wisdom and goodwill. Some of us lost sight of these during the era of so-called neoliberalism. But the state should be kept within constitutional boundaries. This is the perspective from which John Locke propounded his case for monetary integrity. It is a natural accompaniment of a good constitution with separation of powers, as illustrated in England's great settlement of 1689 and the US Constitution of 1790.

A good money constitution reinforces this beneficial separation of powers and serves to limit the arbitrary power of governments. That is another reason for seeing it in moral terms—members of a society should support it as desirable and necessary for a good society, beyond being merely efficient in fulfilling monetary functions. Only then will they be sufficiently on the alert to detect moves that may undermine it; only then will they be able to appeal above the heads of the schemers and manipulators to a public sensitised to protecting the general interest as distinct from their own private interests. It is true, however, that good constitutions cannot always protect a good money system against a determined despot or Big Government with its network of cronyist links to powerful private interests including banks. Can a myth be revived?

One common objection to resurrecting the idea of money as a standard linked to a commodity such as gold is that, historically, any achievements that it had rested on a myth—the myth, or rather pretence, that a precious metal (silver in Locke's day, gold in the nineteenth century) is itself money, and linked to this the idea it is sacrosanct. The argument is that such a "myth" (the idea that money is by nature gold), once demolished, cannot be artificially resuscitated. It is dead and buried. Or is it? One answer to this is that it has been revived in the past. Indeed, John Locke's classic exposition came against the background of frequent debasements, bankruptcies and tampering with the coinage by royal prerogative. Merchants at the time fully expected such a "flexible" standard to continue—so they could go along for the ride. They were outraged when the British government accepted Locke's view. But Locke understood that it was an unavoidable implication of his theory of constitutional government. The control of arbitrary power, rule of law and social order depended on the sovereign also being subject to rules. Only in this way could money serve its social functions a bridge between classes and generations.

To be sure, creditors liked the good money as described by Locke and Mill. It protected them from continual losing out to debtors, including powerful debtors such as the state. No financial system can fulfil its economic functions well without the trust of creditors. When depositors, investors or lenders commit their money, they are at risk of losing it. They can lose it basically for either or both of two reasons:

a. the borrower does not pay it back as the income stream out of which the debt was to be serviced (interest and repayment of principal) fails to materialise (in the case of government, this income stream includes hidden forms of monetary taxation);
b. the money in which they made the loan—say, the pound sterling—loses its value or even becomes worthless. Unless they are forced to do so, people will not put their own money at risk unless the value, the standard, of the money is itself expected to be "stable". (For some, "stable" may mean permanent "low inflation" matched by nominal interest rates which "discount" such stable inflation expectations). Even modern states pretend to accept this. In practice, we all know how this has ended up.

Locke's call for a fixed monetary standard, reflected in the US Constitution, and reinforced by Mill and others, reaches some of us still. But it has become muffled. His spirit lacks the clout that he carried in life.

The Theories Compared

In modern monetary systems, where fractional reserve banking and related legal flaws are pervasive, along with lenders of last resort, too big to fail and deposit insurance, as we saw in previous chapters the constituents of high-powered money (monetary base) have largely lost any super-money quality which is the basis of their enjoying strong, broad and stable demand. This is a natural accompaniment of the view, according to which the unit of account (what is a pound, euro or dollar) is and has always been defined by a state or other competent authority. Keynes insisted that the unit of account function is the primary concept of a theory of money. Even commodities, when used as money, have to bear a fixed relation to the standard, and it is the state that decides the rate (e.g. the state decides how much gold equals a pound). The monetary standard established by that ratio is an abstraction produced by human imagination or consciousness. Whereas, for statists, value is given to money from the top and trickles down, under the classical, liberal view value swells up from below, from the people as and when they decide that they want to hold it. In principle, money could be wholly private, with issuers competing for custom based on trust, skill, and satisfying customers (for example as regards preference of coin sizes, type of notes and geographic location for clearing houses and mints).

Thus the state theory diverges radically from the classical. Instead of elevating money into a standard of invariant value—mythical or not—state theorists draw the inference that, once established, money is just another public utility set up by governments for the general interest as defined by them. Hence, the idea emerges that the public should be allowed just the right amount of money, not too much and not too little. This "heterodox" theory is carried forward in the twenty-first century by advocates of Modern Monetary Theory, which argue that governments spend money into existence and that "the value of taxes gives value to money". Governments are in command. Modern money is "backed" by a state's "enforceable tax debts"; it can coerce citizens into paying taxes. This power ensures that every taxpayer needs its money or risk being sent to prison. "Taxes drive money" (Wray 2012). This mechanism gives value not only to the money that the state issues but also to the money created by commercial banks in its domain.

This accompanies a corresponding difference in their respective ideas of what is involved in a monetary transaction. Is it the settlement of a debt or does it involve handing over something of value in exchange for a good or service? The state view, which corresponds closely to what is often called the credit view of money, is that it is the first—settlement of a debt. These two concepts are linked to two incompatible theories of banking. On the commodity view, banks are intermediaries connecting borrowers and savers. On the credit theory, banks are creators of money as the loans they make become money as deposits in the accounts of customers, which are in turn claims on banks. On this view, terms such as "monetary disorder" are misleading. Deflation and inflation are products of a disorder of the state and/or in the rules about monetary policy. These in turn are the outcome of a power struggle for control over money, notably between creditors who wish to make it scarce, even at the cost of a damaging deflation, and debtors who prefer a plentiful supply even at the risk of inflation. There is no single, correct answer to the question: "How much money is too much?" It all depends on a shifting balance of power. On this reading, a good money regime is the product of a stable state. Hence, the adage: "Inflation is everywhere and at all times a political phenomenon".

Was There a Golden Age of State Money?

Just as advocates of a gold standard look back to the decades before the First World War, which facilitated the first age of economic globalisation, so statists look back nostalgically to a period they regard as a Golden Age between 1945 and the 1970s. During those years, across much of the Western world, the role of creditors and money markets in channelling capital resources was checked by state controls. Money was seen as a tool of government policy—no more and no less. At last, national governments could set interest rates at a level designed to stimulate activity and employment rather than being bound by "golden fetters". If necessary, interest rates in one country could vary from those in the outside world; financial markets were suppressed by rigid rules governing what banks could do; physical controls limited capital movements, exchange rates could only be changed by international agreement and the allocation of bank credit was guided by central government. The way was thus cleared, according to the statists, for expansionary fiscal policies to secure full employment. This period saw what they, the statists, viewed as a proper balance between markets and state, creditors and borrowers and adequate social control over the production of money. In fact, it required the forcible suppression of markets. The US was a partial exception to this in allowing greater freedom for money markets though even here a panoply of restrictions left over from the 1930s kept banks and finance institutions in separate compartments under supervision.

Supposedly, this "Golden Age" broke down in the 1970s because power over money was taken away from governments and shifted to banks and money markets. The statists blame excessive and unwise bank lending for triggering multiple financial crises and inflation. They claim that the attempt to combat this by a "monetarist" experiment limiting the supply of money predictably failed because the quantity of money is determined mainly by bank lending ("loans create deposits") which was free of official controls. Money is hard to define precisely, they said (ignoring the reasons we have advanced in this volume—see Chapters 1 and 2—why it had lost its distinctiveness). Finally, the statists continue, governments, rather than leave money as the plaything of markets saw no alternative to setting a credible commitment to controlling inflation—notably through granting central banks a degree of independence and a mandate to pursue price stability. (There is much falsehood and inaccuracy in this storytelling by the statists; we give our account of the story of modern money in Chapter 8).

In reality, the so-called golden age of state money was an age of state planning, credit rationing, artificially low interest rates, an uncompetitive financial sector and many restrictions on personal liberty; through much of the 1960s and 1970s, for example, Britons were allowed to take a maximum of £50 when travelling abroad—to cover all lodging, meals and entertainment costs; the figure was entered into your passport.

Time to Ditch the State Concept

In sum, advocates of the The State Theory of Money are intellectual and political pygmies compared with the giants of the classical school. The latter knew full well the dangers of inconvertible money. They warned us off it and the founders of the US insisted that the dollar be defined as weights of gold and silver—a foundation of the constitution of the new independent country. Yet their warnings have been cast aside. Instead, the world has adopted a concept of money that has been and continues to be used as a cover for mistakes causing great damage. It provides a false air of legitimacy to monetary regimes that have repeatedly resulted in money losing value much more rapidly and completely than any metal-based money ever has and that have presided over vast asset market inflations which end in

Crash and Great Recession with devastating economic, social and political consequences. The greatest avoidable monetary disasters in history have occurred under fiat money regimes or under quasi-gold standard regimes heavily distorted by state intervention (an example of the latter which haunts twentieth-century history and beyond is the Fed-led monetary inflation of the 1920s coupled with its follow-on implications for monetary conditions in the Weimar Republic—as discussed in the next chapter). More examples are produced frequently—almost every year it seems there is another Zimbabwe, Venezuela, Argentina.

Why then do economists now generally embrace the statist theory? One answer is simply to say that we live in a world of nation-states and that such a theory fits that environment. In practical terms, it gives economists and editorialists status and influence—official manipulation of interest rates makes those that set short-term rates in their "monetary policy committees" (MPCs) into rulers of the financial universe, inside players in "the only game in town". Many are also politically naive. Supporters of state theory assume far too lightly that democratic states will remain politically stable despite letting loose destructive *tsunamis* of money. In reality, policies adopted under cover of the state theory of money weaken the liberal-democratic foundations of the states that pursue them. Despite efforts to protect society from the ravages of unfettered discretion by giving central banks mandates to pursue objectives with a degree of independence, this concept of money promotes greater concentration of power. It opens the highways for insider trading, front running, crony capitalism, monopoly capitalism and all manner of abuses. The very weakness of the current 2% inflation standard facilitates the continuation of ultimately destabilising monetary policies and inhibits any pullback from these. Some members of the so-called monetary policy committees may at some point favour a pullback but would seldom voice such a recommendation—perhaps fearful of bringing the whole debt-laden edifice down, a collapse of markets and deep recession or perhaps just cynically out of self-interested loyalty to the president, prime minister and/or parliamentarians who together appointed them. In summary, fiat money regimes lower barriers to monetary debasement and raise the likelihood that the production of money will be abused by overmighty private interests (see Chapter 10).

References

Knapp, F (1905, UK edition 1924), The State Theory of Money.
McMaken, Ryan (2022) "Why did the World Choose a Gold Standard instead of a Silver Standard?" Mises Wire, January 5.

Mill, J.S. (1848) Principles of Political Economy.

Shelton, Judy (2011) *Fixing The Dollar Now: Why US Money Lost Its Integrity and How We Can Restore It*, Atlas Economic Research Foundation.

Wray, L.R. (2012) *Modern Money Theory: A Primer on Macroeconomics for Sovereign Monetary Systems*, Palgrave Macmillan.

8

A Short History of Modern Money

It would be hyperbole to describe the collapse of the international gold standard at the outbreak of the First World War as Man's exit from the monetary Garden of Eden. Yet, we can make two observations. First, the gold standard was doomed, being incompatible with the politics of the twentieth century—with its world wars, communist revolutions and its nationalist and socialist ideologies, any one of which would have broken it. Democratic states had to try the experiment of managing money through central institutions and regulators. Second, in monetary terms what has come since has been on balance worse. Yes, there have been some bright interludes and fiat money has not prevented a great advance in living standards during the last 100 years as a whole, but promises of a better monetary future have ultimately proved hollow. The gold standard was destroyed by outside forces it could not control. Modern money is being destroyed from within.

Gold Standard's Record Re-Examined

We are not blind to the occurrence of monetary problems under the pre-World War I gold standard. There were bubbles and crashes galore; and there were sustained episodes during which goods markets experienced a moderate degree of monetary inflation or deflation.

On closer examination, however, many of the episodes of asset inflation followed by crisis were related to suppressions of the automatic mechanisms

© The Author(s), under exclusive license to Springer Nature
Switzerland AG 2022
B. Brown and R. Pringle, *A Guide to Good Money*,
https://doi.org/10.1007/978-3-031-06041-0_8

of the gold standard, interruptions in the gold standard's functioning and, in the US, endemic instability in the banking system originating in President Lincoln's banking legislation passed during the Civil War (see Rothbard 2010). Yes, we should mention the potential for internal flaws—the bunching of new gold discoveries or of mining technology advances on the one hand (promoting rapid growth in the money supply, or monetary inflation) or, on the other hand, excess demand for gold, often due to a large country joining the gold standard (indicating monetary deflation). But we have to go back to the gold imports from Latin America in the seventeenth century to find an epic example of asset inflation due to such potential flaws—then in the shape of the great bubbles in Amsterdam in the 1630s. And it is far from clear that the charge of global monetary deflation related to Germany adopting the gold standard in 1870 really sticks (see Chapter 12, p.).

Consider booms and busts during the period of the international gold standard starting with America's Great Panic of 1873. This had much more to do with the fact that the monetary inflation unleashed by the Civil War was coming to a close than sudden changes in the global demand for gold. The US was making its way back from the Greenback—the irredeemable paper issued during the Civil War—to gold. At the same time, the US simultaneously suspended the monetary role of silver whose price in global markets was already falling in response to Germany's move to gold in 1871 (while demonetising silver). Earlier, the railway bubble of the late 1860s had occurred under conditions of fiat money (Greenback) inflation.

Fast forward to the crash of 1893. This followed several years of monetary inflation as the Administration and Congress defied the constraints of the gold standard by embarking on a spending spree (the so-called "Billion Dollar Congress" of 1889–1891) while simultaneously placating the silver miners by passing the Sherman silver act of 1890 under which the government in effect bought silver with gold at a high floor price from Western producers. When the Cleveland administration came into power in early 1893, there were less than 100 m dollars of gold in the official reserves. The public had lost confidence in the capacity of the Treasury to honour its pledge to convert dollar banknotes into gold. As the new Administration cracked down (for example ending silver purchases), panic spread through the banking system where the previous monetary excesses had stimulated so much reckless lending. Banks called in loans, causing bankruptcies of banks, railroads, steel mills and many others. Unemployment rates soared to 20 per cent or more. This signalled the start of a long depression.

Then we come to the great boom and bust of 1907 again rooted in the US. The Treasury Secretary Leslie Shaw, appointed by President Teddy Roosevelt in 1902 (through to 1907) aimed to create a virtual central bank within the Treasury. So he deployed the large holdings of cash of the Federal Government in the banks to that end, exempting them from deposit requirements for this amount. By increasing the rate of monetary creation beyond what would have happened under the gold standard, this set the stage for the bubble that emerged in US asset markets up until 1906 (see Bruner and Carr 2007). The San Francisco earthquake of that year set off huge volatility in money, foreign exchange and credit markets. Background factors included growth in gold mining supplies amidst technological advance in the mining industry and new discoveries.

In general, the international gold standard era, which lasted from the early/mid-1870s to 1914, witnessed some periods of pervasive price decline and others of price increase. In some part, these were totally consistent with the pattern one should expect under sound money. For example, during the 1880s, prices were falling by 1 to 3 per cent annually. But this was a natural accompaniment of exceptionally rapid growth including rising productivity in the US economy, coupled with similar economic miracle in Continental Europe especially Germany, against a background of globalisation driven by early telegraphy and the steamship.

In short, many of the great panics came after periods of monetary/asset inflation which only occurred because the gold standard had been suspended or its rules suppressed/interfered with or due to the perennial instabilities of fractional/reserve banking with its flaws—particularly in the US.

The Advent of the Federal Reserve....

We come next to the era when the US was the only large country to remain on a full gold standard which included circulating gold coins—1918–1932. The period of US neutrality in World War I (up until March 1917) had seen massive inflows of gold into the US as Britain and France stripped their monies of their one-time gold backing by using gold to pay for huge armaments and other imports, notably from the US (see Brown and Simonnot 2020). The US money supply soared as the US Treasury/Fed purchased the gold and this in turn caused a surge of consumer as well as asset prices, led by a speculative boom in war stocks. By the end of the war, US reserves of gold were well in excess of what was required to back the supply of high-powered money (banknotes, bank reserves with the Federal Reserve) in accordance with the founding law of that new entity (which opened its doors in 1914).

So as peace dawned in 1919, the US was the only large country with its currency fully convertible into gold including gold coin. The Federal Reserve, with a surfeit of gold relative to legal requirements even despite rapid wartime inflation (extending back into the period of US neutrality)—explained by the huge sales of gold in the US by Britain and France to pay for munitions, etc.—had a considerable degree of freedom to steer monetary policy. This meant that the Fed could in effect decide on a path for monetary base growth or short-term interest rates intended to satisfy various policy objectives. These, it decided, would include stabilising prices in the short or medium term and supporting the stock market—aims that ran contrary to the spirit of the pre-1914 international gold standard.

....Stirs Asset Price Inflation

Indeed, over the decade 1919–1929, the Fed was to make ample use of its new discretionary power. Soon after the war, it tried to bring prices down, reversing in particular the further run-up of prices in the first year of peace. It raised its key "discount rates" sharply (from 4.75 to 7%), thus contributing to the Great Recession of 1920–1. This proved traumatic. The political push-back against that experience, critically in Congress (see Meltzer 2002), was so great as to turn the Fed from the early 1920s onwards into a price stabiliser. In particular, it fought against any tendency for prices to decline. That was, however, fatally destabilising for the "machinery of money", as it coincided with what was in effect a second industrial revolution; the period saw the rapid development in America of many new production techniques and a whole array of new products, with automobile mass assembly lines, electrification, radio, etc. This brought huge gains in productivity, while primary commodities' prices fell—due in part to a build-up of excess capacity around the world during the war.

Under a good money regime, prices would have been falling by 2–4% per annum through the 1920s. Instead, the Fed held down interest rates in the pursuit of stable prices. The new central bank carried out its novel interest rate policy (under the gold standard there was no such thing) by steering the supply of monetary base on a path which meant it was always veering ahead of underlying demand. "Steering" here meant episodes of large open market purchases of government paper so as to inject reserves into the banking system. These episodes fitted the objectives set by the de facto Fed policy chief, New York Fed President Benjamin Strong, over the decade included assisting recovery from the 1920/1921 recession, giving a helping hand to the struggling UK pound sterling, and giving a *coup de whiskey* in 1927 to Wall Street when the stock market seemed in danger of falling back. These objectives were used as justifications for low rates. The efforts to avoid any risk of "deflation" set the stage for an asset inflation of historic proportions, with red hot markets in US stocks and real estate. Cross-border capital flows (dominated by US lending) in search of apparently high yields, a characteristic of asset inflations, soared from 1925, including huge flows to Weimar Germany where a speculative boom emerged in the midst of an apparently miraculous economic expansion (*Wirtschaftswunder*) following the end of hyperinflation.

We conclude that between 1921 and 1928, the dollar was not a good money. And that had big consequences globally given that the US had emerged from the World War I as the dominant monetary power.

A Bad Scene in Europe

To get a full picture of the monetary scene in the aftermath of World WarI, we have to look also outside the US, where conventional opinion favoured a return to gold at the 1914 gold parities. But prices had everywhere risen substantially, while gold stocks (coin and bullion as held by the public or governments) in all the belligerent countries had dwindled, meaning that a far-reaching deflation would be required for a return. In Britain, as illustration, no serious thought was given to a possible alternative route to sound money—returning to gold at a higher official gold price (in terms of sterling). This alternative route was problematic in any case. Some modern estimates show that sterling's exchange rate by the mid-1920s was not far from so-called "purchasing power parity" with the dollar (see Gerlach and Kugler 2015). A devaluation of sterling (together with all those currencies in the world then pegged to sterling) such as would have enabled the UK to amass gold reserves to back a reincarnated gold pound via a huge balance of payments surplus would surely have exacerbated the protectionist tilt of US trade policies under Republican Administrations from 1920 onwards.

Anyhow in 1925, sterling "returned to the gold standard" at the pre-war parity, as conventional opinion expected, but the return was mythical. With the UK gold backing for the currency sorely depleted by wartime sales, sterling only became convertible into gold for 400 oz (12 kg) bars; there was no return to a full gold standard in which gold coin was the core of monetary circulation. In effect, we should think of sterling at that time as returning to its pre-war parity against the US dollar of around 4.80 dollars to the pound rather than as "returning to gold". And there was no political possibility of allowing the automatic mechanisms of gold (stunted in any case by the absence of gold coin circulation) to regain their force; the authorities completely avoided the logic of gold, failing to allow monetary conditions to tighten when gold and foreign exchange drained out. Instead, they pleaded with the US to ease monetary conditions. As in the US, though in a different form, we see here an early example of a "managed monetary regime".

In Germany, an international treaty (the Dawes Plan) in 1924 made the new currency created after the hyperinflation, the Reichsmark, convertible into the US dollar at a fixed exchange rate. Although there was an indirect link to gold in that dollars were fully convertible into gold, there was no effective market brake on the huge flows of capital into Germany as driven by US monetary inflation. To complete the picture, France moved to a gold bullion standard in 1926/1927, but only after the franc had been devalued to far below its pre-war parity (The new franc Poincaré was equal to one-fifth of the previous franc Germinal).

The Great Crash

The origins of the Crash of 1929 and the subsequent Great Depression are to be found in the monetary inflation led by the US through the 1920s. This was far from being an inevitable tragedy—there were several points when alternative monetary policies, especially in the US, could have averted it. An example was the action of the Fed in 1927 in sharply easing US monetary policy in response to a passing economic lull and a modest stock market pullback (and a plea for help from the Bank of England), despite the Reichsbank President imploring the US not to ease policy for fear of sparking new waves of capital into Germany (see Voth 2003). Then, there was the tightening of US monetary policy through 1928 and1929 ahead of the October Crash, an action that ignored warning signals in Germany (red flags that turned out to be crucial in what followed), as well as evidence of a US economic downturn (from August 1929) and the end of the domestic real estate boom (from late 1928).

From Autumn 1928, the German economy had already entered recession and was in political turmoil about the new proposal for settlement of war reparations (the Young Plan) as the Nazi Party mounted a propaganda campaign against any such deal. This unsettled US investors (including US banks) at the forefront of the international lending boom into Germany; a stop to capital inflows caused by a sharp tightening of US monetary policy could only make matters worse. Then, a German banking crisis during Spring and Summer 1931 culminated in a standstill on payments due by German institutions to foreign creditors; at the same time, the German government introduced exchange restrictions on outflows of capital. The UK authorities, confronted by a gold drain triggered by awareness of British banking exposure to Germany, suspended the gold bullion standard (July 31) and let sterling float sharply downwards against the gold currencies. This set off waves of speculation against the dollar, largely in the form of a gold drain (holders of dollars converting these into gold) driven by fear that the US might abandon the gold standard. In response to this, the Fed tightened monetary policy far beyond what was required by the actual US gold position where there was still adequate coverage (in legal terms) of Federal Reserve notes. The final straw, after an interim easing of US monetary conditions (including large-scale bond purchases by the Federal Reserve) in Spring and Summer 1932, was speculation through late 1932 and early 1933 that the new President elect (Roosevelt) would take the dollar off gold; this prompted a new abrupt tightening of US monetary policy.

So the proximate causes of the Great Depression were monetary policy mistakes driven by politics including alleged cronyist connections of Benjamin Strong with Wall Street institutions who were minting it in making loans to Germany and with Wall Street firms who stood to lose from a bursting of the bubble already in 1927 (Rothbard 2010). While society was no longer ready or able to follow the unyielding disciplines of gold, politics dictated that attempts should and would be made to restore the good money of the world before World War I. The climate of opinion and the simple fact that the European belligerents had sequestered then liquidated the gold backing to their monies so as to pay for the war constrained the freedom of action for alternative choices to be made.

The Monetary World After World War II

Fast forward to the new shape of dollar hegemony. After World War II, legislation in the US made full employment the aim of economic policy including the Fed's conduct of monetary policy. And the dollar remained inconvertible into gold for US citizens (banned from holding gold since 1933), although it was convertible for foreign monetary authorities at a fixed price ($35 per ounce) since 1934. Then in 1961, following the election of John Kennedy as President and his promise to end the stop–go policies of the previous decade by implementing Keynesian policies—the gold price in the London bullion market started to sporadically rise above this official price. This reflected growing demand by non-official entities (these did not have access to the US Treasury "gold window") and were surely influenced by the inflationary direction of US monetary policy. The revaluation of the Deutsche mark and Dutch guilder by 5% against the US dollar in March 1961 demonstrated that the US dollar was no longer unambiguously the safest monetary store of value. The leading central banks joined in a new arrangement to prevent such spikes in the gold price above its official level. This arrangement, described as the "Gold Pool", collapsed in March 1968.

In line with the Treaty obligations the US had assumed in setting up the Bretton Woods System as mentioned in Chapter 2, foreign central banks could present dollars and receive gold at $35 an ounce and there was a large rebalancing of official reserves with a rise in holdings of European countries as they recovered from World War II. Meanwhile, exchange controls widely prevented non-official entities and individuals from buying foreign currency or gold. In the world outside the US, exchange freedoms did increase through the 1950s. Canada abolished exchange restrictions and then floated its currency, and the Swiss franc remained free of restriction (except when subject to US freezing action during the war and its immediate aftermath), and then in the late 1950s, Germany removed all exchange controls. Other countries simultaneously abolished controls on current account transactions but maintained them on capital flows meaning that monetary conditions in their countries continued to have significant shelter from US monetary hegemony. In principle, US monetary conditions should have tightened in response to the rundown of US gold reserves and pressure on the official gold price so as to sustain the convertibility pledge but there is little evidence of Fed policy in the critical 1960s having such sensitivity (see Meltzer 2010).

Given the rapid productivity growth of the 1950s and 1960s, both in the US and even more so outside the US where economic miracles were occurring notably in Germany and Japan, under a sound dollar regime US prices of goods and services on average would indeed have been falling (matched by an expected tendency of prices to rise during far-off future periods of sub-par productivity growth whose timing was unknown). It gradually became apparent however that US monetary policy was not constrained by the ultimate convertibility pledge. Two per cent a year actual inflation in the second half of the 1950s, for example, reflected strong monetary inflation. Indeed during the 1950s as a whole, the Fed rode roughshod over the natural rhythm of prices (see glossary). This rhythm was surely already strongly downwards in the aftermath of the Korean War (1950–3) as resource shortages and other dislocations faded. The "Eisenhower boom" in the stock market had some embryonic characteristics of asset inflation but these did not develop fully. The natural rhythm downwards was not reflected in the actual course of consumer prices as the US money supply and the nominal value of output expanded strongly together from the mid-1950s on.

William McChesney Martin, the then Fed Chairman, became renowned for his dictum that the task of a central banker was to take away the punchbowl just when the party got exciting, although he was always rather late and abrupt in doing this, causing in the process three recessions within 10 years. This helped the Keynesians come to occupy during the 1960s the chief economic policy positions in the US, following the victory of President Kennedy's Democrats in the 1960 elections. Inflationary pressures rose further in the 1960s though this was not obvious in the goods and services markets until the middle of the decade; symptoms of asset inflation were evident earlier (see Brown 2017). Kennedy's tax cuts, signalling the political triumph of demand management, flattered only to deceive.

The remedy worked like a dream—or seemed to. Monetary inflation was, however, stronger than recorded goods and services inflation suggested, given the rapid productivity growth as described above (see concepts of "goods inflation" and "monetary inflation" in Glossary). Meanwhile, economic miracles were emerging overseas—first in Germany and Japan, followed by Italy and France. If we group these countries at the time as in a dollar zone overall prices should have been falling across this area as a whole—by more on average in the US than in these foreign countries. (It is an established hypothesis in growth economics—the so-called Balassa-Samuelson theorem—that countries in economic miracles almost always concentrated in export sectors will tend to have strong relative price rises in their so-called non-traded goods sectors (see Chong et al. 2010)). The economic policies of the Kennedy and Johnson administrations were, however, formulated by economists who believed they could achieve lower unemployment at the cost of only somewhat higher inflation, and they were determined to avoid the recessions and pullbacks of the 1950s—not to mention the horror of returning to the1930s. While Martin, the Fed Chief until 1970, was no Keynesian, these economists at the Federal Reserve Board influenced the "climate of opinion" there (see Meltzer 2010). Moreover, Martin did see it as his responsibility to help "contain" the cost of government financing—for him the Federal Reserve was "independent within government but not independent from government". This became a more critical issue when, following Kennedy's assassination in 1963, the Johnson administration increased government spending both for the Vietnam War and the Great Society reforms.

Asset inflation, whose symptoms were already building in the early 1960s (see Brown 2017) was duly followed by higher goods and services inflation. Strikingly this inflation gained strength through the second half of the 1960s without the fillip of currency depreciation or collapse. Historically, high inflations have often been led by currency depreciation (In terms of US experience, we can trace that observation back to the Civil War) (see Wesley Clair Mitchell). In this case, the dynamics of inflation included strong external as well as domestic demand in US goods and services markets as revved up by the monetary environment described throughout the dollar zone. Given the inexorable rise in goods and services prices, gold at the fixed price of $35 an ounce became increasingly cheap in real terms by any standard of historical comparison.

While dollar devaluation was not an original cause of the inflation, it came to the fore when President Nixon broke the residual US convertibility pledge to maintain the peg to gold in August 1971 (since 1968 there had been a free market gold price for non-official transactions) in an aggressive manner, imposing an import tariff whose removal was conditional on other countries revaluing their currencies. As a politician, the short-term needs of the domestic economy trumped any long-term rationale—hard to detect—in maintaining an international system that no longer seemed to demonstrably serve the US interest. Not least with the 1972 elections on the horizon, devaluation was preferred to disinflation. The so-called "Nixon shock" was followed by eighteen months of sustained US currency depreciation stage-managed by Paul Volcker who served as under-secretary of the Treasury for international monetary affairs from 1969 to 1974 (President Nixon's Treasury Secretary until 1972 was Democrat John Connally). According to his biographer, Volcker considered the suspension of gold convertibility, of which he approved, as "the single most important event of his career" (Silber 2013).

De Gaulle's Gold Play

Before reviewing the new phase in the history of dollar hegemony after 1971, and the challenges to it, we should note a previous challenge. This came from France in the mid-1960s when General De Gaulle, advised by Jacques Rueff, a monetary conservative, complained of America's abuse of monetary power and advocated a return in some form to gold as the base of the international monetary order. And in an important respect, gold did become more feasible as a base through this period and further ahead to the closing of the US gold window in August 1971. As the European governments of France, Germany and Italy, in particular, converted the dollar inflows during these years into their reserves into gold, the distribution of the yellow metal between them and the US became more equal relative to their size of monies than at any time since 1914. The depletion of gold holdings in Europe due to belligerent government sequestration during World War I was at last being rectified, courtesy of the US Treasury in keeping convertibility of the dollar for foreign central banks/governments. (More than courtesy here: in fact the US was selling the gold to the Europeans at an increasingly bargain price as calculated in dollars of constant purchasing power). It became possible to imagine, as Rueff did, that a new international gold order could be created at a revalued price of gold in terms of paper monies.

Rueff, De Gaulle and the Belgian economist Robert Triffin were all correct in pointing out the inherent deficiencies of the Bretton Woods System and in predicting its demise (The famous "Triffin dilemma" alleged a basic flaw in the system: the world depended on the extra liquidity injected though the US payments deficit as foreign countries built up their dollar assets but the counterpart to this—the growth of huge US short-term dollar foreign— liabilities gradually undermined confidence in the dollar; while if the US took action to eliminate its payments deficit, the world outside would suffer a contraction leading possibly to a depression). In the US, however, political support for strengthening the link between money and gold or in prolonging gold's role was weak. Anyhow, the student uprising of Spring 1968 in France ignited social and economic turmoil, ending De Gaulle's presidency and with it France's gold-plated defiance of the US. Germany, dependent on a US security guarantee in the context of Cold War, had no inclination to provoke the superpower.

Although it would have been quite possible to reformulate a gold link for the US dollar by raising the price of gold and starting on a new gold-based system, the Nixon Administration not only "suspended" the "convertibility" of the dollar but also embarked on a crusade to expel any vestiges of gold from the international monetary system (while carefully maintaining the world's largest official reserves of the metal).

Germany's Bid for Monetary Freedom

Though Germany had not joined France under De Gaulle in mounting a gold challenge to the US dollar, already two years before the Nixon shock (August 1971), it had started to navigate a monetary course which would provide shelter from rising US inflation. Even before the end of Breton Woods,

Germany took the lead in resisting the inflationary policies of the Fed. This was the first time since the US became monetary hegemon, a power whose policies shaped and dominated the entire global system (which we can date from 1919) that it faced foreign defiance. True, in 1927 Hjalmar Schacht, the famous Reichsbank President, had complained about what we would today describe as the export of US monetary inflation to Germany—the role of Fed policy in promoting the loan and wider asset boom there (with goods and services inflation not apparent in either country due to the surge in productivity growth). But that complaint was ignored and there could be no follow up. Apart from De Gaulle's gesture already noted, in the 1960s, there was no real objection in Europe to the export of asset inflation by the Fed. The European challenge emanated from other considerations.

In West Germany, the danger of "importing inflation" from the US did produce eventually a strong political reaction—though this took the form of fiat monetary nationalism rather than advocacy of a global gold standard. When the Social Democratic Party and their Liberal Democrat allies (FDP) won the 1969 Bundestag election, they quickly revalued (raised the external value of) the Deutsche mark, in line with their campaign rhetoric. This made imports cheaper and promised big gains for the middle classes (for instance, the German currency would buy more dollars and other foreign currencies, making foreign travel cheaper). In May 1971, as Arthur Burns was stoking up US monetary inflation, ostensibly so as to accelerate recovery from the 1970 recession (which has now been revised out of existence), Germany again defied the US monetary hegemon by floating the Deutsche mark which promptly appreciated. Dr. Otmar Emminger, who was then Vice-President and would later become President of the Bundesbank, West Germany's central bank, was a key intellectual influence behind this "declaration of monetary independence" for the Deutsche mark (see Emminger 1977). Although the new government had given the top job at the Bundesbank to a long-time Social Democrat, the Hamburg-based Karl Klasen (a jurist who had climbed to be co-head of Deutsche Bank), economics minister Karl Schiller and Otmar Emminger were in the driving seat.

The idea behind their concept of a hard DM was that Germany could escape the most damaging impacts of US monetary inflation by pursuing monetary independence. Its monetary system would have a national anchor to replace the US dollar (see Chapter 3). This was a bold idea—ever since World War II all countries had tried to maintain a fixed exchange rate to the US dollar. Devaluation was to be avoided if at all possible (in British political circles, the City and the media it was a "dirty word" until market pressures emanating from continuing monetary inflation forced a devaluation of sterling in 1967). A component of this national anchor for Germany would be setting targets for the growth in the Deutsche mark monetary base. There were at least two crucial assumptions needed for the idea to work. First, the demand for monetary base in Germany must prove to be broad and stable; second, the new, potentially large, fluctuations of the Deutsche mark in the foreign exchange market must not themselves damage German economic prosperity.

On the first point, high legal reserve requirements imposed by the Bundesbank on the banks ensured a strong and stable demand for monetary base, albeit artificial and corruptible in nature. Also there was broad demand both in Germany and outside (including on the other side of the "iron curtain") for the popular 1000 DM note. There were seeds here, however, of a longer-term problem. If reserve requirements forced banks to hold larger reserves than they would prefer or deemed necessary, then they would put pressure on the authorities to reduce them. The banks could also find ways round them. Through the 1980s and 1990s, both forces were in action. Even so, demand for reserves proved for a time quite stable. On the second point, exchange risk created for Germans from floating of the DM would turn crucially on how far other European countries followed the German lead in adopting hard money policies and even turned themselves into satellites of the German monetary area within Europe. Some countries including Holland, Belgium, Luxembourg, Austria and intermittently France, did indeed follow such a strategy. As a result, the hard DM inflicted less damage in the form of exchange rate volatility than it would otherwise have done. Over time, the DM became a "hard currency", i.e. a good store of value to Germans and the other countries of the wider DM-zone.

The DM was rather less attractive in view of exchange rate volatility as a store of value for residents outside the DM-zone. Even so, the widespread conviction that exposure to the risk of monetary inflation was much less if you held assets in DM rather than the dollar supported its use by global investors with a long-run perspective. Given the high reputation of goods "made in Germany" for quality, there was a strong demand for goods and services from suppliers in the DM-zone even if they seemed "expensive". Thus, while the hard DM was far from fulfilling all the qualifications needed for an ideal money, for many years during the 1970s, and again in the mid-1980s, it became highly popular in Europe and beyond. Its attractions were such that (West) Germany often attracted flows of capital, destabilising the currencies of other European countries. It showed what a medium-sized but determined country could do to win independence and a degree of monetary stability.

Living with a Weak Dollar

The dollar was beset by episodes of weakness, some sharp and extended, through the last three decades of the twentieth century. However, there was a period when it looked as if it might undergo metamorphosis.

The US experiment with monetarism from 1980 to 1984 showed there was a large potential demand for a hard US currency. At best, though, we could describe Paul Volcker's anchor during the monetarist experiment as semi-solid. (Whether or not Volcker was a genuine convert to monetarism or just used it as a way of escaping blame for high interest rates that the tightening of policy would cause is another matter. Nonetheless, we can refer to this period as a monetarist experiment, whatever the private views of the experimenter-in-chief may have been.) The trouble was that demand for monetary base in the US monetary system was not stable. It might have been more stable given time and skill on the part of monetary system architects. One way to do that would have been to reintroduce gold into the US monetary system, but that course had been rejected by the Gold Commission (reporting in 1982). An alternative way would have been to pass legislation to subject the US monetary system to constitutional rules, while rolling back regulations and various forms of back-stopping for banks which impeded the constituents of high-powered money gaining super-money qualities; as outlined in Chapter 5 such action would have helped to build a solid anchor. Fundamentally, there was simply not sufficient appetite in the US political system for such a fiat money constitution and related reforms. That would have needed a capacity to tolerate economic pain during the re-anchoring phase and to withstand the protests of special interests harmed by episodes of currency strength.

Paul Volcker, head of the Fed from 1979 to 1987, had by 1984 come to share the growing concern about the damaging trade implications of the super-strong dollar. The following year, the incoming US Treasury Secretary James Baker determined to push the dollar lower and stimulate the economy ahead of looming mid-term elections in 1986 amidst growing concerns across the "Rust Belt" about competition from cheap imports. The new dollar deval-uation offensive was launched at Plaza in Autumn 1985, and the Volcker Fed supported this by easing policy. The Deutsche mark came back into focus internationally as a hard currency. Would (West) Germany defy the US hegemon?

This time, political forces in Germany were not so favourable to this as previously. While they were not powerful enough to stop Bundesbank's defiance at the time, opposition to its policies grew. Complaints from the export sector resonated with the government of Helmut Kohl, not least given the strains on his CDU party's funds and its dependence on contributions from export businesses. (see James 2014). Such resentment reduced domestic opposition to the Kohl Government joining the train to European monetary integration. A few years later, the institution of the hard DM was to suffer a turbulent storm with German Monetary Union in 1990 and then a shipwreck with the launch of European Monetary Union.

The rise of the Swiss franc followed a somewhat similar history to the DM, albeit with some significant differences and a totally different denouement. Like Germany, Switzerland in the early 1970s started on the course of monetary independence, anchoring its monetary system by the setting of strict rules relating to the growth of the monetary base according to monetarist principles. As a small economy with no power to influence monetary policy beyond its borders, the exchange rate costs of monetary independence were potentially greater, at least for the export sector, than in Germany. The monetary control as pursued by the Swiss National Bank (SNB) was indeed stricter than in Germany: it did not even try to peg short-term interest rates.

The pure monetarist experiment only lasted, however for four years: by 1977, the damage done to Swiss exporters by the spectacular rise of the franc, now renowned as the safe-haven hard currency, triggered a sharp reversal of Swiss policies. The SNB sales of Swiss francs to the market in an attempt to stop the rise in its value caused a huge rise in the money supply, swamping official targets for monetary base expansion. There were subsequent attempts to revert to strict monetarism, but defects in Swiss monetary base control as a key component of the anchor proved to be too great, in particular following a computerisation of inter-bank clearing which suddenly reduced bank demand for reserves. By the late 1990s, Switzerland had formally scrapped the anchor based on monetarist principle and switched to an anchor-less form of control, inflation targeting, albeit supplemented by intermittent and sometimes persistent resort to a foreign currency-based anchor. This took the form of monetary policy dominated by an objective for the franc-euro exchange rate.

These stories illustrate the difficulties facing any country, large or small, that tries to stand out from the crowd and resist the inflationary policies of the leading currencies and currency areas. More and more countries are drawn into the "gravitational fields" of the dollar and—later on a much smaller scale—the euro. Though apparently independent, they become satellites.

How Tokyo's Bids to Resist US Monetary Expansion Failed

That failure to achieve monetary independence of the US is illustrated by our next exhibit—the spectacular monetary path of Japan from the 1980s to early this century. When the dollar devaluation policy was unleashed at the Plaza Accord of 1985, in an effort to reduce the US trade deficit, the yen soared. The so-called Louvre Accord of February 1987 (in which the US, Germany and Japan agreed to take actions to stem the decline of the dollar which had now "got out of hand", one could say in the 18 months since Plaza) was a catalyst to Japanese monetary and credit policies becoming even more inflationary. This badly affected Japan's exporters who in turn complained about the strength of the yen. The huge rise of the yen and a bout of productivity growth did keep the lid on consumer prices. And so the Bank of Japan within a far from transparent political system got the green light to pursue new aggressively easy policies; these included structural reform in the financial industries long advocated by politically powerful groups there. Controls restricting banks' competition for deposit and loan business were scrapped. This combination of policies triggered one of the biggest asset price booms of the twentieth century, which we should view as part of a global monetary inflation as unleashed by the Volcker Fed in the wake of the Plaza Accord. The Nikkei stockmarket index rose sixfold during the decade of the 1980s to reach 38,975, a peak it has never regained.

Finally in 1989, the Bank of Japan and Ministry of Finance, concerned by the crazy speculation in equities and real estate, and evidence suggesting that consumer price inflation was at last emerging, sharply tightened monetary policies, with the new BoJ Governor Mieno personally advocating a strong yen in part as a matter of national prestige. This tightening occurred simultaneously with a belated tightening of US monetary policy by the Greenspan Fed in response to an alarming increase in US CPI inflation (year-on-year above 6% through large parts of 1990). The Japanese action was not accompanied, however, by any new model or concept for monetary control, just "old-fashioned" interest rate management. The recession of 1990–1991, which coincided with the US downturn, was followed by a profound multi-year banking crisis, a mountain of bad debts and several years of sub-standard economic growth by international comparison, even after making correction for growingly important demographic factors. Critics blamed Mieno for persisting with high interest rates for too long. But the huge mal-investment and credit bubble inevitably left an economy in trouble, and their roots can be traced back to the destabilising effect of the Plaza Accord including the US monetary inflation which accompanied and followed it. Any serious attempt to anchor the Japanese monetary system would have sent the yen even further to the sky for some transitional period—always a short-term side-effect of re-anchoring or anchoring for the first time.

The pity is that there was no re-anchoring plan, just empty talk of benefits of a strong yen, some of which seemed to reflect nationalist pride—vying with the hard DM but with not even an anchor in design stage. Anyhow from 1995 to 2007, there was a new spell of a soft yen accompanied by monetary policies which led the US in terms of radical ease—QE and zero rate policy were Japanese innovations. The severe banking crises in Japan during 1996–1997 were a catalyst to this change in monetary direction. Even so, advocacy of a strong yen based on pride in Japan and on its pursuing a distinct path related to its own economic model, was taken up during this period by Eisuke Sakakibara (previously renowned as Mr. Yen during his spell as Vice Minister of Finance (1997–1999)). Subsequently Professor Sakakibara sided with the breakaway factions from the LDP which gained considerable political power, and which formed a government under the DDP coalition umbrella from 2009–2013. His considerable influence there coincided with the term of Masaaki Shirakawa as Governor of Bank of Japan—a second brief spell of a hard yen in Japan.

Between the hard money spells of Mieno (1990–94) and Shirakawa (2008–12), Japan had become a pioneer of "soft money" support for "bad banks" (banks saddled with huge non-performing loans) and massive fiscal "stimulus"—a policy combination that was later to characterise the reaction of Europe and the US to similar problems (Himino 2020). None of this spelt high goods and services price inflation in Japan—in fact prices remained stable or even fell slightly as Japan became subject to very strong downward pressure on prices stemming both from rapid integration with China and from the IT revolution. Hence, Japan illustrated the way in which what central bankers termed "price stability" could go along with and indeed provide cover for a bad spell of asset inflation—this time, through the period 2000–2007. The lack of serious asset inflation in domestic Japanese markets was widely attributed to the recent experience with the giant boom and bust of the 1980s and early 90s. Japanese investors, many of whom were nursing big losses, were less likely to become entranced by a new narrative concerning those same bubble assets (domestic real estate and equity markets) that had collapsed so recently. Also Japan had nothing to compare with the promise entrancing Europeans of an Eldorado on the back of European Monetary Union or an American housing Eldorado on the back of rising home-ownership. Thus for Japan, asset inflation manifested itself primarily in cross-border capital flows (the so-called yen carry trade). Japanese investors developed a huge demand for foreign assets while foreign investors queued up to borrow apparently low interest cost yen which they then sold to finance investment globally. Thus was reflected in a weak yen through 2003–2006.

Yen loans—like Swiss franc loans—became a hugely popular way of financing investment globally, whether this took the form of corporate take-overs or purchases of real estate. Let us clarify this story, which can be confusing! Noticing that Japanese interest rates were much lower than those in the US, investors all over the world borrowed yen at low interest rates, and then sold the yen in order to go into much higher-yielding investments denominated in dollars and other non-Japanese currencies. They could profit from the interest rate differential—paying lower rate on their yen borrowing than they were earning on their dollar and other currency assets. But this profit depended on one critical assumption. They assumed that they would not lose this benefit via adverse exchange rate fluctuation (yen rising); some subscribed to stories as to why the yen would now be much cheaper for a long time than in the past. (One such story was that Japan had continued into a second "lost decade"; in fact most would now agree (in 2022) that there was at most a lost half decade which came to an end by 1998). Because if the yen were to rise in value strongly, then when they came to repay their yen borrowing, they would have to purchase the much more expensive yen and so lose all (or most of) the profit they thought they would make—or end up with an overall loss. In normal sober-rational mode, they would not have believed those stories about how the yen would remain weak. That is how the "carry trade" business became part of the asset inflation phenomenon.

A final point to note here is how the soft yen period of 1995–2007 fitted into developments in US policies, starting with the pursuance of monetary inflation through the IT "economic miracle" of the late 1990s; then with a second lap starting in the aftermath of the 2001 attack on New York and continuing into the preparations for the 2004 elections. The monetary infla-tion which took off at Plaza (Autumn 1985), had continued through to 1989, pursued in its second half by Alan Greenspan (Alan Greenspan was chairman from 1987 to 2006). Volcker, who had been outvoted by Reagan appointees on a monetary policy vote in February 1986 (they forced through a cut in rates in advance of the mid-term elections) had been replaced. The White Houses (most important, Texan lawyer James Baker, now President Reagan's chief of staff, and close friend to then Vice-President Herbert W. Bush who was preparing his candidacy for the 1988 presidential election) had become impatient with Volcker's renewed resistance from early 1987 to soft money and his opposition to letting banks conduct securities business. Symptoms of asset inflation were evident in equity markets, real estate markets and risky corporate bond markets. The asset inflation experienced a quake with the Wall Street equity market crash of Autumn 1987; as already mentioned, the Greenspan Fed rode to the rescue with a stepping up of monetary inflation—the first and most important example of the "Greenspan put", with its ancestry in the Benjamin Strong put of 1927 (see Chapter 3).

This 1987 episode was indeed a key turning point. It caused huge moral hazard and heralded an extended monetary inflation. It was followed by another not much more than a decade later. By 1989, US consumer prices were again rising strongly. The Greenspan Fed reacted firmly in the end; its sharp policy tightening of 1989–90 explains the timing of the recession (1990–91) which followed the great monetary inflation of 1985–89. This was followed by an extended weak recovery through to Spring 1993. This experience illustrated the fact that the end of the monetarist episode of 1979–1984 had left monetary policy in the US without any clear steering concept. The US and the world economy had wandered again into a high inflation episode—featuring both persistent asset inflation and (with a lag) high goods and services inflation. It was surely time for a new approach to monetary control.

Why Governments Chose a Compass, not an Anchor

At this fork of the road in the early 1990s, there were two stark alternative directions for controlling the machinery of money. We should note though that there was no debate on these in the US Congress or in the wider US political arena.

The first was to build on the monetarism of the 1970s and early 1980s, setting strict limits to monetary growth, moving further in the direction of good money as defined in this volume. The second was to throw overboard the traditional concept of an anchor and redefine it to suit a new politically fashionable doctrine.

Governments, central bankers and legislatures in together forging the monetary regime chose the latter. The idea of an anchor still resonated with some in the corridors of monetary power but in general even they rejected its traditional meaning so they redefined it. Henceforth, it would be used to refer not to controlling the machinery of money via constraints which would prevent the supply of money veering ahead of demand but rather a delegated authority to the central bank to use its instruments (most of all fixing short-term interest rates and increasingly with time manipulating medium and long-term interest rates) to achieve a stated aim for consumer price inflation over the medium-term (say two years). At the start of the age of inflation targeting, most people assumed success or failure would be judged by factual outcomes (whether stability was actually achieved in terms of statistical outcomes, though this itself had many possible interpretations) but later this evolved into a criteria whereby the state of consumer *expectations* would be critical. Success would be measured by whether or not a target rate of increase of consumer prices (as defined by the central bank) was *expected to be achieved*. (In the US, as already noted in Chapter 1, objectives also included "maximum employment" and "moderate long-term interest rates"). Later still, this was reinterpreted (in the US) as applying to the *average* of inflation outcomes/expectations over a long period of time.

At its best, this was more like a compass than an anchor. Setting a course for this new voyage in monetary practice depended on input from econometrics. The Federal Reserve would steer the path of interest rates in accordance with guidance from its econometric model so as to achieve just the right mix of a stable low inflation rate and low unemployment. Successful implementation required the Fed and other central bankers not only to know enough about the economy and how money works to be able to achieve their target but also to have the tools to do the job and the freedom to take whatever action would be needed to bring about the desired state of expectations. The central bankers claimed that they had sufficient knowledge and that their ability to set the path of short-term interest rates while strongly influencing long-term rates provided the means to achieve the targeted low inflation outcome. Adequate weapons existed. Yes, they needed sufficient protection from executive pressure. No automatic mechanisms; no anchor; just good statistical models operated by qualified economists—Follow the Science!

....In the US...

Yet as always personalities mattered. This story started in 1997 when Fed Chair Alan Greenspan endorsed a paper by the then Governor Janet Yellen which argued in favour of sustaining inflation at around 2 per cent rather than trying to bring it down further (see Brown 2017). The US was basking in an IT-boom and Greenspan was unwilling to derail this despite warning against the market's "irrational exuberance" in late 1996. To be precise, Greenspan did not endorse the 2% inflation standard or sign up to it; but he did decide (in line with the Yellen paper) that the Fed "for now", given that inflation had already fallen to around 2%, should not try to push it lower. This was gobbledygook according to sound money principles. At a time of sustained productivity spurt such as the US economy was enjoying through the second half of the 1990s (and into the early 2000s), prices should have been falling as competing firms passed on cost savings. The Fed in effect had stimulated monetary forces which had resisted this fall and indeed brought about a moderate rise in overall prices of goods and services. An accompaniment of this was the rampant asset inflation about which he had complained obliquely in late 1996 when citing "irrational exuberance" without making the obvious connection to monetary inflation.

Anyhow, Greenspan's term as Fed Chair was up in early 1999 and towards getting re-appointed by President Clinton, it was surely important to keep the economic good times going, not least given the approach of the 2000 elections. As an astute Washington insider, Greenspan was aware of the influence of the neo-Keynesian economic advisers surrounding the President. Hence, in so far as Greenspan was at all inclined to cool overall monetary inflation at that time, he would have perceived political obstacles; one such moment might have been in late 1996. Beyond then, however, the public record suggests that his monetary policy decisions were driven by a growing conviction that continued low consumer price inflation justified calm on the monetary front. The next stage came in Autumn 2002 when President George W. Bush nominated Professor Ben Bernanke, a neo-Keynesian monetary expert renowned for his advocacy of inflation targeting and work on how to avoid an economic depression, as a governor. Greenspan's tenure was only renewed for a further two years in 2003 on the implicit understanding that a policy of monetary reflation to fight "deflation" would be pursued. We should understand this in the context of the looming 2004 Presidential and Congressional elections and the concern that economic weakness had lingered into early 2003, long after the brief "recession" of 2001 had ended (a recession now ironed out by data revisions). Then came the appointment of Bernanke to the head of the Fed in early 2006—and it was full steam ahead to inflation targeting becoming the established creed of monetary policy.

....And in the Euro Area

In Europe, the European Central Bank (ECB), which opened its doors in 1998, adopted a "twin pillars" model of policy in managing the euro when it was launched in 1999. In a faint echo of Bundesbank monetarism, this required policy-makers to pay due attention to monetary developments, with a monetary target alongside the inflation target set at "close to but under 2%" from 2003. However, this model did nothing to stop the monetary inflation, which built up in the US through the late mid-1990s and into the 2000s, being transmitted to Europe. The global financial crisis (GFC) of 2007/8 ended all hopes of the euro developing into a European successor to the hard Deutsche mark. The euro found no model of soundness to guide its path during its early years and build a distinctive reputation. Yes, the ECB reacted strongly when goods and services inflation did pick up in 2005–2006. Indeed, both the ECB and Fed, fixated by inflation targets, overreacted, failing to take proper account of the credit market deflation already evident from Summer 2007. This excessive late tightening contributed to the violence of the subsequent bust. In the recovery from that bust, the Trichet ECB did make a last attempt to diverge from the Fed's monetary inflation, but it was too late; its ill-fated raising of interest rates in Summer 2011 was overtaken by the eruption of the Euro-area sovereign debt crisis.

This debt crisis—the denouement in Europe of the virulent asset inflation through the years 1997–2007—turned the ECB into a transfer tax authority. As such, it proceeded to levy monetary repression taxation on Northern Europe, especially Germany, transferring the proceeds to weak banks and weak sovereigns throughout the union, but with a bias to the South. Mario Draghi, appointed as the "fixer of the euro" (meaning the defender of the status quo) in 2011 used the ECB's balance sheet to effect these transfers. Salvaging Italy's membership of the union—and political cynics would say while sustaining the status quo there at the same time rather than precipitating fundamental reforms allowing free market capitalism to triumph—was central to the ECB's purpose under Mario Draghi, one that was fully endorsed by the German Chancellor. This distorted the ECB's balance sheet. Its assets were weighted with bad loans to weak banks and weak sovereigns while its liabilities were swollen with reserve deposits owed to German banks.

The situation remains delicate. German banks are disproportionate holders of these reserves (at the Bundesbank as part of the European System of Central Banks) because investors place their funds in Germany to gain greater protection thereby against an ultimate default by Italian banks or the Italian state and similarly weak entities elsewhere in the monetary union. Crunch time will come when market interest rates rise substantially to control inflation, as they will have to eventually. Will the ECB be able to raise interest income (to match payments on its liabilities) from its portfolio of loans to weak banks and governments (as in its holdings of bonds)? The danger is that this would trigger widespread bankruptcies. To avert this would require big transfers of funds to these deadbeats; but could this be done surreptitiously? The simplest "solution" would be to kick the can down the road by letting consumer price inflation rip and holding interest rates down. Note that the road back from unsound money would involve shrinking the ECB balance sheet—but first it would have to sell off the junk.

"Not Our Job to Target Asset Prices?"

Although the leading central banks conducted regular surveys of possible emerging risks, they failed to understand the implications of the growth of massive financial imbalances, the new financial instruments, the build-up of bad real estate loans, speculation and bad banking before the GFC. They certainly did not admit that these phenomena were fundamentally reflections of monetary inflation which they had generated. When the crisis broke, they denied responsibility. But why did they not face a post-mortem challenge? The most obvious answer is that they carried out their policies with the full acquiescence and indeed encouragement of the Parliaments/Congresses and Presidents/Prime Ministers to whom they answered. They then rescued banks deemed too big to fail; let the get-rich-quick speculators get away with their loot; and created money while desperately trying to persuade people to borrow and spend more. They all doubled down on their existing "inflation targeting" model, averting blame by pointing to bad or inadequate financial regulation as the cause of the disaster, not their own policies. All wrapped up in talk of reforms and new regulatory bodies and expanded global "safety net" of resources to "provide stronger protection from crises" basically all funded by taxpayers (See IMF 2021).

What happened? Although goods and services inflation was lower on average than in the past from say 2013 (the end of the global debt crisis with its last instalment in Europe), largely reflecting economic sclerosis and weak investment spending, asset inflation continued through this long cycle (from say 2012 to the eve of the pandemic at the start of 2020) and this had several adverse effects as explored in other chapters. Indeed, the "low" inflation outcome in this long cycle up to the pandemic was a conservative influence, cementing the status quo. The system operated in the interests of existing large asset holders, private equity, monopoly capitalists such as the big IT/social media groups and governments which benefited handsomely from monetary repression tax (as did people who can raise this tax for themselves as discussed in Chapter 6).

Did central bankers turn a blind eye to the implications of their policies for asset inflation? Not in all cases, but they invariably concluded they neither could nor should do anything about that, at least in terms of monetary policy (they can now assign any role in that to their so-called macro-prudential tools such as variable capital asset ratios and macro taxes). They pointed to evidence that sharp asset price rises are typically due either to "irrational exuberance", or technological breakthroughs. Few acknowledged at least publicly a connection between easy money and asset inflation. Just as, in the run-up to the GFC in 2007, central bankers insisted that any rise of interest rates sufficient to prick the bubble in real estate would also bring on a recession and that this would cause much greater damage than letting the bubble burst and "cleaning up afterwards", now they claimed that banks were adequately capitalised so that monetary policy could and should continue to underpin demand during recovery from the pandemic. They had the range of new tools and powers accumulated in the past decade, including unprecedented interventions to serve as market-makers, as lenders-of-last-resort to a range of institutions outside the magic circle of the big banks, and steer flows of credit in the economy, with subsidised loans to selected range of clients deemed economically vital (while in practice having the political clout to tap flows of state-directed money).

"We delivered sound money!" Really?

We recognise that there is a strong view, perhaps even approaching a consensus, among central bankers and the mainstream economics profession that the inflation targeting regime operated over the past 30 years or so was successful. With a few honourable exceptions, criticisms centred on specific alleged "mistakes" of judgement in particular interest rate/monetary policy decisions by particular central banks' rate-setting bodies rather than the policy-making model itself. Hence, the lack of any real interest in fundamental reform. The shock and destruction of the GFC should have been a wake-up call. Is it not obvious that the incentives given to asset inflation build-up in the form of extended spells of ultra-easy money sow the seeds of future financial crises? And is it not clear that these are of ever-increasing magnitude? And that they have ever-rising costs to society? With benefits going to a few people? But central bankers and governments persisted in their set course, eventually steering their monies and economies as buffeted by pandemic and war into the Great Inflation of 2021–2 - as analysed in later chapters.

References

B Brown (2017) Goods Inflation, Asset Inflation, and the Greatest Peacetime Inflation in the US American Economic Journal 45 429 442

Brown B. and Simonnot P. (2020) Europe's Century of Crises under Dollar Hegemony. Palgrave.

Bruner, Robert and Carr, Sean (2007) *The Panic of 1907: Lessons Learned from the Market's Perfect Storm*. Wiley.

Emminger, Otmar (1977) *The D-Mark and the Conflict between Internal and External Equilibrium 1948–75*. Princeton Paper.

Gerlach, S. and Kugler P. (2015) "Back to Gold: Sterling in 1925" CFS Working Paper No. 515 Goethe University.

Himino, Ryozo (2020) *The Japanese Banking Crisis*. Springer, Singapore.

IMF (2021) *The Global Financial Safety Net during the COVID-19 Crisis: An Interim Stock-Take*.

James, Harold (2014) *Making the European Monetary Union*. Harvard University Press.

Meltzer, Allan (2002) *A History of the Federal Reserve* Vol. 1 (1913–51). University of Chicago.

Meltzer, Allan (2010) *A History of the Federal Reserve* Vol. 2, Book 1 (1951–1969). University of Chicago.

Mitchell, Wesley Clair (2011) "A History of the Greenbacks" Books on Demand.

Rothbard, Murray A. (2010) *History of US Money and Banking in the United States*, Mises Institute.

Silber, William L. (2013). *Volcker: The Triumph of Persistence*.

Voth, Hans-Joachim (2003) With a Bang, not a Whimper: Pricking Germany's Stock Market Bubble in 1927 and the Slide into Depression, *Journal of Economic History*, Vol. 63, no. 1, March, pp. 66–99.

Yanping Chong, Osca Jorda and Taylor Alan M. (2010) The Harrod-Balassa-Samuelson Hypothesis: Real Exchange Rates and Their Long-Run Equilibrium, NBER Working Paper, 15868 (April).

References

9

Symptoms and Consequences of Bad Money

Here we summarise the harms of "moderately bad" money regimes in modern democracies. These are not necessarily present in all cases of bad money but they are typical and common. In what follows, we have in mind regimes currently operating in the world's major economies.

Mega Boom-Bust Cycles—

The overriding feature of such bad money regimes is a mega financial boom-bust cycle. The boom phase can be highly elongated and conjures up illusions of prosperity. The bust phase is on such a scale as to set off economic, social, political and geopolitical devastation. The busts may be very far apart (sometimes decades) and so we should also be on the alert for other, immediately recognisable, features. Typically, under current moderately bad money regimes, a government authority (albeit "independent") conducts monetary policy without any significant reference to, or consideration of, the outstanding money supply. Instead, it sets the path of interest rates so as to achieve objectives expressed in general macro-economic terms. In implementing this policy, the authorities claim to have good estimates of the so-called "neutral interest rate" at which the economy would be "in balance". They use a range of techniques to help ensure that their control of the short-term interest rates (often indicating their intentions of where to set these in the future) will influence substantially longer-term rates. Sometimes

© The Author(s), under exclusive license to Springer Nature
Switzerland AG 2022
B. Brown and R. Pringle, *A Guide to Good Money*,
https://doi.org/10.1007/978-3-031-06041-0_9

for extended periods, they manipulate interest rates down to abnormally low levels—in some cases well into sub-zero territory.

Short-Term Investment Horizons

Other prominent features of "moderately bad" money regimes include short-termism and trend-following in investment strategies (whether of individuals or businesses). This short-termism stems in part from an awareness that the next big crash and great recession—payback for a long period of monetary inflation especially asset inflation—looms as a larger risk the further we look into the future; the short-term seems safer in this important respect than the long term. The impact of this short-termism on the economy is magnified by widespread financial engineering which means essentially high debt and camouflaged leverage. Using debt to leverage up short-term investments so as to increase expected rates of return is often a more attractive strategy than striving to get higher returns by assuming the risks of long-run investment.

Given the widespread search for yield on the part of interest-income starved investors, market and legal discipline deteriorates. This gives increased scope for dishonesty whether on the part of financial managers or on the part of individuals accounting to themselves. Robert Shiller (2000) cites such dishonesty as a characteristic of "irrational exuberance". Cumulative and prolonged inflation in asset markets entails serious corruption of the price-signalling function there in a climate where speculative narrative-telling is highly contagious. There are no effective barriers to these stories in the form of investors' rational scepticism.

—And Other Damaging Effects

These include, in addition, the following:

- Cumulative serious loss in the value of money, as seen especially in soaring prices of residential real estate which is in effect the largest consumer durable
- A lack of trust in money as shown by the demand for hybrid assets which are widely perceived to combine safe-haven qualities with limited monetary functions
- Growth of zombie companies kept alive by handouts and bank forbearance

- Increasing inequalities of wealth as stemming from dubious practices (including the abuses of financial engineering, monopoly capitalism, and cronyism) and asset inflation.
- Outbreaks of international currency wars, as discussed in Chapter 2
- Manias in assets or goods which are not at the core of the economy (tulip bulbs, golf clubs, tokens, cryptos, the art market, Iceland bonds)
- Increasing fears of government default, whether involving actual repudiation of the debt or huge write-down in real terms by inflation
- Breakdown of market discipline on banks to efficiently and cautiously allocate credit
- A compulsive, obsessive and even hysterical chorus of commentaries in the financial media on what central banks will do next, however fundamentally trivial
- A tolerance by the economically mighty of ever more detailed and wide-ranging regulation, as if this were a price worth paying to make their vast profits acceptable socially. This regulation deflects pressure for more fundamental reforms that would threaten their profits bonanza. Banks employ armies of box-tickers and form-fillers with "generals" in charge lest huge reputational damage and fines result from lapses in compliance.

We note that booms and busts in themselves do not necessarily imply that a regime of bad money has taken hold. Indeed, economic cycles are part and parcel of capitalism. Yes, the most violent cycles historically have featured stories of monetary inflation (and related to this a boom and bust in credit), but we can identify more modest cycles without an obvious source in great monetary disorder. Investors can spontaneously fuel a boom—e.g. when they are over-optimistic about the potential for a new burst of technological progress to deliver income or profits.

High Profits, Regulation, Debt and Depression

Under even moderately bad money regimes, huge trading profits typically emerge in parts of the banking and/or near-banking system as an accompaniment to the asset inflations which they generate. Some of this financial profits bonanza may be transitory, related to the climb in underlying leverage during the asset inflation, and turn into even larger losses during the asset price deflation phase, especially if this is severe. Other profit sources may not subsequently turn to loss, if stemming from large volumes of deal-making and market turnover matched by highly variable costs; and some may be at least semi-permanent if they are derived from grown monopoly power which can survive or even increase during downturns. Anyhow, the bottom line is that the financial sector profits of the boom phase ultimately imply large extra costs or losses. Sometimes these costs and losses are born by the general public in the form of hidden and/or official taxes to compensate victims and sometimes by the financial firms themselves (as explained in Chapter 6), all par for the course when frenzies die. Considerable losses are usually borne by amateur speculators drawn in by the publicity that reaches a peak typically during the last stages of a mania—when some insiders and professionals have already taken profits and closed their positions.

The *huge profits* typically emerge first in the mainstream banking system. Typically, after a severe cyclical bust, governments move to regulate this sector more strictly, usually in a way which promotes monopoly and monopoly profits. Risk-taking moves in part to the less regulated shadow banking or near-banking sector. This sector is not typically suited or set up to finance traditional business. Thus small and medium-sized businesses (SMEs) are in some cases cut off from their normal financing channels although venture capital at high rates may be available especially for projects promising high near-term profits. Longer-term projects may suffer in consequence of the high degree of monetary uncertainty as described, though some admirers of the venture capital industry would point out examples here of backing start-ups without any intention of making a quick kill through the sale of equity at an early date in the public markets. In the United Kingdom, bank lending to SMEs has collapsed since the global financial crisis; now the banks play a minimal role in allocating credit to SMEs, which account for 99% of companies, 60 per cent of the employment and around half of turnover in the UK private sector.

In such ways, the damage of inflation becomes apparent. This is true even if the annual rise in consumer prices, as officially measured, stays below the target of about 2 per cent. Sometimes the result of excessive money and credit growth does not immediately show up in retail prices. These may be held down by non-monetary factors, such as cheap imports from China and other places. But the accompanying asset inflation is a big problem—once people look beyond the immediate excitement of capital gains. Asset inflation carries high economic costs through inducing *misallocation of capital*. In the long run, people are poorer in consequence. And along the way, many may experience damage to their wealth despite the froth of bubble periods.

Another result of bad money is seen in a massive build-up of public and private sector debts. In part, these occur because during the inevitable downturns, governments and central banks try to encourage growth by borrowing and spending more themselves and inducing citizens to follow their example. This brings forward spending at the cost of increasing future debt repayments. But there is a natural limit to this process. Later, talk of the need for debt reductions on a vast scale becomes commonplace (See White 2021).

The burden on younger people in particular grows rapidly. First, they will eventually bear the burden of the taxation needed to pay interest on the debt and close the budget gap, and secondly they will live long enough to suffer the loss of prosperity which will eventually be the result of bad money. They could suffer for a long time from the economic sclerosis which bad money can induce (see glossary). Low interest rates with monetary expansion diverts capital to poor investments with short-term payoffs or promises of monopoly profits; rampant speculation and the emergence of manias might do much to undermine confidence in capitalism—especially once these move on to the next phase of crash, recession and exposure of fraud and criminality.

Such policies distort market prices and undermine their signalling function while increasing taxation without representation through monetary repression tax and inflation tax (as explained in Chapter 6). Some of the spending projects financed by higher public borrowing attracts fraudsters, as seen during the pandemic (and earlier during the Obama mega fiscal stimulus of 2009–11); it often goes to enrich narrow special interests ("pork-barrel politics"); huge gaps in the public finances tend to discourage private investment, as capital spenders (and their equity holders) fear future tax hikes. Numerous examples throughout modern history illustrate how easy it is to slip into an unsustainable build-up of state indebtedness that quickly becomes impossible to reverse in time to avoid a crisis—as seen for example in Greece in its decade-long sovereign debt crisis (2009–2018) where real GDP fell by more than 20% due to a build-up of public debt.

The Damage to Daily Lives and Growth

Modern money is not a secure basis on which people can plan their lives, buy a house, get married, raise families and save for retirement. Bad money has corrupted and lamed competitive capitalism. For many citizens, fortunes and life chances depend far more on networking through cronies and affiliation to powerful groups than on their enterprise in "delivering bread to the customer" (as Adam Smith put it, not out of love, but from enlightened self-interest).

Governments have degraded money under the guise of supporting employment. In fact, longer-term employment prospects suffer from this, as does lasting economic prosperity across society as a whole, notably due to bad money corrupting the price signals in asset markets, most of all the long-term interest rate market. More regulation to protect society from bank failures usually just causes excessive risk-taking to move outside the heavily regulated sectors. So the economy is weighed down by too much regulation, too much deposit insurance, too many "too big to fail" banks, not enough anti-trust action. This beefed-up regulatory regime therefore comes with very large costs (direct and indirect) and a heavy burden on business.

How Bad Money Raises Uncertainty

One contribution that money should make to society and our individual lives is to reduce uncertainty. By allowing us to vary the timing of our sales and purchases, to save for a rainy day, money enables us to plan how we can best meet our needs now and in the future. It does this while meshing and reconciling our individual preferences with those of other people. To do this effectively, it needs to instil in us confidence that the machinery of money will not get out of control and unleash inflation in goods and asset markets. Whereas a good monetary regime will offer a credible means to prevent this happening, the current regime fails on this score also. This spoils one of the main contributions money should make to human well-being.

Social Harm of Zero and Negative Rates

While zero or negative interest rates allow governments to borrow at zero cost to them, the costs to society of the entire monetary regime of which these form part are heavy: at one level, these include the costs of regulating banks, the costs incurred by financial institutions obliged to comply with regulations, the subsidy involved in the government guarantee of banks' liabilities, the costs of subsidising mortgage interest and allowing tax deductibility of some interest payments by businesses; and the monetary repression tax. Then, there are the costs of sorting out the financial system after each crisis. At another level, there are the costs of all the bad investments made in the over-optimistic mood during the asset inflation—money spent on capital projects to produce goods or services we do not need or want. Such expenditure results from—and represents—wasted resources either from government spending on bank rescues, etc., or from private sector's capital investments that are not economic for society.

Finally, heavy monetary taxation, whether in the form of monetary repression tax or inflation tax, and as symptomised by low, zero or negative interest rates, ultimately depresses productivity and growth.

How Inflation Targeting Detaches Money from Value

We now turn to another damaging effect of modern monetary doctrine—how it leads the public to confuse prices and value.

In orthodox economic theory, given competitive markets, prices reflect the value placed (in economic jargon "at the margin") on a good or service by consumers. When people expect prices to be reasonably stable over the long term (while varying quite a bit even from year to year), consumers will develop a sense of the "right" price for something. Making adjustments for perceived quality, this helps them decide whether to purchase the item or acquire the asset in question. Consumers will send signals in aggregate via their purchases, through the impersonal mechanism of the market, to producers whether to increase or reduce supply of that product. This does not mean that producers can just "declare" what an item is worth. Nor does it imply that work or goods that are not traded have no value. Just because housework for example is not priced and does not enter into GDP statistics does not mean it has no value—that would be an absurd conclusion. Economics does not insist that only goods and services traded in the market have value. But for goods and services that are traded, prices indicate the value consumers place on them, given costs of production.

When a central institution like a planning body or a monetary policy committee is given discretion to adjust short-term interest rates with the aim of achieving some combination of objectives, the path of prices of goods and services depends (in ways which the committee often cannot possibly judge or forecast well and therefore come as a surprise) on whatever policies that body decides on. Suppose it steers the machinery of money so as to achieve a target for some definition of prices. Even though it may succeed, by clever manipulation of rates, to hit the target, the course of prices of other goods not to mention unpriced goods, may bear little relation to the prices of stuff in the index. This is a version of Goodhart's Law, which states that when a measure of something becomes a policy target, it ceases to be a good measure.

We can see this in the history of fixing the appropriate price index to be targeted under the 2 per cent inflation standard. Should the index exclude items where the price changes are (often or actually) outliers? Should the price of residential accommodation be included and if so by including house prices or rents? If the latter, how to treat the imputed rental equivalent of home ownership? Should an implicit price be included for government output and more generally for public goods? There is also a tendency towards "index-picking" to suit the policy aim. And then, there is the huge topic of hedonic price adjustment—adjusting prices down to take account of quality improvements—which so obviously can become abused in a monetary system where the aim is expressed in terms of the path for the general price index. All the more reason why a good money has a solid anchor which works on money supply, not directly on prices.

Where the value of money is inherently unstable, investors and consumers—anybody spending money on anything—will have a tough time working out whether the price they are asked to pay represents value. The evidence suggests that under modern monetary management some prices, including for that giant consumer durable good which is also an asset—housing—often become detached from people's ingrained sense of true value. They just do not have the time and effort available to continuously re-assess the additional (or "marginal") amount of satisfaction or enjoyment ("utility") of extra consumption of particular items and judge whether this is in line with the latest price.

Don't Blame Liberal Economic Theory

Rather than blaming monetary systems, some economists accuse the economic theory of value itself for the lack of an obvious connection between the price of something, or the income somebody makes, from the real value it has (Mazzucato, 2018). The idea that some activities "create value" while others "extract value" has—according to this thesis—been misapplied by modern free market economists to glorify so-called "wealth creators" in the private sector because they produce goods and services traded and priced in markets. This leads free market economists to undervalue and even vilify people in the public sector whose work is financed by taxation while over-valuing others. Surely, prices ought to reflect value—economists would say here "at the margin"—not the other way round. Recalling Oscar Wilde's quip that a cynic is somebody who knows the price of everything and the value of nothing, prices should reflect what work is worthwhile and which products ought to be valued.

Yet, such critics have no solution. Economists who criticise traditional economics on such grounds fail to produce an alternative theory of value.

They also pass over the solution proposed by the neo-classical economists who reconciled value and price via the marginal revolution—price equals the additional satisfaction (utility or equivalent) a buyer obtains from an object or experience purchased when in an efficient market, the price will equal the marginal. Yes, this approach values subjective, individual satisfaction—the additional satisfaction or benefit (utility) that a consumer derives from buying an additional unit of a commodity or service. But progressive economists from the left ignore such subjective measures of value at their peril. For the alternative is to judge the value of an object or experience on behalf of somebody else, assuming "we" know what "you" want or "need".

The Left also Should Condemn Bad Money

Left-of-centre economists and commentators should focus their criticisms of right-of-centre policies not on the bogeyman of "neo-liberalism" but on bad money's effect on the social fabric and the lives of voters. An analysis by *Labour Together*, which describes itself as "a network for people from all traditions of the Labour movement, organised to explore new ideas and thinking on the left" offered an interesting analysis of the new model of economic growth. It argued persuasively that this was driven increasingly by inflows of financial capital, rent extraction (diverting rather than creating wealth through obtaining grants, subsidies, sweetheart contracts, etc.) and debt-financed consumption. It recognised that government policy increased the return on assets such as equities, housing, land and pensions, outpacing the rise in wages:

> The new model of growth was underpinned by a cross-class electoral coalition of interests including the financial sector and asset-wealthy citizens, who would become increasingly concentrated among home-owning, older generations.

Certainly, the debt-driven growth model has slowed economic growth. But the analysis could have gone much further. Bad money as we, the authors, define it has also contributed to growing inequality, monopoly power, a bias to short-term and speculative investment over longer-term investment in productive capacity, the swollen size of the financial sector and the shibboleth of "shareholder value" which in fact has many dubious meanings including the application of financial engineering, pursuit and use of monopoly power, and much other camouflage. But, in pursuit of a progressive agenda, many economists wrongly identify free market, "neo-liberal" theories as the cause of such distortions. In other words, they overlook one of the really powerful influences at work—which is the distorted way money itself is created and managed. In this book, we hope to demonstrate the close links between modern monetary policies (including the ideas and theories that support them) and the very social diseases that she and other commentators rightly condemn.

In short, the public and the political class should become more aware of modern money's dangers, its bias to short-term gratification, its link to cronyism and monopoly power (see Chapter 10) and its links to technologies that threaten human liberty including right to privacy). We should reflect on the way money policies have arbitrarily rewarded those who already have much and take away from those that have less.

Illustrating "the Essence of Bad Money"

Let us illustrate "the essence of bad money" with the help of two contemporary phenomena—one is an idea of economists, the other an experiment in cryptocurrency. Both of these draw passionate supporters as well as equally passionate critics. They are Modern Monetary Theory and Bitcoin.

Modern Monetary Theorists Want Even More Bad Money

One of the most important post-pandemic issues is whether we can pay our way out of the economic mess. The answer is yes, according to the advocates of Modern Monetary Theory (MMT). They say that scare stories about budgetary deficits, adorned with claims that such deficits constitute a debt that our grandchildren will be forced to pay back, lack rational foundation. This way of thinking, the MMT supporters say, is a hangover from the old days when money was thought to consist of things like gold coins with intrinsic value. Given such a wrong idea of money, it was intrinsically scarce, so governments had to be sure they did not run out of it. And they had to pay back what they borrowed. The new and more accurate idea is that money is a unit of account represented by tokens with no intrinsic value. In order to give value to the token, the central authority demands the return of some of these tokens at the end of each year. This gives value to the token.

The government with its own currency can always create money—it can never run out of money and need never default. If, therefore, taxation is nothing to do with financing government expenditure, why do we tax? There are several reasons… redistribution of wealth, adjusting relative activity in different branches of the economy, reducing greenhouse gases……. but the major reason is that taxation gives value to the currency (token).

Politicians have been reluctant to use this ability to create money because they have been convinced that increasing the money supply automatically causes inflation. But creating money does not need to cause inflation. So now, we arrive at the heart of the matter. Under President Barrack Obama, the United States created massive quantities of new money to combat the Global Financial Crisis. The EU did the same and so did the UK. Yet, say MMT supporters, there has been very little inflation. Why not? Because the resources available met the demand for goods and services without the need for sharp increases in prices. In other words, pouring money into an economy does not cause inflation if it is done correctly. The process has to be regulated by monitoring inflation in great detail. This, they say, is a crucial point that governments have been getting wrong. MMT says that to determine whether it is safe to increase the money supply, we should monitor inflation itself, not employment. Governments should not be worried about borrowing in their own currencies. If debt cannot be issued, print money. If excess expenditure leads to inflation, increase taxes.

Whereas proponents of MMT advance this as a radical cure for economic depressions, critics dismiss it as an old idea—deficit spending financed by taxes—wrapped up in a new guise. The critics are right—there is no magic money tree. But what both proponents and critics miss is that MMT offers a quite accurate account of what governments are actually doing. They already are creating as much money as possible; they already do in practice look to inflation and expected inflation in setting rates. Indeed, this "theory", in flesh-and-blood reality, is the essence of bad money ideology.

Bitcoin—A Red Flag for Fiat Money

The early twenty-first century saw a revival of privately issued monetary assets—this time in crypto form. Central bankers said the cryptocurrencies should not be called currencies and warned society of the risks, albeit in some cases welcoming "private monetary innovation" in principle. To rival state currency, private currencies not only have to perform the basic functions of money as well as state money, they also need qualities superior to state money. This is challenging.

Yes, Bitcoin shows that a would-be form of money can still arise through private initiative. At present, Bitcoins are accepted only to a limited extent as a medium of exchange/payment for a range of goods and services and experts doubt that their infrastructure could cope (at acceptable cost) with a much greater role here. At the present stage of technology, there are user complaints about money transfers involving long times to be confirmed (which in the decentralised ledger system requires at least two "nodes"—in fact also "miners"—to vet that the funds are in fact there on the blockchain). Some users have to hire experts to deal with these issues—more costs adding to the spectre of rising costs as "miners" seek to sustain profits. The "coins" are not a reliable store of value. There is no solid anchor to Bitcoin feasible in the terms of our earlier discussion (see Chapter 5)—other than a crude prospective limit to total supply. The merchants who advertise themselves as accepters of Bitcoin do not use it as a numeraire currency to express prices of goods, services and assets. The unit of account function is the most central and critical quality of money. Unless goods and services are priced in Bitcoin, it has to be exchanged into another medium of exchange—such as dollars or pounds—first, at a cost.

However, Bitcoin has had remarkable power to entice and excite. Its price soared from $12,000 to $68,000 in the thirteen months to November 2021 (collapsing to below $20,000 barely six months later), and several major firms were accepting it, albeit most ostensibly where this might facilitate purchases made with "black or grey" funds, whether to pay for a luxury car, a watch or fine art. Without doubt, Bitcoin has strong appeal in enabling people who have no reason to trust each other to transact with each other in confidence without the intrusion of a third party, usually the banker, who increasingly in our age is partly an agent of government. That quality derives from the use of blockchain technology. As we shall see later in this volume, the quality of dispensing with the third-party "overseer" could in principle be added to established fiat monies and gold if regulations were lifted to permit this in safe forms but all of this remains hypothetical.

Bitcoin lacks the suppleness required in a good money. According to the "prospectus," total supply is fixed once 21 million outstanding, and in mid-2021 already almost 19 million had been issued cumulatively. Will close substitute cryptos develop? But the outcome in terms of reliability as a store of value might be acceptable to some of us relative to all the bad money alternatives. The speculation built up in Bitcoin, huge uncertainties as to when and how this would be liquidated and the actions of regulatory authorities mean the journey ahead will be bumpy, to say the least. (At the time of writing, the most visible crackdown outside China had been on a conventional financial institutions competing with crypto by using blockchain technology to develop digital versions of fiat monies.) It is possible also that hackers armed with new technology succeed in breaching the vaunted invincibility of the blockchain.

On a more positive note, there is no denying its at least passing achievement from the perspective of monetary history. The total market capitalisation—the sums held in the form of Bitcoin—had reached $1.16 trillion in November 2021, more than double the value of the US official gold reserves. The total of crypto assets at their peak valuation of October 2021 amounted to over 40% of the US monetary base (a sensible basis of comparison as there was as yet hardly any "broad money" forms in which to hold crypto) and was not far behind the amount of gold held in monetary form outside the central banks/governments (and excluding jewellery). This is a stunning record for a new form of investment/currency asset. On the other hand, its market capitalisation collapsed to only some $750 billion in March 2022, illustrating vividly its speculative nature.

To understand why Bitcoin has any value, our focus should be on two big marketing points—its "limited" supply and its capacity to function as a medium of exchange without the intrusion of the now widely distrusted "third-party" banker (or by extension credit card or payment card company) who loom so large in the established monetary systems. Bitcoiners infuriate many central bankers, commercial bankers and economists. Benoît Coeuré, a eurozone central banker now at the BIS, famously described Bitcoin as "the evil spawn of the financial crisis". Yet, the market sent a different message: wait and see. From the start, when anonymous founder "Satoshi Nakamoto" issued his challenge to conventional money in 2009, demand for the cryptocurrency has been fuelled by mistrust of state money. It still is. It is up to money and market critics to judge whether Bitcoin in fact lives up to the aspirations of those who have embraced it or whether its flaws—including the environmental costs of the mining process—are too manifold and serious. Critics are concerned that the waves of speculation that have dominated the Bitcoin space have fatally damaged what was a promising innovation. It needs a lot of courage for serious potential adopters of this money to maintain their convictions about it as a good money when its market value can drop 50 per cent in two months.

Is the fiat money order so rotten that progress is still possible for the Bitcoiners beyond the crypto-winter which descended in Spring and Summer 2022? Supporters believe that issuers of state money can be relied on to abuse their monetary prerogatives. Some defenders and advocates of Bitcoin still firmly hold to the view that its market price will become more stable over time. If more people use it to make payments, its market price should become less subject to wild swings, because this aspect of the demand for money is more broad and steady than demand for a speculative asset. If it did, this would advance its claims to be money. These remain unpersuasive. But remember, its benefits and costs should be viewed not alone but relative to those of fiat money. As long as we fail to reform our "moderately bad" monetary regimes, as long as they continue to have such damaging effects, so long will alternatives with any plausible claims to be money attract a following—all the more so if they are not subject to the prying compliance departments which populate the fiat money systems.

Preserving the Appearance of Normality

While all these damaging effects are unfolding, politicians and officials strive to preserve the appearances of normality. Mistakes may have been made in the past, they will acknowledge, but "we" have learnt from them; core services are not under threat; the central bank will provide an ultimate means of settling payments (when banks settle outstanding debts to each other across the books of the central bank). "We" will continue to oversee the banking system. "We" will provide liquidity to ease the daily functioning of money markets as well as in their capacity "lenders of last resort" in a crisis. Meanwhile, we will fuel the boom with money and credit, because to raise interest rates "abruptly" would "cause a recession".

Take for example a speech to the Economic Club of New York on 10 February 2021, by Federal Reserve chairman Jay Powell, just a few weeks on from the inauguration of President Biden and the start of a new Congress. With stock market prices rising to peaks that many observers regarded as unjustified, given the real dangers in the outlook, Powell stressed that the Fed would maintain a "patiently accommodative" policy stance until the economy hit "full employment" and inflation has been running above 2 per cent for some time. Such reassurances are not just public relations. They are crucial. They must convince. The slightest doubt, even about the very long-term future, could trigger big pullbacks in asset prices and raise fears about money itself. But look behind the facade and everything will have changed.

That concludes our survey of the costs and consequences of "bad money" regimes.

References

Labour Together (2022) Labour's Covenant: A Plan for National Reconstruction.

Shiller, Robert J (2000) Irrational Exuberance.

White, William (2021) http://williamwhite.ca/2021/11/15/monetary-policy-and-the-everything-asset-price-bubble/.

Part IV

Vested Interests, Politics and the Pandemic

Introduction

Two thousand five hundred years ago, the Greek historian Thucydides said there were three great causes of wars: self-interest, fear and greed. Today, these same passions are still at work, but now they are tearing our societies apart from inside. Who controls money and how its supply is regulated are at the centre of the struggle. If the world is to restore good money regimes, it is vital that we grasp the dangers of current trends and learn the right lessons from them. We should, however, go even further and ask: given the evidence of economic and financial crises and their harmful effects, why has there not already been such outrage as to generate the backlash needed?

Demand for reform should have been raised further by the pandemic, yet its effect has rather been to stifle unrest under a false comfort blanket of money. Vested interests, intense lobbying by monopoly capitalists in technology and finance, and the establishment media have all played parts in the betrayal. And we should not overlook the fact that even amidst the middle classes, there are many people who rightly or wrongly think they are gaining from asset inflation until it turns to asset deflation (as discussed in Chapter 6). In this chapter, we point to the forces and actors that keep bad money systems going. In the next (Chapter 11), we explain why the pandemic has strengthened these malevolent forces by raising super-monopoly profits of the pressure groups, raising the state's tax revenues and showing politicians how easy it is to curtail civil liberties when people run scared.

Part IV

Vested Interests, Politics and the Pandemic

10

What Keeps a Bad System in Power?

Cash for Cronies

Part of the answer is cronyism. We must take one step back to understand this. The severe crises may be decades apart and estimating the cumulative cost of lost prosperity over the long-run from what we call "bad money" is challenging. It involves counterfactual analysis (what would have happened if we had had good money rather than bad). And of course there has always been controversy among the economic experts as to whether bad money was responsible for the crises or for the loss of prosperity. So the status quo establishment in power can find leading experts who reject pinning blame on bad money and they may be surrounded by powerful interests.

As illustration, the big banks and big non-bank financial institutions, which may in any case take government bailouts in various forms during the crisis, have no fondness for a narrative that places their reckless lending powered by an inflated asset market at the heart of the problem; let's rally instead around the economists who say that the problem was a lack of investment opportunity, excess savings and a failure of economic policy in the sense of a refusal to stimulate demand in timely fashion and perhaps lack of international policy coordination. The big financial institutions and the monetary establishment usually can appeal to a bad luck story involving some official bungling (the bunglers now being out of office) with some conviction—such as the OPEC cartel action in 1973–4, or the "bungled and avoidable" bankruptcy of Lehmans in 2008. In the next big crisis, the excuse narrative will surely include some combination of pandemic woes, the Russia-Saudi

© The Author(s), under exclusive license to Springer Nature
Switzerland AG 2022
B. Brown and R. Pringle, *A Guide to Good Money*,
https://doi.org/10.1007/978-3-031-06041-0_10

Arabia oil market "grip" of 2021-, the Biden/Yellen mega fiscal stimulus of Spring 2021—and of course the Russia war in both its dimensions of military operations and US/EU-led economic sanctions.

Let's consider the present alliance of forces for bad money. This includes Big Tech and Big Finance, not friends of good money and other allies in what we can describe broadly as the "cronyist state". Big Tech owes much of its present financial might including the accumulation of vast monopoly power to virulent asset inflation; yield-hungry investors in the midst of interest income famine had lust for paper which seemed to promise monopoly rents now or in the future.

If instead competitive capitalism had been stronger in resisting the assault of budding monopolists (which might have been the case if they had not benefited from such a low cost of equity capital due to asset inflation), then we could have imagined several competing Googles and Facebooks and Apples and Amazons—meaning that the individual platforms of any of these would have had much less comprehensive private data on any individual, less valuable thereby for advertisers, less potentially abusive and less fertile ground for the emergence of surveillance capitalism..

Big Tech also makes big profits from Big Government, whose growth in turn has been enabled by bad money; one component here has been the "war against terror", with one report putting revenues for Big Tech from this at near $50bn between 2004 and 2020 with the US Defense Department and Homeland Security in the lead (Acron 2021). The sums may not seem vast in the Big Picture but we should note that, at the stratospheric P/E multiples typical of virulent asset inflation, prospective profits from Big Government make a substantial contribution to the giant market capitalisations of Big Tech. Though the war on terror may have wound down, other military prospects of Big Tech are winding up, many of which remain below the radar screen (see Glaser, 2020).

How Big Tech works against the cause of Good Money is illustrated by the case of Amazon—but others, whether for example Apple, Microsoft or Alphabet, could demonstrate similar points. Asset inflation has done wonders for its stock price through all these years of meagre if any profits on its core retail business (at first in absolute terms and then relative to its market valuation). The magnificent stock price performance, reflecting in part speculative expectations that in the future the core business would have sufficient monopoly power to raise profit margins and in part actual huge profits in cloud computing where it has achieved market dominance, has been crucial to its success in financing what looks like widespread predatory action against new entrants and competitors, albeit well-camouflaged by client-friendly services. All of this will most likely be the subject of long-running litigation, with the FTC pushing forward at end-2021 in this process with its investigation into anti-competitive practices by Amazon's cloud computing business. Amazon has already opened its defence, asking that the FTC chair, a leading academic legal critic of the company, to recluse herself from the case (see Khan, Lisa 2017). In the public space, the evidence against Amazon mounted with charges of systematic snapping up of former government officials (see Lippman, 2021).

Of course cronyism itself is not an offence (though it may of course spawn behaviour which does cross the line in terms of legality), and so news in late 2021 that Amazon founder Bezos had donated $100 m to the Obama Foundation was par for the course, as was the long-standing charge that Bezos and President Obama had made a sweetheart deal much earlier under which Amazon obtained enviable terms for distributing its parcels (see Morris, 2017). The media is also full of stories about cronyism related to the saga of Amazon's AWS so-called JEDI contract with the US defence department on cloud computing (Weinberger 2017). (Amazon Web Services, Inc. provides on-demand cloud computing platforms and APIs to individuals, companies and governments.) Finishing where we started, all this alleged cronyism and anti-competitive behaviour fits in with Amazon's place in the coalition of forces against good money. Certainly, Amazon would be no friend of efforts to restore cash as a payments medium including high denomination notes as this would benefit in-store vs. online business; ditto with efforts to strengthen laws safeguarding competition which meant that users of cash would get cheaper prices than those using payment cards (at present monopoly power enjoyed by credit and payment card companies and their effective lobbying mean that the cost of cards is usually shunted onto cash purchasers who in a fully competitive level playing field should pay a lower all-in price than the card user, given that the merchant must pay fees to the card companies). Lower prices for cash would be an incentive for the public to shop in brick and mortar stores rather than online.

Amazon's inherent co-interest with bad money extends far beyond these points. Amazon would greet cautiously an extension of crypto monetary systems which dispense with third party overseers; the implicit anonymity could mean no information for it to track towards winning business. But presumably Amazon could have a strong interest in promoting its own crypto money network in that it could glean information from the total technological space created. An Amazon crypto token, most plausibly a stablecoin based on the US dollar or other fiat monies, could allow Amazon to pick up information about its clients and in some way tie these to its businesses. This could be a huge profit-spinner, as commented on by BIS authors (see Auer and Boehme, 2021), and viewed as a danger of crypto development in some forms. This interest of Big Tech giants in promoting some forms of crypto payments, with clients tied into their "eco-systems", has long been recognised in the case of Facebook (now Meta) regarding its proposed but ultimately aborted (in the face of regulatory and Congressional hostility) development of Libra currency.

Big Tech poses obstacles to the advance of good money ideas in the political system in ways which depend on the nature of its growing influence in particular in Washington (see Krishan, 2021). Big Tech funds political action committees (PACS) which in turn support candidates in US elections, whether in Congress or for the White House, and also which support specific causes. A candidate keen to push good money ideas would not get a great hearing from such PACS, unless perhaps he or she had some offsetting promise to offer—for example, an offer (as some conservatives favour) to go easy on anti-trust action or step up crime surveillance programs of military programs which would see much new business for Big Tech. Suffice to say that Big Tech would be unlikely to sponsor think tanks or research by groups or individuals pursuing a good money agenda. There are cruder and more direct channels of influence; for example, firms can pay high rates for speeches of former officials, including central bankers, who might soon assume positions of power (e.g. Janet Yellen's speaking fees from Alphabet during her career between heading the Fed and then the Treasury, see Walsh 2021). Big Tech may join with Big Media in hushing up voices calling for monetary reforms. And of course Big Tech firms have large captive markets for their distributed news from which certain material which could promote public interest in good money (e.g. direct criticisms or attacks on cronyism in the monetary bureaucracies) could be purged by their internal "censors".

Back to Big Finance as a key element in the cronyism which among other concerns blocks opportunity for good money. Big Finance has found Eldorado in the leveraged products and deals that flourish under soft money and political corruption (see below regarding private equity); the credit card monopolists certainly would not look kindly on a potential challenge to their business from good money. The private equity industry plays a critical role here (as shown, for example, by Stockman 2013). This industry thrives by selling over-priced high-risk debt to investors desperate for income. And the investors in private equity funds look forward to continuing profits from the leveraging up of take-over targets (once taken private) and then resold later in the public equity market where prices are expected to rise for ever powered by monetary inflation. This process of taking over companies and/or building them up is heavily concentrated in the government contracting area, where streams of fixed income are a perfect fit for their financial engineering skills. Globally, a focus of their activity includes operations (many under the heading of venture capital and usually highly leveraged) with public and semi-public sector institutions in the emerging markets, especially in Asia and China.

The biggest US private equity fund, Blackstone, for example, is strongly entrenched in the Chinese market, having had a Chinese state entity as a stakeholder until 2018; its Chairman and founder Stephen Shwarzman has been an important financial contributor to the Republicans and President Trump's campaigning; and there has been speculation on how his Trump ties influenced the interim trade truce deal between the US and China concluded in January 2020. This apparently opened up new opportunities for Wall Street in the Chinese market. More generally, for private equity firms naturally attract well-connected people vital to their business. We can see this in the form of a two-way flow of private equity barons into the US government, including the Fed and Treasury, and of retired top officials in all walks of government back into private equity; alongside private equity personalities have become notable in entering Congress and private equity financial contributions to Congressional races are sought after.

Question marks arose about all this in the pandemic financial/economic crisis of March 2020—with ex-private equity guys at the top of both the Treasury and the Fed, one of which subsequently returned to the private equity fold reportedly with a whole new range of "contacts", including in Saudi Arabia and the Gulf States. No surprise, then, that 2021 was a bumper year for pay-outs to the private equity barons based on the stellar performance in 2020 as generated by the Fed's pandemic emergency monetary policy (Indap 2020). Suffice to ask, that with "friends" like this—by reputation pro-business and pro-market—how could good money need enemies?

Once crony capitalists infiltrate the corridors of power, they legitimise their privileged position by enlisting the aid of existing elites and their ideologies. As discussed in the previous chapter, such ideologues insist that the state, through agencies such as central banks, can and should lead the drive for growth. Cronies love this. This should be led, according to many, by an expanding public sector. Experience and theory both show the hazards of such policies. Yes, the public sector has a role to play in free market capitalism; Milton Friedman, great champion of free markets as he was, fully recognised this, as had Adam Smith 200 years before him. But this role must be clearly defined and limited. It must be restrained from doing things, to curry favour with special interests, that corrupt the economic system. Going for growth at all costs is one of them. But it means more money gushing to the cronies' pet projects.

Global Corruption

Unaccountable political interests exercise undue influence on monetary systems throughout the world. Flows of international aid combined with cronyism in Washington and in the host countries have spread corruption globally. Perhaps one of the starkest examples of this was the IMF lending program to Russia under the regime of Boris Yeltsin (see Florio, 2002), a key element in President Clinton's policy with respect to that country in the aftermath of the Soviet Union's collapse. Accordingly, the program was presided over by Robert Rubin at the US Treasury and Stanley Fischer at the IMF (nominated as deputy chief there by the Clinton administration) both of whom ended up with top jobs at the main US bank lending to Russia, Citibank. The journey along the way included Fischer's notorious memo about the Russian economic miracle in early 1998 (see Fischer 1998), Russia's financial collapse later in the same year, and a savage IMF program of austerity which finally dashed hopes of Russian democracy. Earlier, there had been the allegations that Larry Summers (deputy Treasury Secretary under Rubin, then his successor) in his role as coordinator of the Harvard professors advising on Russian economic reform back in the early 1990s had been careless in allowing corrupt elements to penetrate the US-funded programs in which they were involved. These allegations centred around the role of an "intimate" of Professor Summers and Professor Schleifer, and culminated in a $26 m settlement between Harvard and the US Department of Justice (see Douglas 2009). US officials from the top down, including their colleagues at the IMF, gave no indication of knowing that most of the IMF loans were going to criminal associates in and around Yeltsin's family (see McClintick, 2008), and there is no reason for doubting their ignorance—a case of ivory tower economists having no knowledge of what was happening on the ground, especially in a grimy newly liberated property market such as that in Russia.

As more than a footnote, we should point out that this episode of the Russian lending scandals occurred in the early years of the great monetary inflation starting in the mid-1990s, interrupted by the Global Financial Crisis of 2008; this monetary inflation and particularly asset inflation facilitated the marketing of Russian bonds and other Russian paper during the Yeltsin bubble to global investors and foreign banks, including as mentioned

Citibank whose shareholders were apparently enthusiastic about the great new opportunities in their bank's Russian portfolio.

The inexorable rise in financial corruption globally has accompanied apparently well-intentioned efforts to support countries suffering from financial crises and most recently the pandemic of 2020–22. A startlingly high proportion of the massive aid/grants/loans flooding into emerging markets from international institutions is being recycled back to the main financial centres where it is laundered and re-invested by political leaders and their cronies in "safe" assets such as real estate. This typifies the ways in which powerful forces and actors keep a bad money system going. Corporate monopolists and bad bankers feed on the healthy parts of the economy while, like a virus, they weaken the body and, once allowed in, they are well-nigh impossible to get rid of. Politicians, like monarchs of old, dispense favours while courtiers manoeuvre for their place in the queue of supplicants. Given the political connections, anybody can protect his or her family and descendants from the dangers and risks of old-fashioned market capitalism (Vogl 2021).

There is little pushback. It may be said that the media—where it is free to do so (and press freedom itself is on the decline)—are already decrying the injustice of such a system. Yes, they decry ever-widening inequality. What such articles often lack, however, is any explanation of the forces that support such unjust systems or how they can be brought to an end. One has to question the extent to which even ostensibly independent non-profit institutions including think tanks, being reliant on the donations of the private equity baron philanthropists or other members of the bad money "establishment", give honest analysis and objective recommendations. In practice, the media is often complicit in support of the status quo (see below).

Consider the ways on which financial crises are used not to reform or raise fundamental questions about the system but rather to entrench it; in that sense, they have a systemic role as part of the system and should not be viewed as "shocks" from outside it. Economies weakened by structural flaws are considered (by those claiming expertise in such matters, governments and their advisers) to need constant injections of funds. Without such life support, it is asserted, they would suffer sudden relapses. In effect, crises serve to enhance unaccountable political power—no surprise, then, that they come along frequently. This is what happened after the financial crises in the last quarter of the twentieth century, again after the global financial crisis in 2008, and is likely to occur again in the denouement of the Great Pandemic and War Inflation. Some neo-Keynesian economists got behind the doctrine of "fading investment opportunity", "secular stagnation" and the related problem of the zero rate boundary to monetary policy (see Summers 2016). They never confronted the issue that the economic sclerosis disease had its roots in the bad money which they had advocated—and why should they have done given the promising career opportunities at the top of government that came along from sticking with their viewpoint, which is perennially popular with the ruling presidents and prime ministers?

Plainly, bad money has deep political, ideological and social roots. That explains why revelations by investigatory journalists of scandals—which have included vivid accounts of corruption at the highest level of states—have little impact, and why the finance and political elites use crises to keep the essentials of the system in place, while giving it an occasional face-lift.

Muscular Lobbying

By the late twentieth century, the buoyancy of markets was due in no small degree to the notion that central banks would respond aggressively to any serious threatened downturn. Led by the Fed, they came in to put a floor under stock markets (see Chapters 6 and 8). It started under Alan Greenspan in 1987 and became an established feature—something market participants "learnt" they could count on. But the relationship went deeper. In addition, major institutions were bailed out—including notably the 1998 rescue of the hedge fund Long-term Capital Management. Commercial bankers around the world noted this, as they strove to imitate the stunning success of the great (and less regulated) US investment banks. These bankers worshipped at the altar of Goldman Sachs. Former employees of Goldman Sachs took key policy-making positions in countries around the world. The notorious "revolving door" applied here. Some members of this alumni might still have had personal interest in aligning their policy-perspectives and policy-making details in line with "what is good for GS"; this could include prospects for post-office employment in Big Finance perhaps where GS alumni called the shots and still had big personal interest in GS stock, or perhaps just where the likely employer would be more likely to employ "one of us" than someone who had had a Damascus moment in favour of sound money. Variations on such themes are multiple. In any event, when threatened with extinction in the 2008 crisis ("our business model is no longer viable"), this investment bank smoothly transformed itself into a proper, respectable, bank eligible for Fed lender of last resort assistance, when former Goldman alumni Hank Paulson was Secretary of the US Treasury. A massive salvage operation was organised for AIG, whose downfall could have been fatal for Goldman Sachs given its exposure to derivatives positions with that entity (see Greider 2010). The new bank status for Goldman Sachs dismayed the widely revered central banker Paul Volcker:

> If you want to be a bank, follow the bank rules. If Goldman Sachs and the others want to do proprietary trading, then they shouldn't be banks (Reuters interview, 2011).

That pointed to just one of the links between the financial crisis and the spread of crony capitalism. But it is only a small part of the total picture. Take perhaps the most blatant example of cronyism in the "European space". This starts again with a Goldman Sachs connection. Enter Mario Draghi, PhD dissertation student of Stanley Fischer at MIT, and in the 1990s top official in the Italian Treasury. Recall at that time Italy and PM Prodi were striving to become a founding member of EMU and as such had to meet the Maastricht criteria for its public finances. As unmasked subsequently (see Story, 2010), key swap transactions entered into by the Italian Treasury with Goldman Sachs and one other US leading investment bank were used to massage the Italian debt figures down. The same technique was used subsequently at the start of the 2000s in massaging the Greek debt figures again with Goldman Sachs as the principal counterpart in the swaps. When in 2001 an Italian academic expert in swaps, Professor Piga, was due to present his paper on the subject of the Italian swaps, to a conference organised by ISMA (International Securities Market Association) and Council for Foreign Relations (who had published his research report), death threats forced a cancellation of the proceedings (see Alloway, 2010) and Euromoney (1 September 2001).

Anyhow in 2002 Mario Draghi joined Goldman Sachs as its European chief and in subsequent revelations about the Greek swaps that institution denied that the Italian economist had any responsibility for those deals—a claim disputed by some (see Johnson, 2010); in any case, the claims about the Italian swaps would still stand. Fast forward to 2011, by which time Draghi had made it back to state office, this time as Governor of the Bank of Italy (appointed in 2005); he also becomes head of the G-20 governments' task force on Financial Stability. As such, we should hardly have expected him to examine whether the main force behind the financial instability of the previous years had been central banks! i.e. the long-running monetary infla- tion as driven by the Federal Reserve from the mid-1990s to the early to mid-2000s—(subsequently reversed suddenly and sharply through 2005–6/7 in response to a spike in CPI inflation), a monetary policy sequence largely copied by the ECB; nor would he have turned attention to the question whether it had been asset inflation that in turn formed the fertile ground for such financial extravaganzas as excess leverage in which the Draghi-Goldman Sachs couple are an example. Was the success of Goldman Sachs and others in marketing huge amounts of Italian state debt alongside loads of risky debt during the first half of the 2000s part and parcel of this asset inflation? There is no evidence that Mario Draghi ever entertained such questions. Historians must.

Into the third decade of the twenty-first century, the combination of the digital revolution, asset inflation and advancing monopoly capitalism has spawned new ways to use political power to make money and insulate the economic powerful and their dynasties from society. Actual and would-be monopolists lobby politicians to make life difficult for competitors, provide lucrative state contracts, dispense special tax favours and provide permits or other kinds of state intervention. Such special interests then subvert the public sector and make it serve private ends. This is to them the natural state of affairs. Unless the institutions of civil society are extremely robust and make full use of rights under the law—with an independent judiciary, freedom of speech and people realise what is at stake and have the courage to fight, then the infection of corruption will spread rapidly through the organs of government. It is then but a short final step up the kleptocratic ladder to appoint a head of state or prime minister who will manipulate the law courts and system of justice on your behalf. This gives you immunity from prosecution. You can even obtain court orders banning journalists from reporting or investigating their misdeeds. Kleptocrats then control the main channels of mass media communications.

Why Money is so Vulnerable to Abuse

Why is modern money so vulnerable to abuse by private interests, even in otherwise well-ordered democracies with constitutional guardrails to protect liberty? We would point to two key features.

Firstly, modern monetary and supervisory policies are centralised—conducted by the relevant official bodies—and highly discretionary. The institutions charged with carrying out policy are accountable to parliaments or governments; independent central banks are given their mandates by a political authority and their key senior officials nominated by government, and subsequently subject to approval by a legislature. The thoroughness and extent with which these institutions are "audited", however, are often poor. So there are considerable channels for cronyism to influence official regulatory and wider monetary policy outcomes, and a huge premium on inside information. Some have alleged that Chair Powell in implementing his pandemic policies (together with Mnuchin) was influenced by the interests of the private equity people (he is of course one of them)—and private equity was a huge gainer from his package. If there were proper accountability, a Congressional committee or even court would have had authority to delve into all this. But in the present set-up—no accountability.

Secondly, modern state money foments monetary phobias. That's built into the adoption by central banks of a target of 2% annual inflation rate. This is the modern monetary standard, albeit now seriously undermined by the pandemic "break-out" inflation of 2021–2. So whenever actual inflation rises above or dips below target, commentators quickly sense an unfolding panic. If inflation falls—or is expected to fall—below target people ask: "Have the central banks got enough ammunition?" "Can they print enough money?" "How can the policy-makers persuade people to spend more?" When inflation rises, equally, commentators whip up fears that it may be difficult to stop price rises or prevent inflation from accelerating; the high inflation of the 1970s is back, and they warn.

Such easily stirred-up questioning shows our fear of what money has become and what it might do, or not do. This is harmful in itself. To be sure, it is normal for individuals to worry about money. But it is harmful for society as a whole to be in a constant state of angst such that they are scared by variations in its rate of inflation and of expected inflation or whether there's another financial crisis round the corner. Yet in the financial and economic media, we are continually exposed to extreme fears of deflation and another Great Depression on the one hand or 1970s style high inflation on the other—and both of these possibilities are well within the range of possible future scenarios which could become reality under present bad money regimes.

A Money Crew Powered by Self-Interest and Greed

In 2020–21, the world's central banks and governments, led by Washington (the Federal Reserve and the US Treasury first under the Trump administration and then under the Biden administration), set the stage for what they hoped would be a rapid economic expansion. Their monetary and fiscal efforts combined would supercharge the natural economic rebound following the end of the pandemic. It is hard to find a more dangerous time in the past

100 years to apply the doctrine of contra-cyclical stimulus. Powerful forces moved large sectors of the asset market in ways that could suddenly reverse.

Self-interest and greed helped to power these bad ideas. The "revolving door" is not new. Wall Street bosses had gained lucrative positions of political power under a long string of presidents. But President Trump's and subsequently President Biden's fiscal and monetary bonus came after 20 years of consistent stimulus, camouflaged consumer price inflation (rising only about 2% a year on average) and powerful asset inflation (US stocks rose nearly 9% a year on average or 300% between 2000 and February 2021). The misguided policy prescription applied during the pandemic—to combat the economic supply pullback with a mega-dose of fiscal and monetary stimulus—would be sustained. (The story is brought up to date in Chapter 11 on the Pandemic.)

Gambling on a Growth Spurt

Could virulent asset inflation lead in due course to a spurt of growth that would in some senses justify such sky-high valuations? This is indeed possible in principle; for example, speculative booms accompanied the steam and railway revolution in the nineteenth century, the electricity revolution from the 1870s to the 1920s, the oil, car and mass production revolution in the first half of the twentieth century and the information technology revolution from the 1990s (see also Chapter 8). They were accompanied by surges in economic productivity and growth (see *Technological Revolutions and Financial Capital*, by Carlotta Perez). But this link to productivity gains did not apply to the long asset inflation process from 2012 to 2021. The problem through this period was that many investors were reluctant to buy into long-term investments, preferring instead the potentially quick gains from chasing the financial engineers' output, including momentum trading and camouflaged leverage. There were exceptions, such as the enormous investments in the US in aircraft construction, shale oil and gas production as well as shopping mall construction boom. It is plausible that this latest episode of asset inflation focused particularly on pandemic stocks could produce a capital spending boom in some fields (e.g. think of Tesla, Amazon and more generally, cloud computing).

A Complaisant Media…

One reason why bad monetary regimes persist and spread is that so much of the mainstream media no longer hold policy-makers to account. Journalists do not gain advancement in their careers by seeing the harm; nor do they connect it to policy. They usually endorse the view of those economists who claim that easy money helps cure the ills of society. They applaud the aim of "stabilising financial markets" and combating the danger of asset deflation. The main media outlets/publications dutifully send their journalists along to Fed policy briefings (virtual these days) to ask respectful questions about the latest dot plots or plans for interest rates and balance sheet size. If this means unlimited purchases of assets, so be it. This is called "fiscal" and "financial" *domination*; official policy is geared to satisfy the needs of the tax authorities and/or by the special interests of the finance industry.

This is ironic. Journalists believe that they can be critical when this is justified. They certainly have the legal space to voice contrary opinions—always excluding infringements on press freedom in countries such as Hungary as well as the autocracies. There are indeed always exceptions. But, in general, mainstream media has chosen to employ a journalist herd which has endorsed policies of continual stimulation and low rates, seemingly oblivious to the damage done to the mechanisms of market economies. And we are not just talking here of Bezos-owned Washington Post! In other words, the mainstream media in its reporting on the present monetary regime is far from fully independent and critical, instead becoming strongly biased. The direction of that bias can change in response to a shift in popular and political currents as occurred during the pandemic-war inflation, The sudden surge in consumer prices provoked a public reaction such that inflation and what to do about it became the top election issue. A media which had long been a key part of bad money propaganda suddenly gave a platform to those criticising a set of bad money policy-makers and their past flawed decisions.

Behind the (Lack of) Political Demand for Reform

Given the damage inflicted by numerous financial crises and the litany of harms summarised in Chapter 9, why has there not already been such outrage as to generate the backlash needed? Where do we look for the political fuel to power demand for reform? If the situation is really as bad as we paint it, why has discontent not already risen to a level that policy-makers could not ignore?

Even before Russia's invasion of Ukraine in February 2022, people have seemingly much more pressing issues to worry about, ranging from the rolling epidemic to the harm of social media, Global Warming, racial and gender discrimination—the whole diversity and "woke" agenda—and the spectre of massive occupational job losses from artificial intelligence and robotics. Remember too that many benefit under monetary inflation from the (relative) impoverishment of others. With so many fears and anxieties jostling for our attention, why get worked up about our money? We have described in Chapter 6 many of the illusions of asset inflation, whereby many people feel wealthier than they are fundamentally. For most people, in most states (except for the likes of Venezuela and Turkey), money appears to be working (kind of) most of the time. Even if some sections of the public worry about inflation, and they are intuitively sceptical about central banks and their so-called independence (whether from government or cronyism), there is no reform agenda in the mainstream of political choice that they can rally around. Central bankers strike a chord, it seems, when they insist that money is a public good that now more than ever must be safeguarded by trusted agents—themselves; indeed, any development, such as cryptocurrencies that challenge the official concept of money by offering to take money private again, is a threat: "It is undesirable to rely only on private money", says the head of the Bank for International Settlement (Carstens 2022):

> "Users may initially find great convenience in paying with a Big Tech global stablecoin. But in doing so they may be handing the keys to our monetary system over to private entities, driven by profits and accountable only to their shareholders and other insiders. Such an arrangement could erode trust. A public good like money needs oversight with the public interest in mind".

We have explained why such claims are misguided and misleading.

References

Action Center on Race and the Economy (2021): "Big Tech sells War".

Alloway, Tracy (2010) "More on that mysterious counterpart N" Opinion FT Alphaville March 1, 2010.

Carstens, A (2022) Digital Currencies and the Soul of Money; Speech as Goethe University's Institute for Law and Finance (ILF) Conference on "Data, Digitalization, the New Finance and Central Bank Digital Currencies: The Future of Banking and Money", 18 January

Douglas, Rachel Berthoff "Summers Hated in Russia" Executive Intelligence Review, April 10, 2009.

Euromoney (2001) "How Italy Shrank its Deficit" September 1.

Florio, Massimo (2002) "Economists, Privatization in Russia, and the Waning of the Washington Consensus" *Review of International Political Economy*, Vol 9, issue 2.

Fischer, Stanley (1998) "The Russian Economy at the Start of 1998" *Speech*, January 9.

Glaser, April (2020) NBC news, July 8 "Thousands of Contracts Highlight Quiet Ties between Big Tech and US Military".

Greider, William (2010) "The AIG Bail Out Scandal" *The Nation*, August 8.

Indap, Sujet (2020) "Private Equity Chiefs Get Bumper Pay-Outs on Back of Fed stimulus" FT March 2, 2020.

Khan, Lina M (2017) "Amazon's Anti-Trust Paradox" *The Yale Law Journal*, February. pp. 126–710.

Krishan, Nihal (2021) "Big Tech Companies Ramp up Spending on Political Influence Groups" *Washington Examiner*, August, 11.

Lippman, Daniel and Birnbaum, Emily (2021): "The Secret Behind Amazon's Domination in Cloud Computing" *Politico*, April 6.

McClintick (2008) "How Harvard Lost Russia" *Institutional Investor*, January 15.

Morris, David Z (2017) "This Analyst Claims the US Postal Service is Giving Amazon a Huge Subsidy" *Fortune*, July 16.

Raphael, Auer and Reiner, Boehme (2021) "Central Bank Digital Currency: The Quest for Minimally Invasive Technology" BIS Working Papers, No. 948, June.

Stockman, David A (2013) *The Great Deformation: The Corruption of Capitalism in America*. Public Affairs.

Story, Louise; Thomas London and Schwartz Nelca (2010) "Wall Street helped to Mask Debt Fuelling Europe's Crisis" *New York Times*, February 13.

Summers, Lawrence (2016) "The Age of Secular Stagnation and What to do About it" *Foreign Affairs*, February 15.

Vogl, F (2021) *The Enablers: How the West Supports Kleptocrats and Corruption—Endangering Our Democracy*. Rowman and Littlefield.

Walsh, Joe "Yellen Earned $7mn in Speaking Fees Over Last 2 Years" *Forbes*, January 1, 2021.

Weinberger, Sharon (2017) "Meet America's Newest Military Giant: Amazon" *MIT Technology Review*, Vol. 126, October.

11

Bad Money's Pyrrhic Victory Over the Pandemic

Even before the COVID-19 pandemic spread from its origins in China towards the end of 2019, the virus of monetary inflation was already circulating around the world. When the pandemic struck (say February/March 2020 in the case of Europe and North America), eminent economists urged governments to combat it by taking strong action including lockdowns, stepped-up monetary growth and massive fiscal "stimulus". The right course of action, we argue, would have been the contrary to this. There should have been the utmost care, at such a dangerous time, to prevent money from slipping even further out of control.

This chapter is in three sections. Firstly, we give an account of the official response to the pandemic, focusing on monetary and economic policies. Secondly, we compare this with the counterfactual case—what would have been the outcome, or range of plausible outcomes, under a good money regime? Thirdly, we present our view of the implications of pandemic inflation for our monetary future. We conclude that the much-touted initial success of the "bold" monetary policy response to the pandemic was a pyrrhic victory.

Fear Recession? Inject Cash…

Although the Fed had returned to easy mode in Winter 2018/19, when the Trump administration viewed the devastation of the pandemic in early Spring

© The Author(s), under exclusive license to Springer Nature
Switzerland AG 2022
B. Brown and R. Pringle, *A Guide to Good Money*,
https://doi.org/10.1007/978-3-031-06041-0_11

2020, the monetary easing so far did not seem enough; another Great Recession seemed all too probable. As Alex Pollock reminds us in his study of pandemic, governments are pre-programmed to respond to adverse shocks with bold (meaning interventionist) actions—they must be seen to be "on the case" and "caring" (see Pollock, 2022). A slump in equities and spike in credit spreads during February and early March 2020 called attention to the dangers. In retrospect (and, some would say, at the time), the officials did not need to worry so much; a big economic rebound was always likely on the other side of the supply shock unleashed by the pandemic; we would do better to think of the plunge of output during Spring 2020 as a spasm with an in-built tendency to be followed promptly by a re-breathing in economic life rather than a recession. True, the timing of recovery from the Great Pandemic Spasm was uncertain, not least as regards medical progress in terms of vaccinations and cures, or the public health interventions of Big Government notably in the form of lockdowns and travel restrictions. A wide range of services to consumers became liable to serious infection risk while infection-free supplies suddenly shrank. Individuals across large parts of economic activity became subject to infection risk in delivering their services in the workplace. On the political left, critics seized on the chance to ridicule the pro-market "neo-liberal" theories that had, they asserted, served us badly for a generation. Big government was back—sometimes under new labels such as "levelling up". Many economists itched to wrest back controls over the economy just as governments had imposed new and intrusive rules over personal behaviour during the lockdowns. (Of course, some argued in the opposite direction, see for example Feguson (2021)).

No surprise, then, that in Spring 2020, a US election year, the Federal Reserve decided in close coordination with the Treasury on applying a completely inappropriate remedy—a sustained mega-dose of monetary inflation. This was the wrong remedy as the US and other countries were confronted not with a shortage of aggregate demand but with an enforced cut in supply. Absurdly, the Keynesian mindset had so permeated public debate and the economics profession that nobody in or around the corridors of power was crying this out loud. The White House and Congress applauded. Other central banks followed. In treating this economic spasm in the same way as a Great Recession, the Federal Reserve administered even more powerful stimulus drugs especially out of their so-called non-conventional box than during the last Great Recession and Crash and its aftermath (say 2008–11/12). The Fed's new policy instruments included funding facilities for non-financial firms and state and local governments. This at once raised

questions as to whether the Fed should be conducting such lending policies or whether that should be done by the fiscal authorities (the risks were
backstopped by the US Treasury). And early on there was an aggressive use of
dollar lending to foreign central banks (under swap arrangements). This official credit extension vastly expanded the Fed's reach into the economy—yet
it could not wipe away bankruptcy risk. In a bankruptcy, the Fed as a holder
of corporate paper or as a direct lender would not forego its claim in favour
of other creditors. Yet the story that the Fed would be a big buyer of such
paper including junk bonds set a light under the high-risk credit markets.
Prices of high-risk debt soared. And in Europe it was another version of the
same story; the ECB showed it was ready to lend to weak, highly-indebted
governments and banks, prompting a jump in the prices of their bonds. The
central banks were in effect bypassing the system, assuming high-risk roles
(in terms of the possible cost to public finances) normally reserved for bodies
answerable to taxpayers through Congress or parliaments.

There was another, little-noticed, factor at work—a spreading realisation
that the Fed's stepping up of monetary inflation meant not only a surge
in monetary taxation for governments but also a rise in quasi-taxation to
the benefit of private sector borrowers such as private equity. For the latter
would gain both from an unexpected acceleration in CPI inflation (reducing
the real value of loan principal outstanding) and/or from increased monetary
repression (suppressed real interest rates).

The resumption of asset inflation occurred quickly in the US in conjunc-
tion with a strong economic rebound from the extreme spasm low point.
As lockdowns were eased, spending bounced back. True, this was not across
the board—spending on services widely subject to infection risk remained
depressed. But households, most of all in the US, stepped up purchases of
goods, especially consumer durables. Austrian School economists tell us that
the influence of money creation in an economy is not neutral (even across
all sectors)—but can enter in a highly uneven fashion; that has certainly
been the case during the pandemic. In the context of supply disruptions—
whether dislocation of ports, coincident crisis in microchip production and
haywire container traffic—this meant severe bottlenecks with correspondingly spectacular upward pressure on some prices. Business spending rose
overall, most of all in digitalisation which got big fillips from the stay at
home boom and associated need for technological support, including cloud
computing. (Huge demand for cloud computing also came from the Bitcoin
miners—an example of mal-investment stemming from asset inflation in so
far as the Bitcoin boom was indeed a function of monetary inflation.) That
constellation together with monetary inflation underpinned a huge boom

in "pandemic stocks" (the stocks in businesses which would do well out of the pandemic). Hence asset inflation directly powered a business spending spree in some sectors, most notably digitalization. Leading examples included Amazon, gaining from both the online spending boom and also the surge in spending on cloud computing where it had secured a near-monopoly position (of course not absolute)—subsequently to come under potential challenge in late 2021 from the Federal Trade Commission; similar stories could be told for other Big Tech monopolies.

The bottlenecks described above which accompanied all of this originated in part from mal-investment during many previous years of monetary inflation but mainly from the obvious fact that rising monetary demand bounced back off supply constrained by the impact of Covid and lockdowns. Many companies had joined the craze for building global supply chains including their "just in time inventory management", encouraged by inflated equity markets which embraced a narrative about the profits from "globalisation" (including often a key role for China in the chain); corporate management and their shareholders ignored doubts about whether those chains would work under stress and their possible costs compared to production nearer to home. The crisis in these supply chains which erupted during the pandemic (and earlier in weaker form under the US-China "tariff war"), aggravated not just by the US consumer durable spending boom but also by China's zero-tolerance policy on COVID-19, illustrated the big costs of earlier mal-investment in terms of economic prosperity.

Sit Back and Enjoy the Profits Boom

Investors in the US equity market, though, understandably, were not thinking much if at all about mal-investment. Instead, for them the continuing star performance of equities had a solid foundation in an accompanying widespread profits boom—far beyond just the pandemic stocks—which became evident through 2021. One part of this story was the strong demand for home digital technology coupled with monopoly power in some cases of the suppliers of this—one could think of Microsoft, Apple and Amazon web services in this regard, among others. There has also been the boom in digital advertising translating into *big profits* gain for the near-monopoly suppliers of this, though there could be offsets in loss of advertising revenues for alternative media. The scale of the profits boom overall, however, went well beyond this core, as evidenced also by stellar earnings growth say for the universe of US small and mid-cap companies in general.

How did monetary inflation drive this profits boom?

Quite simply demand across an array of business sectors surged. The new money demand entered the system in a way which drove up profit margins and corporate revenues. We should include here the spending out of fantastic wealth gains, whether in equities, real estate or the crypto space, even if much of this is ultimately illusory.

In a competitive capitalist system, forces of competition would erode profit margins. Demand does not continue to far outstrip supply. As prices adjust upwards across an increasing range, the real purchasing power of the new money created diminishes. As expectations of high inflation broaden out, or alternatively more economic agents become fully aware of the inflation environment in which they operate, firms that had been able initially to drive up their profits will find they cannot do this owing to rising pressure on their costs.

However, the asset inflation process as intensified by the monetary response to the pandemic led equity investors to assume continuing abnormally high profits and margins. But we know that such assumptions are typical of asset inflations and these usually end in asset deflations! Think of the famous US economist of the early twentieth century, Irving Fisher, who two days before the Wall Street Crash in October 1929 wrote that high profits of US companies should now be regarded as permanent and that US stocks were correspondingly cheap. This is therefore another red flag.

There was an element in the monetary response to pandemic that had antecedents in wartime monetary experiences—direct financing by the central bank of government spending. The operation to combat COVID-19 involved massive government expenditures. These included compensation payments to labour made idle in consequence of disease risk, together with aid to front-line medical services and pharmaceutical development; more broadly, there was a whole range of expenditures related to, for example, COVID-19 testing and implementation of new safety rules for mitigating exposure to the disease including the enforcement of restrictions on international travel and enforcing isolation requirements. (All of this incidentally "boosted" reported GDP.) As in wartime, central banks held down the apparent cost of government borrowing, buying large amounts of government bonds and often increasing the government's overdraft limit on their books; in turn, the central banks credited the reserve deposits held by banks to match these purchases, thus increasing the monetary base. A big counterpart to this finance to governments was a rise in bank deposits.

The official authorities levied monetary taxation in the two forms described in Chapter 6. The central bankers and finance ministers—working in new intimacy—claimed victory over the forces of "recession" which, they alleged, would have occurred in the absence of their joint "bold" action. First, they reversed a fall in asset prices through February/March 2020 and empowered asset inflation. (Please note that central bankers avoid talk about asset inflation; they prefer to picture themselves as "supporting markets and market liquidity" at times of "stress" and rising "vulnerabilities"; in this tautological language, a widening of credit spreads, for example, indicates "rising stress" even if it looks to everybody else like the bursting of a bubble.) Second, they financed vast government spending especially on transfer payments, borrowing the money at ultra-low rates. This was presented as a means to alleviate suffering at an individual level, but was also intended to provide a stimulus designed to underpin the rebound at a macro-level. Yes, the spending bills were duly passed by legislatures and approved in the case of the US by the White House, but all of this might not have been politically possible if governments had had to levy explicit taxation (both in the present and future) rather than relying so much on hidden forms of monetary tax. Anyhow, the NBER (guardian of the US records of recessions and business cycles) called the US pandemic spasm a recession, commenting that as such this was the sharpest and shortest ever; the trough came as early as April 2020, the previous cycle having peaked only in the last quarter of 2019 (and on a monthly estimate it came only in February 2020!).

To summarise. The official response to the pandemic was misguided. It was wrong to react to enforced shortfalls in supply by administering a huge dose of monetary inflation and fiscal stimulus. This was to be financed by monetary taxation coupled with mega-borrowing from debt markets where the Federal Reserve had manipulated rates down to extreme lows and correspondingly "printed" money in the form of creating reserve deposits (as described above). The official aim was to support economic recovery. Severe symptoms of asset inflation, however, were quick to appear as evident in speculative fever across a wide range of asset and credit markets with dangerous high temperatures. Goods inflation, the twin of asset inflation, was slower to develop severe symptoms.

What Would Have Happened Under a Regime of Good Money?

Let's turn to the counterfactual experiment.

All such thought-experiments are notoriously difficult, especially when the results of the actual history to date are not yet in. At the time of writing (summer, 2022), the Powell Fed has been broadcasting a "hawkish turn" in monetary policy aimed to prevent the rapid CPI rise through the second half of 2021 and early 2022 becoming the precursor to a sustained high inflation spell. Chief Powell promises that the Fed will continue to "tighten monetary policy" untill success in ending high inflation is assured. The political forces influencing this turn had become strong, with general polling showing that high inflation had become issue number one in the falling popularity of the President and the Democrats ahead of the looming mid-term elections. All judgements or predictions about this "hawkish turn" are highly conjectural in our unanchored and deeply corrupted monetary system. We should not allow ourselves to be led astray by media and market trumpeting of equivalences between the number and cumulative extent of official rate hikes on the one hand and the extent of monetary tightening on the other. We should also beware of hype about the significance of temporary pauses and even rever- sals in rapid expansion of high-powered money which is not "super" in any respect and for which there is correspondingly no strong and stable demand.

Anyhow, with all these forewarnings, back to the counterfactual!

Suppose that the pandemic shock had erupted at a time when the US and much of the world were under a regime of good money, as outlined elsewhere in this book (see notably Chapters 4 and 5). Would there have been a better economic outcome? Did monetary taxation levied under the actual money regimes enable governments to pursue a war against COVID-19 which was more costly than it need have been?

There are grounds for believing this is the case. If, for example, govern- ments had not been able to expect to raise monetary taxation on such a vast scale, they might have done more to build anti-pandemic defences before COVID-19 struck. During the years prior to the outbreak of the pandemic they would have had more incentives to put in place contingency measures to deal with the threat if they had known that, once this threat became reality, they could not resort to hidden taxation. There is no a priori basis for saying whether, when the pandemic struck, interest rates (short-maturity or long-maturity) would have risen or fallen under a good money regime. Even there, scope would exist for an elastic increase in high-powered money components during an emergency. It is plausible that long-term rates would have come under upward pressure in the context of a good money regime and its tight constraints on Big Government with no possibility of mone- tary financing. The affliction of a pandemic means an unavoidable loss of real economic well-being across society as a whole, and under a good money regime, there is less scope for governments to hide this and indeed foster illusions of increased well-being in general. Many households likely would have reduced their spending in reflection of their loss of economic well-being, though not entirely in step, drawing down their savings to some extent.

Under a good money regime, fewer households would have felt better off in consequence of the pandemic. Yes, there are always some gainers from bad news events. But scattering money like confetti made a much wider group of households feel they were better off, at odds with reality for society as a whole. Much of the household borrowing to sustain consumption under our actual money regime was done with the government as intermediator. In effect, it handed out relief payments or grants or soft loans to individuals and enterprises; in turn, the debt issued by government in connection with these is to be serviced by tax collections. Many people expect to escape being caught at the paying end of those and do not recognise the extent of monetary taxation to which they are subject.

There would have been nothing to stop governments, under a regime of good money, from raising social insurance payments to those adversely impacted and mobilising defences against the disease. We are not at all claiming that the government would or should have been passive in the face of this threat. The overall scope of its response would, however, have been constrained by what was democratically approved and financially possible without resort to the illusion factory of monetary inflation. As illustration, the pandemic spending bills would have been accompanied by finance bills providing for a "solidarity tax" to be levied at specified dates in the future. The prospect of this tax would have contained to some degree spending by those not receiving the hand-outs. Without the central bank buying government debt at super-low rates, yields on such paper would have been set in the market such as to reflect individual savings and spending decisions. Pandemic spending packages would not have come under the guise of Keynesian "stimulus".

Let Invisible Hands Work

Under a good money regime, invisible hands operating in credit and equity markets would have cushioned the economic shock effects of the pandemic.

For example, many businesses would have found that the destruction of the pandemic caused a fall in their ratios of equity to debt. The need to raise equity would have produced more companies offering so-called debt equity swaps, where equity is issued to debt holders so as to reduce leverage at present market values.

Under a good money regime, equally, emergency legislation could have been passed to provide humanitarian support and prevent exploitation of labour under the pandemic conditions. Accordingly, workers would have the right to exit employment temporarily during the pandemic rather than suffering a high infection risk at their place of work (if that were the case and no alternative lower-risk place of work including home feasible) without sacrificing longer-term rights to re-employment, while meanwhile becoming entitled to unemployment benefits. Hence, wage rates would have risen in some sectors where inputs of labour were subject to infection risk and there would have been matching incentives for firms there to lower risks in the workplace while having scope to pass on temporary cost increases to customers.

The market would have continued to provide signals of shortages and excesses in the multitude of specialised sectors that make up a modern economy. Under a good money regime, the pandemic would have created sharply divergent price moves for individual commodities and services, given the disruption to supply and demand across the economic space. The concept of a "general level of prices" would have been even more hazardous than usual, not least given the whole new gradation of product and service quality according to degree of infection risk, not previously or even now included in the shopping basket used for estimation purposes by the official statisticians.

For example, during the height of the pandemic, one would have seen price spikes for infection-free delivery of goods and services to households and a surge in wages for workers in workplaces liable to infection. Disruptions in chains of supply due to the infection would add to this price experience. It is not possible, a priori, to say whether, under a good money regime, prices on average would have risen or fallen at specific stages of the pandemic—only that there would have been much more variability than usual both within an overall CPI index and in its movement through time.

Futile Chase of Arbitrary Target

The attempt to restore an arbitrary inflation target (the 2 per cent inflation standard) as the pandemic receded was worse than futile. It defied the now downwards natural rhythm of prices. The episode of sustained upward pressure on prices resulting from all the cross currents on the way to the peak of the pandemic in a monetary system with a solid anchor would have triggered automatic mechanisms such as to thwart the machinery of money from getting seriously out of control (in the sense of causing monetary inflation).

The high prices of goods and services which might have occurred during the pandemic reflecting shortages would not have become locked in. Solid anchoring would not prevent a surge in the CPI reflecting real shortages and dislocation, Indeed a surge would have been fully consistent with the natural rhythm of prices being upwards (see glossary). Solid anchoring, however, would mean that this climb in prices would be reversed as markets adjust and the shortages plus dislocations eventually resolve themselves. Money would not suppress the natural rhythm of prices downward at that stage.

With a solid anchor in place, the supply of high-powered money will be restrained so that over the very long-run money retains its purchasing power. As people anticipate this, they adapt their spending when faced with sharp price moves in either direction. There is nothing mystical or mysterious about this! The severity of bottlenecks would have been less under a good money regime. Instead of monetary inflation unleashing a consumer durable boom, households and businesses would have been spending less—in anticipation of lower prices in the future. Further, international supply lines would have been less vulnerable to shock if it had not been for all the mal-investment in these which had occurred during the long asset inflation in the years before the pandemic.

Medium and Longer-Term Downsides of Policies

As promised at the beginning of this chapter, we now discuss the longer-term monetary implications of policies. We select three "downsides" of actual pandemic monetary policies for further examination—mal-investment, hidden taxation and additional inflation risk. All interfere with the necessary function of the price mechanism to match the forces of supply and demand.

More Mal-Investment

One cost of policy-makers so-called "courage" in unleashing even more virulent monetary inflation during the pandemic was a further distortion of new capital investment—the accompaniment to the advance of monopoly capitalism and the speculative wave of digitalisation as ignited by the pandemic stock boom. As already mentioned, online shopping and work at home gave a new impetus to the digital economy while monetary inflation created a speculative market in stocks related to this—the equivalent of war stocks in the inflation of wartime. The speculative story of monopoly power and the Eldorado of profits that this would bring shone in Big Tech—also in other areas where competition could now be enfeebled further by the passage of the pandemic which knocked out or lamed the smaller and weaker brethren. In turn, the sky-high price of monopoly and potential monopoly stocks allowed these businesses to finance further predatory action to destroy competition.

A key narrative this time has been that the fillip to technological change as brought by the pandemic has resulted in faster progress than otherwise would have occurred. This is a highly dubious proposition; history and theory suggest that technological change as turbo-charged by monetary inflation, instead of occurring in measured steps, causes greater economic waste and adoption of sub-optimal change. This might be costly to reverse in favour of delayed and measured change which would have been superior. As a symptom of the growth of financial dangers as a consequence of virulent monetary inflation during the pandemic, look at the sharp increases in corporate leverage—the opposite to the equity debt swaps that would have emerged under sound money.

Prior to the pandemic, much of the focus of those searching for financial fragility had been on corporate sector indebtedness in the emerging market economies including China—and in most cases, this became more perilous during the pandemic; stepped-up asset inflation amidst huge monetary interventions postponed some debt crises. In the US and elsewhere, the fastest growth of indebtedness was in sectors hurt most by the pandemic (including airlines and more generally the travel sector), raising concerns for financial stability in the future.

More Hidden Taxes

Turn next to the hidden increases in tax burdens related to the further growth of Big Government which the pandemic victory of bad money spawned. During the two years from the start of the pandemic in early 2020, general government debt to GDP ratios across the OECD area increased widely in a range of 20 to 40%. Superficially, this seemed burden-less to many at the time—as zero or negative short-term interest rates coupled with long-term rate manipulation meant that the apparent servicing costs of debt did not rise and in some cases fell. And there was much chatter about how households were in aggregate better off as a result of the pandemic given the accumulation of forced savings which had occurred in its early stages when households had stopped spending on infected services and had not yet ramped up their spending in other areas.

How could it be that many if not most people felt better off in consequence of a pandemic disaster during which cumulative national incomes (measured say over a total 2-year period from early 2020 to early 2022) fell by 10% or more compared to where they otherwise would have been? Did individuals believe that somehow they would not be paying the increased taxes in any form that would finance this magic? Did they think either that by then they would be dead or by political calculation it would be some other group in society who would pay for it (fallacies of composition as this could not be true for all)? Perhaps there was a widespread reluctance or incapacity to reckon with current and future monetary taxation. Contributing to such delusions were the policy-induced price gains across a range of asset classes, which made many individuals willing to treat these forms of monetary taxation, even supposing they were aware of them, as irritation offset elsewhere rather than a real burden.

–Higher Inflation

Rightly interpreted, the sudden jump of CPI inflation across many countries was a "front-loaded inflation tax", as described in Chapter 5. In effect, this surge in prices resulted in a capital levy on all holdings of nominal government paper, whether held directly or in the form of bank deposits (where the banks had piles of reserves at the central bank to match or in the form of banknotes). Under a good money regime, there would have been a more modest price surge, as described in our counterfactual, but this would not give rise to an inflation tax (as individuals would expect justifiably prices to fall back further ahead and the real value of their monetary holdings would be restored). The real value of these holdings fell in step with the levy (a small decline had already been expected as reflected in nominal interest; the levy refers to the unexpected element on interest-bearing deposits or bonds and the total—expected and unexpected—on banknotes). True, there had been a negative inflation tax the year before when the pandemic had caused CPI in most cases to increase by less than otherwise expected; but the negative error then was much less than the positive error now.

Some economists suggested that CPI inflation could be even higher than the Fed's projections for 2022 and that it would remain persistently high for years beyond that, well above the 2% target. Keynesians emphasised the extent of stimulus by fiscal policy coupled with the danger of wage-price spirals triggered by price spikes, while some commentators of monetarist persuasion stressed the explosive growth to date of their chosen money supply aggregate, in many cases M2, together with high inflation expectations now at large (which would make any reining back of monetary growth all the more economically painful and thereby unlikely to happen).

Under conditions of economic sclerosis (see Glossary), overall economic dynamism is enfeebled meaning that "modern" monetary tools of low interest rates plus massive central bank balance sheets fail to ignite demand overall in the economy when the next cyclical downturn emerges. And we are very late on in a very long cyclical expansion (treating February to April 2020 as a spasm rather than recession). The effect of monetary inflation continuing would be that instead of prices in general falling as bottlenecks eased they may continue to rise but at a slower pace, perhaps in line with the 2% inflation target. Picture a hill. Under sound money prices would have risen up a hill to a given level, say x metres high, and then fallen back with ground level again in sight; under the policies actually followed, the ascent of the hill was steeper and longer (as measured at ground level); then instead of a fall ahead, there would be a slow continuing rise thereafter.

Might This Pyrrhic Victory Spur Reforms?

All previous long business cycle expansions since 1919 as extended and fanned by monetary inflation have ended with deliberate and substantial monetary tightening. But suppose that the Fed continues to deny the existence of asset inflation, while recorded CPI inflation, after its bulge of 2021–2, falls back into a "low" range (in line with a loosely expressed target) amidst a "soft" economic landing. In that case, monetary inflation and the far-reaching economic harm of our money regime would continue. Then, the next Great Crisis would feature a severe recession, even depression, and the increases in perceived well-being during the pandemic would be revealed as illusory. Investors would recoil against previously reassuring narratives; consumers, worried about the inadequacy of their savings, would postpone expenditure, while companies would lower new capital investment. This would probably be accompanied by credit crises and defaults of highly-indebted enterprises or states.

It would be highly regrettable if the lesson politicians taken from the pandemic episode (as taught in real time by opinion polls) is that Big Government and interventionist actions are popular. In reality, the claimed success of policy in 2020–21 amounted to a pyrrhic victory. We can hope that this demonstration of the failures of bad money regimes would spark off a movement to reform our money. However, this appetite would need to be sustained. There must also be some kind of plan. These extra elements are the subject of the remaining chapters in this book.

References

Pollock, Alex J & Adler, Howard B "Surprised Again! The Covid Crisis and the New Market Bubble" Paul Dry Books 2022.

Feguson, Niail "Doom: The Politics of Catastrophe" Allen Lane (London) 2021.

Part V

Reform, Idealism and Prosperity

Introduction

This concluding part is all about implementation—how our ideas about good money might be realised.

Each chapter addresses a key question facing us as would-be radical reformers:

First, what form would a good, solid monetary anchor take?

Second, what answers can we give to criticisms of our analysis and suggested reforms?

Third, how might the journey to good money begin?

We start by nominating for our readers to consider two further candidates for the crucial anchoring function. Unlike the anchors we reviewed earlier in this volume, which were for fiat money systems, these are for monetary systems based on commodities or real assets.

12

Two Real Anchors

Back to the Future? A Reformed World Gold Standard

Having discussed, in Part Two (Chapter 5), the desirable features of an anchor, and the central role it should play in a good money regime, we now consider how two real anchors might function in practice. In other words, this part of our book is about implementation and reform. We define a "real anchor" as one that operates in a money based on a commodity or real asset. One such real anchor applies to a gold money system. Gold has been money for thousands of years but is now officially proscribed, damned and execrated (under IMF rules, a country may adopt any kind of exchange rate arrangement it likes except it must not link its currency to gold). The other real anchor applies to a money founded on a basket of equities; this type of money has never been tried anywhere.

We start by describing the anchor in a hypothetical new gold monetary system.

Consider a full-bodied international gold standard where leading currencies are convertible into gold at a specified fixed par value. Currencies such as the US dollar, euro, yen and pound are defined as specific weights of gold. Banknotes and the safest category of sight (current account) bank deposits would be backed by gold (the exact details depending on competition) and convertible at any time into gold coin whose weight is consistent with those definitions. There is no need for regulation. There will be a public demand

B. Brown and R. Pringle, *A Guide to Good Money*,
https://doi.org/10.1007/978-3-031-06041-0_12

for safe deposits which under competitive pressure banks would construct to appeal to this market. A well-capitalised bank might find it can market safe deposits where it promises cash backing at say 80%. Whatever it promises would be policed by an independent inspectorate (like weights and measure officers). The cash backing would have to be legally dedicated to the safe deposits, not mixed in with general bank reserves. The public decides how much money to hold in its various forms (coins, banknotes, deposits, digital coins).

Anyone can take physical gold to a currency issuer and get it melted down and converted into the same weight of coins at a fixed low cost. The definition of a money by weight of gold is the first requisite of a standard. (In Britain under the gold standard, the pound coin, the sovereign, was defined as 123.27447 grains of standard gold, that is, 22 carat gold or gold 11/12ths fine.) The legal definition of par value can be expressed in terms of multiple units of money—for example, taking prices at the time of writing we could say 100 dollars equals 1.67 grams of gold. The second requisite is free import and export of gold—this is a crucial element of the regulation of money. Any country that places an embargo on export or import of gold ipso facto departs from the gold standard.

To be clear, not all above-ground gold is actual money. For our analysis, gold jewellery is one step removed from the monetary base; melting down of jewellery or fabrication of raw gold is a source of potential fluctuations in the supply of monetary base. Conceptually, we could describe monetary base of gold monies all considered together as the above-ground stock of gold either in the form of currently used coins (whether dollars, francs, euros or anything else) or of gold bullion. Both have potential super-money qualities—explaining why in a gold monetary system individuals are willing to hold them at zero interest rather than time deposits, bills and bonds, which are re-denominated in the gold monies. The demand for these (bullion and coin) will be strong, broad and stable—if indeed the reincarnated international gold money system resembles the historical one The potential super-money qualities of gold coin derive from its attractiveness as medium of exchange and store of value; for bullion, these potential qualities derive in part from its advantages as a store of value—in large holdings of monetary wealth bullion bars have sometimes considerable convenience compared to masses of coins, especially given that the former can be minted into the latter on demand for a tiny fee—and in part from its use for financial institutions and others in making transactions in the gold clearing house.

Newly-mined gold is the only source of increase in the overall above-ground stock of the yellow metal. The composition of that stock as between jewellery, artistic objects (e.g. the doors in the cathedral at Florence), numismatic collections, plus industrial objects, on the one hand and monetary use on the other is variable, albeit typically not to a degree which destabilises the gold monetary system. In fact, quite the opposite: this flexibility is an advantage in its functioning, a factor in explaining why historically gold has been a good money.

For example, in a recession when there is typically less demand for gold jewellery, its re-sale price could fall in some cases below its value when converted into money; so some items would be melted down by the owners and the gold brought to the mint for coining. This would add to the supply of monetary gold which would help stimulate economic activity and underpin expectations of higher prices further ahead into the recovery and expansion phase of the business cycle (see Chapters 4 and 5 for how pro-cyclical movement of prices—at a below normal level during recession—is a desirable feature).

A critical characteristic of the gold money system is that the annual supply of newly-mined gold is always a very small percentage of above-ground stocks. Geology and the economics of the mining industry exert restraint over the supply of gold. Over the long span of history, the annual supply of new gold averages around 2% of existing stock. Vitally, this supply responds to sustained changes in demand for money (here gold money). Small annual responses add up. As illustration, an increase in the new annual supply of gold from say 1.5% of the above-ground stock to say 3% means an additional 15% stock over a decade. Of course, not all fluctuations in newly-mined gold supplies are prompted by shifts in real demand for money. Some part is related to major new discoveries (well beyond the normal discovery rate) or revolutionary progress in mining technology. By contrast, we should consider gold output enabled by normal exploration results and normal technological progress as contributing to the in-built tendency for gold stocks to increase over time, a desirable property if indeed real incomes are on a rising trend and we take as a key quality of good money that it should maintain (or even perhaps increase) purchasing power over the very long-run.

The in-built tendency of above-ground gold stocks to rise very slowly plus the capacity of the gold monetary system to prompt additional or lesser gold mining output in response to exceptional developments of money demand are key aspects of anchoring in the gold money system. We should be aware though of the imperfections in this anchoring which stem from possible output shocks (e.g. huge new discoveries or sudden and big improvements in mining technology). We can say that anchoring in the gold money system prevents the supply of monetary gold veering far ahead (or far below) under-lying demand for it, albeit not in a perfect fashion. Note further that this constraint is exercised without any discretionary interventions—it depends fully on automatic mechanisms (see Rockwell 1992).

Gold's position as an element in the periodic table (along with silver and copper, it was among the first elements known to man) implies that there will never be another commodity that shares its qualities, including density, malleability (easy fabrication into coin and jewellery) and beauty. Gold is forged in the incredible heat of an exploding supernova, and these occur only a few times every century in our galaxy; it was present in the matter from which the solar system was formed. Gold possesses all these qualities to an exceptional degree. (Some might argue platinum even more so, but the white metal's greater rarity means that it would be impractical in monetary use as coins would be so tiny given the much higher valuations that its monetisation would bring; silver has the opposite problem, and its tendency to much lower valuation that gold means a high storage cost in terms of price.)

Output of newly-mined gold responds positively to sustained rises in real incomes and productivity in the global economy. Rising productivity gener-ally (with much variation between sectors) tends to raise real wages including those in the gold mining industry, where labour competes with other sectors. Higher productivity and wages accompany the trend increase in gold output over the long-run. Technological progress in itself will not cause the supply of above-ground gold to run ahead of demand only if it were to be much faster than in other sectors of the economy.

One criticism of the gold standard points to the sizeable swings, histori-cally, in gold's real value; that is, in terms of the goods and services it can command, and we cannot know for sure how large these would be in a resur-rected gold standard. Spurts of technological progress in the gold mining industry and the geological characteristics of gold deposits within the earth's crust (leading to occasional discoveries of substantial reserves) contribute to occasionally quite sharp increases in its supply. There are no guarantees that the real purchasing power of an ounce of gold will remain constant in the short or medium term—and indeed, as we have seen, some fluctuation is appropriate in line with such factors as spurts in productivity growth and globalisation or as sudden resource shortage.

The balance of historical evidence about how supply and demand has changed in the long-run justifies some confidence in what has been called "The Golden Constant"—its amazingly consistent record of holding its value over the long-run (Jastram 1977). We have been careful to say that in the long-run the average real gold price can change. The "golden constant" is not an article of faith for rational man; the apparent "constancy" of value in the long-run is not pre-ordained.

Some economic historians have suggested that there was a period of serious monetary deflation (see Glossary) under the gold standard during the 1870s and 1880s caused in part by exceptional demand for gold following the newly-formed German Empire adopting gold as its uniform standard and the US abandoning bimetallism. The counter-case is that the "great deflation" of this period on both sides of the Atlantic was in fact a benign fall of prices (not symptomatic of monetary deflation) reflecting a tremendous spurt in productivity growth and overall output (most apparent in the US during the 1870s and 1880s). Indeed, the anchor of the gold standard functions during such episodes in a way to relax its constraint on the supply of money without over-riding a significant and benign downward move of prices. The increase in the real price of gold, which showed up in the form of a generalised fall in consumer prices, creates incentives to miners to increase the supply of newly-mined gold and makes some owners of gold jewellery convert it to monetary use.

In fact, the end of the "Great Deflation" coincided with discoveries of new deposits of gold and advances in gold mining technology which brought about increases in supply of above-ground gold such as to equal demand with the prices of goods and services on average back up to near the long-run mean or higher in the 1900s. However, contemporary observers of the Gold Standard in its heyday (1870–1914) did maintain that there were long-sustained episodes where gold was either over-restraining or inflating the wider monetary system, pointing to sharp fluctuations in average prices that to them appeared to be driven by financial factors or swings in credit associated with the boom and bust of business cycles. As was stated by one contemporary observer just before Britain "went off gold" in 1931:

> The gold standard can easily be shown to be purely nonsensical and yet it is the best method that has hitherto been put into operation for regulating the flow of commerce. (Pringle 1930)

William Pringle (Robert's grandfather) added that while the gold standard was "the best that has been tried", it was "not the best that has been suggested". Observing that central banks were "feeling their way towards certain lines of policy which imply a wide departure" from the gold standard, he expressed the hope that such policies would in future avert "the evil effects of extreme fluctuations in prices and in the volume of trade and employment" experienced under gold: he was a Victorian optimist!

Now, 90 years later, would a return to gold again face the challenge of an unstable real gold price? Does William Pringle's verdict that gold was "the best that has been tried" still stand?

The price has, indeed, been especially volatile in recent decades (this applies to the real or inflation-adjusted price as well as the market price). If such volatility persisted under a new gold standard, this would be transmitted to prices, destroying its claim to provide a reliable anchor. But experience over the past 50 years has reflected exceptional conditions. First, when money broke its last link to gold, in 1971, gold was abnormally cheap. The domestic demand for gold had long been suppressed by President Roosevelt's 1934 ban on private gold holdings by US citizens. Also, heavy interventions by the US Treasury (selling gold to foreign official institutions at the fixed price of $35 per ounce) had kept the gold price down despite a large and sustained rise in the general price level in the US from 1934 to the closing of the gold window in 1971. So gold's value in real terms had fallen far below any presumed long-run mean and was due for a massive upward correction. This came about via a huge rise in the nominal price of gold in terms of say US dollars. Secondly, in the half-century since then, the real value of fiat monies has declined sharply. The US dollar has lost more than 80% of its value (it can buy only 15% of the goods and services that it could in 1971). When the market antici-pates an upturn in inflation in the US, the US dollar price of gold sensitively reflects that, while new expectations of deflation will cause the gold price to fall (other things being equal). Gold has thus served as silent witness and recorder of the wild excesses of paper money.

Indeed, the vagaries of fiat money have been so wide in the decades since 1970 that the demand for gold as a safe haven has fluctuated wildly albeit being on a strongly rising trend; the inflation-adjusted price in US dollar rose fivefold in the decade to 1981 and then collapsed as the Federal Reserve pursued its brief monetarist experiment. A new burst of inflationary monetary policies in the second half of the 1980s led by the US adopting a devaluation policy (starting with the Plaza Accord of September 1985) brought a gold price rebound before a new slide in the 1990s came in line with a decade of international détente and an emerging economic miracle centred in the US (the IT revolution). We should also note at that time a growing volume of gold sales by some central banks including UK. An agreement of central banks to limit their gold sales in 1999 was seen by some commentators as a catalyst to reversing this long downturn in the gold price. Any short-term boost to the gold price from the removal of this cloud (potentially hundreds of tonnes of gold overhanging the market albeit small relative to above ground gold stocks of around 190,000 tonnes) was dwarfed by a crescendo of inflationary monetary policies under the so-called 2% inflation standard. Since then, it is surely plausible that the trend rise in demand for gold (expressed in terms of demand for above ground stocks) has far outstripped the normal rising trend line of gold demand which would have been in place under the counterfactual of an international gold standard; so the real price of gold has soared. This has jolted up production of gold while costs rose steeply at the margin as miners dig deeper into the earth's crust.

Prospects for the Gold Price

What of its future value? If a new international gold standard regime were created, the emergence of broad, strong and stable demand for gold's monetary base (as described above) should mean that the real price of gold in the long-run would be much more stable than it has been during the past half-century. On the one hand, as a fully restored money, the real price of gold might fall (prices of other goods and services would rise relative to the price of gold). This could reflect the loss of the premium in its present price that reflects the market's anticipations of continued monetary inflation, and some of the present hoards that investors keep in gold as a safe haven could be drawn down, leading to an excess supply of gold. On the other hand, there are forces that could sustain the real gold price or even keep it on a rising trend. On the supply side, some experts believe that as more and more gold has been dug out of the earth's crust the real cost of extracting the yellow metal at the margin has risen substantially, even allowing for technological progress in the mining industry. In a world of big brother and mass surveillance, the demand not only for gold coin but also for bullion and jewellery under a new gold standard regime could remain higher relative to real income growth than in the past. Some or perhaps many people would prefer to keep at least some of their savings in the form of gold bars or coins. Also, a modern version of the gold standard would take time to establish itself and build trust; after all, in some countries there could be a build-up of political forces in favour of returning to a fiat money regime especially if the process of fitting a gold anchor had caused much economic stress. The price on average of goods and services in countries or areas that opted not to join the new world gold standard would be determined by their domestic monetary policies, with the exchange rate between the national fiat money and the gold monies being a key intermediary factor.

There is no way of knowing the long-run real price of gold that would form under a newly constituted gold standard; in fact, whatever par quantity of gold is chosen to define the new gold dollar (and it could be that monetary reform goes along with creating a new dollar equal to 10 old dollars say), there is likely to be a large cumulative movement of goods and services prices upwards or downwards in the early years. That can be one of the hurdles in applying a gold anchor to an unanchored monetary system (see White 2011). Given the huge totals of government debt now outstanding at floating interest rates, there may be political advantage in fixing a conversion price for previous fiat money into gold at a level well above the recent market price (e.g. as in early 2022, fixing a conversion price of based on $2500 per ounce of gold, rather than say the then market price of $1800). That high conversion price would cause a once-and-for-all jump in consumer prices on average in the initial phase of the new gold standard. The real value of government debt would be reduced; should this be viewed as a quid pro quo for the subsequent advantages that money and debt holders (creditors in general) would get under a good money regime?

Historically, re-anchoring money to gold has been accompanied by initial price falls, as previous inflation during an interim period of fiat money has been rolled back, though there have been exceptions. Note that during that interim period, if long, a lot of government debt could have been repaid in debased money, meaning a good starting point in terms of low debt outstanding, for the reincarnated gold standard. Indeed, given that a gold standard such as we are describing here will not be starting any time soon, that is how the burden of government debt may be reduced.

Interest Rates and Prices Under Gold

How would interest rates and prices be determined in a monetary system with a gold anchor? The appeal of gold for adornment and as a store of value is worldwide. Despite the fact it pays no interest, most people and institutions such as central banks buy to hold gold for the long term. Virtually all the gold ever mined and refined still exists—hence the notion that an "owner" of gold is more like a trustee or guardian of that amount of the metal, rather than merely an investor. Yes, some holders might sell gold when interest rates on alternative investments rise (or buy gold when rates fall)—and these would include banks managing their reserves; so the demand for gold, as the monetary base, is influenced by interest rate changes. In such conditions, interest rates will help to balance demand for and supply of money in the short-run.

As illustration, an excess demand for monetary base (gold) relative to supply, as could occur in a powerful economic boom, would cause interest rates in the money market to be bid up as people were willing to pay more to borrow money. In turn, expectations that this tightness of conditions in the money markets could persist for some time would push up longer-term rates. As this effect rippled out into longer-term markets, rising rates there would independently exert some downward pressure on demand for goods and restrain the cyclical rise in their price.

Through such channels, a gold standard would allow prices of goods and services to fluctuate widely in quite long swings and this would be in accordance with the natural rhythm of prices as already highlighted in this volume (see Glossary): would there be a tendency to maintain a stable purchasing power over the long-run? Yes. The basis for expecting such a tendency includes a low rate of increase in supply of above-ground gold stocks and a growth in demand for these stocks (monetary and jewellery combined), which is also low and fairly stable (and we have explained the importance of monetary gold's super-money qualities in this regard).

There are two further positive aspects of the gold money system.

First, its in-built contra-cyclical tendencies; under a gold-based system, during recessions, as prices fall to a low level in response to falling incomes and spending, this sets up an expectation they will rebound, which helps to stimulate spending in the present. The gold standard does not inhibit this pro-cyclical move of prices of goods and services (prices rise to a higher level during the recovery and expansion phases of the business cycle and fall to a low level during the recession). In fact, the gold standard facilitates it; the fall in consumer and other prices to a lower level during a recession means the real price of gold rises (relative to other prices), encouraging gold mining production. (We do not imply here that prices are falling throughout the recession; the price experience between sectors is distinct, but in each case the price fall to a lower level might occur abruptly followed by a plateau.) As gold flows into the global economy, people will use it to buy goods and services, reinforcing a tendency of prices to recover into the subsequent expansion. Expectation of a rise in prices encourages consumers and businesses to bring forward spending—spend now rather than later.

Secondly, the gold standard also tends to restrain the growth of public spending beyond what can be financed by tax or non-inflationary borrowing. This also is a foundation of long-term monetary and financial stability. If individuals suspect the government of running excessive deficits, they will convert paper money into gold. This reduces demand for assets not fully backed by gold while increasing demand for gold itself. This reaction will not only drive up interest rates but could also spark a flight from the currency into others where the government was behaving more responsibly. All this is a horror story to many modern economists unused to the concept of monetary discipline. But that is how a solid anchor works.

Shopping with Gold

Some individuals would keep part of their monetary wealth in gold (whether in bars, bullion, coins or digital forms). As far as demand for gold coins is concerned, it is true that if a currency were fixed at a price of $1800 an ounce (or equivalent in local currency) you would need very tiny coins—the weight of a feather, at a thousandth of an ounce—to buy an ice cream! But even under the heyday of the gold standard before 1914, gold coins were not used for such small retail transactions (in some monetary systems silver or copper coins circulated for these). In a reincarnated gold money, a range of monetary instruments (including banknotes, alloy coins and payment cards) would be used for effecting small transactions; individuals could also choose to use these for larger transactions. The smallest gold coin illustratively might have a face value of $500, suitable for purchasing high-value consumer durables and a range of luxury goods and services. Of course, the main demand for gold coins in dollar terms for shopping will be by households at the top of the income and wealth distribution. Yet even if only 5% of households use gold coins (real or digital) for shopping, that would be a large substantial overall demand; and many would appreciate greatly holding an asset that is an excellent store of value that can at any time be used to spend directly (even if they hardly ever avail themselves of that opportunity!).

We Answer Classic Criticisms of Gold Standard

1. *Under the classic gold standard real output and short-term changes in the price level were more volatile than in period since 1945*
   Answer: Under a sound money regime prices and price changes should not be stable but reflect a natural rhythm upwards and downwards for all the reasons we state. Also, the increasing scale and costs of present system, including the much larger share of government and services in total economic activity, make such comparisons of little value. Monetary policies as practised extend business cycles—by central banks flooding the system with liquidity, but eventually this shows up with a big recession

and crash. Even if there has been less real output volatility as measured over short periods since 1945 is that a price worth paying for all the loss of economic welfare along the way from badly-allocated capital investment stemming from distorted interest rates etc.?

2. *The gold standard entails high resource costs—Milton Friedman put it at 2.5% of GDP per annum*

Answer: The real resource costs of the present system are much higher. Just look at the ongoing annual costs of vast central bank organisations (plus the matching commentariat) and the whole regulatory/compliance industry. All this would be done away with under a gold standard. Also, the 2.5% statistic is largely spurious. This estimate assumed that all money (including time deposits) under a gold standard would be 100% gold backed (see White [1999] and that the demand for money in real terms would grow in the long-run at 4% per annum.

3. *No lender of last resort so bank bankruptcies would be unavoidable*

Retort: The taming (and even near-eradication) of monetary inflation would mean a much better functioning market in equity and bonds which would discipline banks and inhibit them partaking in what turns out to be wild behaviour. Yes, there would be occasional bankruptcies, but holders of 100% cash backed sight deposits at these banks would be totally safe. With capital markets disciplining bank behaviour under a good money regime, the financial industry would be put in the same position as the non-financial industry as regards success and failure and why not so? Would banks cooperate in a crisis and even rescue banks under attack? So long as they don't break anti-trust laws, then of course they could combine; but we should not think of this as a main line of defence; the system we are designing does not rely on this.

4. *Causes depression when a central bank has to raise rates to stop gold outflow as the Fed did in 1931*

Retort: We discuss this fallacy in the history chapter (Chapter 8); there was no gold standard internationally in Autumn 1931; the US had not been running monetary policy on the basis of gold in the 1920s. Under a hypothetical reincarnated international gold standard as discussed so far in this chapter, yes, there could be upward pressure on money rates in one centre if the relevant political authority is undermining confidence in its commitment to the standard. But this rise of rates should not precipitate depression but rather cause a lurch into bad money policies to be aborted before they cause long-run damage.

5. *There were wide swings in real value of gold and thus of value of money*

Retort: to be sure, there were fluctuations in gold's real value (see above). Some of these were wholly benign, in line with the natural rhythm of prices (e.g. productivity surges, business recessions causing prices to fall; resource shortages causing prices to rise). But yes, some also resulted from monetary supply overshoots or undershoots of underlying demand for money. But the costs of such episodes pale in comparison with the fantastic losses in real purchasing power which have occurred under fiat money, and these never correct back, unlike what happened after the much smaller losses of purchasing power, under the gold standard.

6. *There would be major short-term gold price changes as big countries join or leave gold standard*
   Retort: Re-anchoring or anchoring an unanchored money will involve costs. They don't have to be huge. Indeed, if the unanchored monetary system has become so bad, they may be small (as when the German currency was re-anchored to the dollar after the 1923 hyperinflation). And transitional anchoring costs should be compared to the benefits stretching far into the future. Moreover, in today's context, it is not clear that a large country joining the gold standard would mean a higher level of demand for gold globally—as some wealth-holders might decide to shift their portfolio composition away from gold bullion to bonds and time deposits denominated in the new gold money. We should concede, however, that a large country or group of countries leaving the gold standard, especially where leaving is coupled with government seques-tering (and subsequent selling) private holdings of gold money, could cause severe monetary inflation for those remaining on gold, as monetary demand for the yellow metal globally falls. That is what happened in the context of US neutrality during the First World War when the European belligerents sold sequestered gold in the US (see history chapter).

7. *Finally, there is the criticism that, given the level of cash holdings, bank reserves and current accounts, the price of existing gold would have to rise by many multiples, implying "unfair" windfall gains to the current holders.*
   Retort: In progressing to a good money regime which takes form of gold much of the present hoarding in gold as a hedge against bad money would decline—making way for increased monetary demand.

Another Anchor Based on Real Assets—The Ikon

Other anchors based on real assets are conceivable. In this chapter, we describe how the anchor works in a money already proposed by Robert

Pringle, one of the authors of this book—developing an analysis by Wolfram Engels—for a money based on tradable claims to real assets (see Pringle 2012; Engels 1981).

The most common form of these is equity shares in companies listed on stock exchanges. These represent legal claims to ownership of real assets—the net amount of a company's assets and liabilities. In effect, the portfolio would be a diversified bundle of such equity shares. One type of this class is familiar to investors as "exchange traded funds" or ETFs. We know from contemporary markets these are widely traded and can be highly liquid. The unit of money could be based on a global index in the case of an international standard or a national index in the case of a national currency, but other combinations are possible (e.g. in Canada a money based on both the Canadian and US equity markets could be considered); the principles involved are the same.

Just as under gold, this would mark a fundamental break with present practice. As with gold, it would represent a new recognition that our concept of money was deeply, irredeemably, flawed. Money must represent and uphold a standard which everybody, however powerful, must follow. It is a rule-based order. It must inhabit a constitutional realm above day-to-day politics of government—we shall realise this is the only way to protect this precious social asset from abuse. Adoption of such an experimental standard would mark a recognition that ad hoc remedies for the diseases of the current system will not work, that our problems go far beyond the pile of excess debt, or unfair wealth distribution, or episodes of asset inflation…to a bad money itself.

The unit would be defined in "physical" terms—in this case claims on real assets. The hypothetical money, let's call it the Ikon, could be defined as, say, a tiny fraction of the basket containing the outstanding share certificates of all equities listed on the New York Stock exchange on a certain date. Alternatively, we could take a basket containing all share certificates outstanding of companies in the S&P 500 index. A share represents a claim to ownership of a real asset. Measured in Ikons, the share price index is constant over time (a formula will be developed to calculate the index). Any solvent bank could issue bank notes in Ikons, appropriately backed by holdings of share certificates. Anyone holding bank notes is entitled to demand conversion of notes into shares and many would do this if the Ikon became less valuable as money than in the market, i.e. its underlying equity content as defined above. They will receive shares valued at the closing price on the last trading day increased by the percentage deviation of the index from its par rate. This reduces the money supply. Conversely, if the index falls below par (for the Ikon), anybody can take shares to the monetary authority and demand money (Ikons) at a value for the shares equivalent to the closing price on the last trading day reduced by its percentage fall from par. This increases the money supply.

The issuing entity would have no discretion over/monetary policy. Its assets would consist of investments representing the market portfolio—in practice a diversified bundle of equities. Its liabilities would be bank notes and reserves of private banks. Private banks would compete to create deposit money in Ikons, extending "loans" and making investments all denominated in Ikons. The all-in cost of these loans to the customer would include bank charges (a margin) and a default risk premium; on top, the borrower's Ikon liability to the bank would tend to rise in terms of consumer prices through time if indeed the underlying equity portfolio is positive-earning. Importantly, though, unlike finance denominated in a traditional money the real value of these Ikon liabilities would fall during economic or social bad times when the stock market is depressed. The assets of the banks in this Ikon system would comprise loans to clients and reserves held against their bank notes and other monetary liabilities so as to ensure convertibility on demand; their liabilities would be deposits from the public, borrowing from the central bank and their own issuance of banknotes (or digital coins as transferrable via blockchain). As described, the issuer would convert on demand its money deposits into share certificates at par—for example so many units of the specified equity ETF for each Ikon. (There would have to be a continuous technical adjustment to par so as to take account of dividends on shares which in practice could not be paid out; the procedure here would be similar to gold ETFs where cost of storage is rolled into the gold equivalent going forward.) The anchoring of the Ikon monetary system as a whole would include "natural" constraints to the supply of equity (the stock of business capital in the enterprise sector) and fluctuations in the ratio of monetary to non-monetary (pure investment) demand for the equity paper outstanding which matches this capital in the enterprise sector. (The analogy here is with fluctuations in the ratio of monetary to jewellery demand for gold in a gold standard system.)

How solid would be this anchor, with its key feature of convertibility of money into Ikons? Most generally, does the convertibility feature into real assets (equities) mean that the machinery of money will not get out of control? And towards that objective, does the suggested anchor have components which would have the desired properties to prevent money supply from veering ahead of or below underlying demand?

On the first question, once the new regime is established in a given state or monetary region, individuals, firms, state enterprises and all other people/economic units would adjust their economic behaviour to the demands of this currency standard. They would anticipate that in line with a tendency of equity prices to rise in real terms over the long-run (not an absolute given, as investors in the Japanese stock market since its peak in 1990 know only too well!), the Ikon's real purchasing power in terms of consumer goods would appreciate. They would learn how to live with a money that would be expected gradually to appreciate in its real value (with ups and downs). It would be an unfamiliar, topsy-turvy world, but it would quickly become the new normal. Yes, there would be economic shocks and painful adjustments. A key political question, if we consider an Ikon money as launched by the state rather than emerging in private markets, is whether people—voters—would be ready to take a longer-term view. The costs of the system could be heavy in the short to medium term as, for example, employees adjusted to a world of a stationary level of general money incomes (falling for some sectors), with falling consumer prices, while the benefits, which may ultimately greatly outweigh them, will come later.

Would people bear the hardships and shock of such an adjustment on the journey to the promised land? The authors of this volume argue that in an ideal world moneys should emerge as successful and popular via a process entirely driven by personal choice in private markets regarding preferred mediums of exchange and store of value, for example. True, we recognise this is not practicable in the real world with all the obstacles there including regulations, legal impediments (such as legal tender laws), and restrictive practices of financial institutions with market power, though it should still be possible for any new money at a broad society level to have been tested first and gained considerable popularity in private markets. Beyond that, we should imagine a situation where people would be able freely to choose a standard to apply to their system in the future. Question: Would a group of potential creditors and debtors entering into a loan/investment contract, given their choice of a standard when they did not know whether the outcome would favour creditors on the one hand or debtors on the other, choose the Ikon? Yes, if they wanted the only measure of value that would not create distributional risk in the contract between these two groups, or No, because its purchasing power value would fluctuate.

Ultimately, the total stock of enterprise capital in quoted form is the foundation for the Ikon, analogous to the total stock of above-ground gold for gold money. The increase in enterprise capital (thought of in real terms as physical units of equipment and goodwill including intangibles) in any period is the counterpart to newly-mined gold. There are the differences that whereas gold exists in identifiable units, infinitely sub-divisible and identical to each, capital stock has no such easy recognition; as against that, there is the guide of market valuations. We should also mention that the above-ground supplies of gold are much smaller relative to the size of potential money supply (for a large country say or the globe) than is the case of the stock of enterprise capital for the Ikon. (Correspondingly the share of enterprise capital held in monetary form—as against pure investment in equity—would be much smaller than for the share of above-ground gold stocks held in monetary form rather than jewellery, artistic or industrial form.) This is relevant, as we shall see below, when it comes to considering the possible patterns, and extent of fluctuation, in the Ikon's purchasing power.

If indeed the Ikon were used broadly as money in at least one large economy that monetary demand would influence the value of equities; as demand for money is normally quite stable, it would, indeed, tend to reduce the amplitude of fluctuations in the real value of equities. The average price level in Ikons would reflect shifts in the relative valuation of goods and services on the one hand and equities on the other. For example, a slump in the stock market would likely trigger huge arbitrage flows out of direct owner-ship of equities into holding Ikons; the resulting surge in the Ikon money supply would raise the prices of goods and services in Ikons. This relationship would not be instantaneous in a medium-sized or large-sized economy with a large non-traded goods and services sector where prices were not immediately sensitive to exchange rate fluctuations (between the Ikon currency, say, and the US dollar).[1]

The fluctuations over time in the stock market would be changed in nature (from the present where there is no Ikon) if indeed the Ikon currency is a substantial money in terms of size relative to other monies; swings of valua-tion, both nominal and real, due to variable central bank policies, QE, etc., would be eliminated; there would be no credit-fuelled booms and ex ante savings would always match ex ante investments. Thus, the change in the real values of Ikon money could be far less than the swings in stock market indices which have been observed historically, though probably larger than the (quite wide) swings in the real gold price. Correspondingly, the average valuation of equities would be higher than now. (We are talking here of valu-ation of 100% equity financed companies for simplicity, though the point is general.)

Our author, Robert Pringle, who has advocated the idea of the Ikon, points out that this expected long-run mild appreciation of the money in terms of purchasing power would be an attractive feature for its holders. Of course

---

[1] In the hypothetical case of a global Ikon standard, the fluctuation in Ikon prices of goods and services as driven by fluctuations in say the S&P 500 would occur under the influence of Ikon money supply on demand rather than via the exchange rate between the Ikon and non-Ikon currencies.

that feature is present also for direct ownership of equity, but the availability of this equity in a highly liquid and transferable form, usable in everyday transactions, adds a new dimension to individual choice. The downside is that this monetised equity unlike the best of traditional monies is not a haven against recession or depression risks and other possible bad events. Even so, people would wish to hold large balances in Ikon cash or sight deposits. They would not have to sacrifice yield to obtain liquidity—the so-called liquidity premium. These super-money qualities might support a broad demand for the Ikon in high-powered money form.

Following the analysis by Engels (1981), Ikon money itself would be expected to have a positive return in real terms. That would be consistent with the positive real returns expected on equity investment and the IKON is an equity money. Of course some investors and borrowers would still like to make use of conventional type debt instruments denominated in monies which are less variable in value at least over the short or medium term. They could still do so, though there may be no such money available in domestic form for the country or countries where an IKON money had become dominant.

At first sight, it might appear that the Ikon as money would have one highly negative feature—that the prices of goods and services as expressed in Ikons would fluctuate inversely with the stock market. So, for example, when the stock market was at high levels, prices of goods and services expressed in Ikons would tend to be low (compared to long-run average) and conversely, and prices of goods and services over the long-run expressed in Ikons would be on a falling trend. A rise in stock prices (as represented in the Ikon index) beyond the par value will result in money (Ikons) being withdrawn from the economy, cooling the boom. Another potential disadvantage of the Ikon anchor, is that it would frustrate—if operating on its own—the invisible hands of free market capitalism as described earlier in this book. Specifically, we argued that under a solid anchor, such as gold was in the heyday of the gold standard, prices are allowed to follow a natural rhythm. During a deep recession (hopefully not too many of these under a good money regime!), prices should be well below normal with strong expectations among business people and households that prices will be higher in the future. But in the Ikon world with the stock market in the doldrums in the depth of recession, prices in Ikons would then be abnormally high, with expectations of lower Ikon prices in the future when recovery comes. Yet many of the causes of booms and busts would no longer be present.

As against these doubts about the Ikon in terms of the business cycle, there are positives to consider. During the recession, there would be a strong tendency for outside holders of stocks (in non-monetary form) to sell them for Ikon, taking advantage of arbitrage opportunity created by the latter having monetary use. So the Ikon money supply would grow strongly together with the rise in Ikon prices during the recession—and in combination, this would give a stimulus to economic activity during recession. This may be the Ikon equivalent of the invisible hand we observe at work under a gold standard. As discussed earlier, the idea is that it is part of a natural rhythm for prices to fall during periods of rapid productivity growth. This property would hold under the Ikon if productivity growth were to be accompanied by a rising stock market. The danger here would be that the monetary contraction brought about by reverse flows out of Ikon money into the stock market could be so fierce as to abort the boom.

Key Properties of Ikons

In this section on the Ikon, we present some more details on mechanics of the proposal and conclude with some reflections on whether this could become part of the global monetary regime.

The supply of money in nominal terms would normally be counter-cyclical. If, for example, in anticipation of recession the index of shares fell below par arbitragers could profit by buying the shares in the marketplace and taking them to the monetary authority for converting into money, meaning the money supply or monetary base would increase in nominal terms (though possibly not in real terms, see above, as the real value of Ikons could fall in this situation of low stock market prices—meaning higher prices in Ikons of goods and services). Holders of shares would have an incentive to have them minted—i.e. present them to the money issuer for conversion into the monetary unit and the issuer/issuing authority would be obliged to do this, i.e. purchase shares from any seller at the market price in exchange for money.

If this money were to catch on in private markets and become dominant, such operations would be on a scale to inject money in nominal terms (but not necessarily real) into the economy. On the other hand, at a time when optimism about business prospects was high, and the price of shares rose, the issuer would be obliged to sell (in exchange for money) any number of shares to stop the index rising above par. This operation would withdraw money from the economy. With the price of shares fixed in terms of Ikon, all other prices would have to adjust. So prices of goods and services in Ikon would rise when stock markets were under downward pressure and conversely. An underlying rise in the real value of shares and thus of the monetary unit would be evidenced by a fall in other prices, including prices of goods and services.

This probable behaviour of goods prices in Ikons, up on onset of recession, and down when stock markets roar ahead, could be problematic but not a sufficient cause to reject this monetary project given its broader advantages. We should consider here that a growing use of Ikons would mean that stocks would enjoy a broader and more stable demand meaning that the so-called equity risk premium would fall reflecting the lower overall volatility of stocks in real purchasing power. Even so, at this lowered risk premium, people who hold cash in this Ikon would in the long term earn a positive real yield. A lower-risk premium due to broad stable demand for stocks would help build long-run prosperity.

There would be a strong portfolio demand for the Ikon, even if it does not necessarily score well on all the monetary tests as described above. It would be inherently desirable, in different ways to gold. There would be no direct counterpart to the jewellery demand for the yellow metal which is important in how the anchor works in the gold money system, as explained above. Nonetheless, we should consider the large non-monetary demand for equities outside the Ikon monetary system—and we have seen that shift between this non-monetary demand into monetary demand during slumps in the stock market plays an important stabilising role in the economic system. In this respect, both gold and the Ikon are at one extreme and say Bitcoin at the opposite extreme (in the latter, there is no non-monetary demand for the codes which are the basis of that money). The value of money would mirror the desirability of claims on assets such as equity shares, real estate, artworks and a thousand other classes. Like gold, the Ikon money would have intrinsic value, but based on real investments (ultimately capital goods and a range of intangible business capital) rather than linked to a partly consumer good (jewellery and ornaments). The money thus anchored would be universally desired. It would have all the characteristics of super-money.

The Ikon would, specifically, have the property that we identified as crucial for a solid anchor; that is, it embodies something of real economic value independent of its use as money. True, as discussed above, the link to capital goods rather than consumption (jewellery) is arguably problematic in terms of the automatic mechanisms of the monetary system. Yes, there would probably need to be a body to ensure that the shares or other tradable claims were representative of the market portfolio as a whole and also assure the integrity of selected shares or other tradable claims, such as freedom from manipulation. If instead several countries all chose a world market index or the S&P 500 as the defining foundation for their real money, they would all be on a fixed exchange rate regime with each other. The choice of an index or bench-mark could emerge from creative chaos. It could start as a private initiative simultaneously in several countries coexisting with present fiat monies. But here we are visualising the contours of a new, unfamiliar monetary geography and there is no need to pick up every stone on our path.

Other Benefits of a Real Asset Money

If this money were to catch on, along with disruption it could confer several benefits.

First, it would promote wider ownership of equity. The returns would be dominantly in the form of movements in the price level as expressed in terms of this money. Whereas, at present, the fruits from equity ownership go to a small minority of equity owners and the intermediaries that service them, fuelling inequality, in the real asset system anybody holding money would benefit from economic advance.

Second, it would boost savings and investment. Consider this question: is it really desirable to provide a money that always needs to stimulate spending, as ours does, with its built-in tendency to increase debt? Borrowing more and more is a condition of survival of fiat money.

Third, this anchor would reduce the bloated size of the financial sector. Bank lending would mainly take the form of short-term advances to credit-worthy borrowers repayable on demand (as indeed was the case in commercial banking for many decades). So banks and other financial institutions that rely on the artificial stimulus of low rates would find demand for their services collapse. Investment houses/advisers who currently charge high fees for advice that just produces average returns would have no clients, since everybody could gain such a return by holding cash.

Fourth, such a money would reflect the changing preferences of society in another way—for instance, the growth in people's preferences for "green" investments. Larger investments in such eco-friendly enterprises and other ventures to sustain the environment or combat climate change would be mirrored in the equities used as backing for the currency, and thus the value of the money people hold.

Finally, like gold and all other forms of good money, it would be inherently desirable and desired. That is what we mean when we say money should have intrinsic value. It would provide fertile ground for the growth of super-money qualities.

In broad terms, the anchoring system to the Ikon would have solid features. Even though the Ikon would fluctuate in purchasing power, it could enjoy considerable popularity as a money, especially among investors willing to take a longer-term view. It is possible that a broad use of the Ikon, going together with a lowered (or indeed zero) equity risk premium, would promote investment and prosperity.

If prosperity is to be maintained or increased, we must plant our money in the real world. That is the lesson that recent crises teach us. Only a money rooted in the real world can provide the framework by which billions of individual human beings can make their choices felt and apply their energies with confidence to improving their material condition.

In short, both gold-based and equity-based standards would give currency the status and attributes of super-money. This concludes our survey of the essence of good money.

References

Engels, W. (1981) The Optimal Monetary Unit.

Jastram, Roy W. (1977) (reprinted with additional material by Jill Leyland, 2009): The Golden Constant: The English and American Experience.

Pringle, Robert (2012) The Money Trap.

Pringle, W. Henderson (1930) An Introduction to Economics, Ernest Benn.

Rockwell, Llewellin (1992) The Gold Standard: Perspectives in the Austrian School.

White, Lawrence (1999) "Theory of Monetary Institutions" Wiley.

White, Lawrence (2011) "Making the Transition to a New Gold Standard" Cato Institute Annual Conference, November.

13

We Reply to Potential Questions and Criticisms

Introduction

In earlier chapters, we made the case for a radical overhaul of our money system and outlined what we consider to be the essence of good money. We now address some of the many questions, criticisms and objections that can be raised against our analysis and call for reform (and see also Chapter 15).

We present our views in the form of responses to eight hypothetical questions and criticisms.

How Should Reforms Improve Society?

Many of us have been badly affected by the financial crises of the past few decades. Unless we change the system, there will be more crises. Tinkering will not do—so far, such piecemeal "reforms" have not solved the problem. They merely put off the day of reckoning.

However, the pain of those who endured earlier crises is not our main reason for urging reform. Indeed, many of those who were affected back in 2008 or in 1990 or in 1980 or in 1973 are no longer with us. There is a whole new generation out there which did not experience this. And we are certainly not saying that the only cost of bad money is the prospect of further crises. The real cost includes all the loss of well-being and prosperity that we have suffered relative to where we could have been with good money as a society

© The Author(s), under exclusive license to Springer Nature
Switzerland AG 2022
B. Brown and R. Pringle, *A Guide to Good Money*,
https://doi.org/10.1007/978-3-031-06041-0_13

as a whole. That far transcends stock market losses or job losses during a crisis. We could have enjoyed a cumulative growth in living standards over a long period of time. And then there are all those benefits of good money that transcend the calculus of prosperity gains or losses, albeit that these latter are important in terms of any election campaign eventually on the issue.

We have argued that on all these grounds this must be a root-and-branch overhaul that goes to the very meaning of money and its role. Such an overhaul is necessary to chart a way out of the money trap; to do that we should understand better how we got into it (Pringle 2012). Constructing and designing a good money system is much more than a technical reform; it will require a complete change in our mind-set. It will need us to understand why, in our efforts to turn money into an obedient servant, we have made it our master. True freedom will come only when we recognise that money works for all of us only when, by consent, its rules apply equally to each of us, without fear or favour—only when it cannot be manipulated by the government of the day or by special interests, governed by law rather than men and women. To put it another way, money should serve as an impartial medium and measure, and link generations across time and individuals across space in the same net of rules. That is a prize worth fighting for on moral as well as economic grounds. And such a money will be far more than a convenient tool. It will have moral authority. It will be talked about with respect.

We need to be clear about why good money matters so much to society as a whole. As already mentioned, a good money should increase well-being over time. It is only through the money and price mechanism that we can find out what people want and how much they want it. The resources available to produce these goods and services are always limited. The market helps us to find out how much it costs to produce what we want. For the consumer, market prices set in money help us to gain the maximum amount of benefit from our resources including our work over time. Even if, as a society, we decided to adopt some form of rationing of basic goods and services, rather than providing them through the market, it is hard to imagine people ever being content to consume exactly or only what somebody else said they should. Thus, money in some form seems to be fundamental if a given amount of production is to give the most satisfaction to the largest number of people. For those of us involved in the production, distribution and marketing of goods and services—whether as employees or owners— money prices and wage rates enable us to specialise in the kind of work we can do best. Money and banking/credit services are the keys to the extensive specialisation and incredible range and variety of occupations in a modern economy. To fulfil such functions, money should be not only widely accepted but also a reliable measure by which to compare prices across a country or region and over time. People start to distrust money when it loses value or when they fear that it will. As they do. So there is a moral aspect.

Distrust eats away at the social bonds holding individuals together. Good money is basic to economic and political stability. A big challenge along the pathway to good money is the need to disseminate in the political arena an understanding of its societal benefits and to build enthusiasm for these.

Is Money Really as Bad as You Make Out?

Yes. It is even worse. It is undermining our society and the proper working of the market economy.

Many observers—especially those in or close to the corridors of monetary power—claim to see the period after the Global Financial Crisis as one of successful innovation in central banking and overall policy-making. In particular, they aver, central banks deployed their balance sheet not only to sustain overall demand and prevent a downward spiral into depression but also to provide a shock-absorber cushioning the impact of market volatility and massive movements of funds. The "unconventional policies" designed by the monetary establishment have been a "great success", never mind the naysayers!

However, this is to see policy through rose-tinted spectacles. Ironically, one of the early critics came from economists at the central banks' club, the Bank for International Settlements. They argued in their published reports from the mid-1990s into the first decade of the twenty-first century that central banks led by the Federal Reserve followed too easy monetary policies—what they called a "Bias Towards Ease". This, they said, fuelled the hot speculative markets in assets and more generally what we have described here as the symptoms of asset inflation including the growth of financial imbalances. They pointed to higher levels of debt, to corporate leverage and dangers of the dollar's dominance as a currency for sovereign borrowing—raising huge default risks for borrowers (White, 2009 and references cited therein).

The regulations and legislation designed since the Global Financial Crisis have not addressed the underlying problem—how to prevent the same degree of monetary excess recurring which was at the origin of these kind of shocks. After all, the failure of markets to discipline the wild and over-leveraged financial institutions in the years up to 2008 was related to the hot markets as induced by many years of monetary inflation in their equities, especially in Europe where many investors were impressed by promises about the new age of financial integration (as spurred by EMU) and what this would mean for profits. Equity investors seemed not to care about or even see the increasing leverage of those institutions, camouflaged as they were by a cobweb of clever accounting devices around so-called vehicles which did not appear directly on their main balance sheets. An example of such nonchalance and illusion-making was the consummation of the Royal Bank of Scotland's take-over of ABN-AMRO and Fortis amidst rapturous shareholder approval in Summer 2007, even as the first tremors of financial crisis were felt. Barely a year later RBS was bust—albeit saved by the British government—and so on to the big crash and subsequent patchwork of "reforms".

This saga should be political dynamite.

Many companies using capital and resources that should be freed up for employment elsewhere have been able to survive only by virtue of ultra-low interest rates. Without this prop, some would increase efficiency sufficiently to survive; others would go out of business, thus releasing resources for use in more productive ways. As regards national debts, defaults or their equivalent in sustained and extreme loss of monetary value would have many damaging effects but may become unavoidable. There is growing recognition among the public that monetary policies under the present regime contribute in varying ways to deepening economic inequality which is at odds with what should occur under ideal competitive capitalism. And many sense that money itself has become in some way they find it hard to describe the source of an underlying economic malaise.

Previous chapters have traced a gradual but, it appears, an inexorable decline in the quality of money. In the US, the attempt under Paul Volcker to build a hard dollar was short-lived indeed as we have seen. Then, the rot set in with the market bail-out orchestrated by the Federal Reserve in 1987, signalling that it would stand behind Wall Street. True, the then Fed Chair Alan Greenspan was not acting just to shore up Wall Street though that was an important objective; he was also concerned that the 1987 crash would bring on an economic downturn. The monetary inflation unleashed at Plaza entered a new lap. The short-lived stop to that monetary inflation at the turn of the decade triggered financial system crashes around the world and subsequent bailouts, including the US Savings and Loans industry, the so-called convoy bank system in Japan (where the government gave uncon-ditional protection to banks ending with the nationalisation of Long-Term Credit Bank) and a Scandinavia saga of bust and bail-out.

While we judge that the monetary actions just chronicled to have involved wrong use of monetary tools, they were widely hailed by the media and by establishment economists at the time. This praise continued into the Great

Asset Inflation starting in the mid-1990s and continuing through to the mid-2000s with a small intermission in the aftermath of the dotcom bubble and bust (1999–2000). Central bankers basked in the respect of the media and politicians. In the same era, there was a global trend towards granting or fortifying central banks "independence" to pursue policies of "monetary stability". But this turned out to be a fig leaf. Globalisation and a surge of cheap goods from China as a billion people joined the world economy brought prices of many tradable goods down from 1990 onwards; such a temporary price deflation would have been natural under a good money regime. But given their brand new inflation targets, central bankers in effect stood in the way of prices falling overall and stimulated asset inflation. As the Fed was backstopping the US equity markets, and given the global influence of the Fed and Wall Street, global markets followed. The media, with few exceptions, purred approval. So here we are; many people are grumpy, unhappy and even angry but the political banking-central banking establishment carries on regardless.

How Is "Bad Money" Linked to Low Capital Investment?

They are deeply connected. As we have said, after each crisis the only way to support the economy as perceived by these monetary bureaucrats is to lower rates still further in order to persuade people to spend more, take on more debt. Symptoms of malfunctioning markets have grown in each cycle. So central banks have been drawn increasingly into using their own balance sheets to fight against the natural course of affairs. They rushed to absorb shocks that would previously have been absorbed by market adjustments. This has exposed central banks' balance sheets to larger risks. While politicians have assumed that the public would not tolerate an economic downturn, continual stimulus has caused larger and larger distortions and a build-up of underlying, systemic risk. For years before the global financial crisis of 2008, and then again in recent years, any person or company, small or large, who did not borrow as much as possible (with a key exception in the case of ever more powerful monopoly capitalists) was made to look foolish.

Low and ultra-low interest rates can depress productivity through many channels. Zombie companies absorb resources that should be available for firms meeting a real market demand. Asset inflation drives accumulation of mal-investment. Dual mandates where central banks are told to pursue maximum employment and price stability are deeply flawed. They do not have the tools to reach these aims other than by luck, and in any case, maximum employment does not mean maximum prosperity (e.g. if the way in which monetary policy induces market forces to achieve this aim in fact ends up distorting demand in the labour market towards low productivity work and stimulates much wasteful capital investment along the way).

No surprise, then, that the overall picture post the 2008 global financial crisis has been slower economic growth, low productivity, deepening wealth inequalities, increasing risk of sovereign defaults spreading from emerging markets to developed countries…ultra-low/negative rates for ever, market tantrums and seizures, a quite stagnant, highly regulated, banking sector, risk moving to unregulated "near banks" and the public sector taking on more and more risk.

As in 2008, so again in 2022, we can see another crisis is coming, but there is zero political urgency to reform.

Is Excess Debt, Not Excess Money, the Real Problem?

No; to focus on debt is insufficient. As long as the problem is defined mainly or merely in terms of excessive debt, then that directs reforms towards reducing reliance on debt, strengthening defences against vulnerabilities, within the existing monetary system. Hence, reforms aim to strengthen defences against shocks, counter the build-up of imbalances and perhaps raise interest rates to forestall a debt-fuelled boom. But these are always contentious. Politicians are reluctant to see their central bank raise rates and thus, they fear, bring the expansion to an end, just because of a fear of debt and excessive leverage.

There is no rule in the current money system that prevents debt from rising to dangerous levels over successive cycles. All the pressure remains on raising debt levels. This is as true of the political pressure to ease access to mortgage finance for house purchase as it is for innumerable other "good causes"—take support for the arts, for the health service, or for education. In the absence of a fixed rule, whichever good cause has sufficient political muscle will get the money—even if the value of that money is immediately less than expected precisely because the aggregate of all the money doled out to all the "good causes" exceeds the real output of the economy.

That is why the diagnosis has to address the failure of the monetary system as a whole, not just the debt component in it. So far, efforts to strengthen the system and forestall another banking crisis have relied on enforcing regulation of banks, bigger capital buffers and so-called macro-prudential policies.

This is supposed to increase the resilience of banking systems so that they can withstand falls in prices of assets on their balance sheet or used as collateral for their loans, such as property, and other macroeconomic shocks. Policies aim to prevent excessive credit growth and leverage, excessive maturity mismatch and market illiquidity, to reduce concentration of risk in a bank's loans and investments. They pay special attention to the potential for systemically important banks to adopt destabilising strategies, as happened in the crisis of 2008. But these have only worked for a time and to a limited extent. They have not allowed full resumption of market activity in finance or in the real economy. Markets must remain suppressed for fear of excessive debt and risk-taking leading to more defaults and losses.

Why Do You Focus on "Super-Money"?

We have explained in Chapter 5 how a credible anchor ensures that money can fulfil its essential contribution to a good society. Money will do this if—and only if—it retains its value over the long term, measured over decades. Thus, a good money will be a trusted store of value—one of its three classic functions. It will also need to perform its other classic functions well—as a medium of exchange, a numeraire (a unit that sellers of goods and services use to post prices on their sales lists) and a standard of deferred payment (i.e. a unit used to denominate loan contracts).

Good money has at its core a group of components which satisfy these properties to the highest degree—we have described these as having super-money qualities. This monetary core performs as a superior store of value and medium of exchange to monetary assets outside this core, and in consequence, they typically are non-interest bearing. They are usable instantly without any hassle. There is no possibility of capital loss in nominal terms and demand for these core assets thrive on the expectation that money will keep value in real terms also over the very long term. In a monetary system where the "ultimate" money is a real asset this might become the most money-like of all assets. This monetary core is essential to the design of a solid anchor.

As we have emphasised, there is no such thing as a perfect anchor—but some are far better than others. When money is tied to, and convertible into, a real commodity or asset, then its real value will vary with the real value of that asset; if that asset is widely held for reasons other than its monetary use, and is widely traded, and when it has an established record of keeping its real value relatively stable or even rising gradually, then there can be confidence that money will also retain its real value (see in particular Chapter 5). That quality of being strongly respected and indeed desired endows such a money with power. On such grounds, we have presented in this volume the case of a real anchor based on equity (see Chapter 12).

To grasp the significance of our concept of super-money, one must get "inside" the minds of holders and users to understand the real motives that make them hold it in such high esteem and that lie behind the strong and robust demand for it. Such a quality eludes statistical measurement but rather gives significance to statistical regularities. However unfashionable it may be to hold such views, we are convinced that the evidence favours such a money as (albeit far from perfect) a big improvement on the present.

"Democracies Will Reject the Rules You Want"

Many critics of a return to gold say it would not be flexible enough to meet the needs of modern governments with greater discretionary spending powers and responsibilities (Schenk 2013).

As discussed in Chapters 2, 3, 6 and 8, monetary discipline has been rare and currency depreciation has been the norm in the US and indeed most of the world. The US inflation rate has averaged more than 3% a year since 1914—and that includes the deflationary episodes of the 1920s and the "lowflation" of the second decade of the twenty-first century, meaning consumer prices have doubled on average every generation. Many other countries have fared far worse, whether democratic in the sense of being also "free societies", or so-called democracies under authoritarian regimes (which can still be ultimately sensitive to public opinion especially regarding economic issues). About the only currency to be able to claim relative (but very far from absolute) long-term stability is the Swiss franc. The temporary success of monetary policies in rolling back inflation in the late 1970s and early 1980s showed the promise of monetary regime change.

The failure to secure monetary stability in the longer term illustrates how difficult it can be politically to persevere on the road to a good money regime. We have to confront the incompatibility between the existing monetary regime centred on discretionary management focused on interest rate control and exceptional central bank balance sheet size and composition, and good money over the long term. As good money is in the long-run a precondition of well-being as we define it (a reasonable degree of freedom-plus-prosperity), then the existing monetary regime will end.

That is why any serious debate has to face up to the question of how democracies can generate the will to formulate and submit to self-imposed rules.

We answer: "Yes we can consent to being bound by rules where it really matters; but we should all recognise the tensions involved". For example,

- A virtuous monetary regime is decentralised and seemingly fragile.
- The money of such a regime is liable to short-term fluctuations in real value.
- Elected politicians compete to offer benefits to particular groups and the self-interest of these beneficiaries can override the collective interest in sound money.
- Political leaders generally promise more than can be collectively financed by taxation and private sector savings.
- Spending pressures lead naturally to a rise in state spending as per cent of output.
- Populist leaders are particularly susceptible to such pressures.
- When policy over money, banking and financial markets is implemented by a body entrusted with wide discretionary powers, it will be subject to irresistible pressures as the epicentre of the power struggle over control of money.

Will a money that allows fluctuations in its value over the short or medium term be so unpopular as to be unusable? That is what defenders of the present system allege. Yet we don't think short-term fluctuations in value such as we saw under gold standard are a basis of huge unpopularity. This is much more likely to stem from the big erosions in value over time which occur under unsound money regimes. Above all, critics should compare a return to a rules-based system not with the ideal "flexibility" of the current fiat money but with its tawdry results.

"There Is No Geopolitical Urgency for Change"

Even before Russia's invasion of Ukraine in late February 2022, we could say: "Yes there is, whether we focus in a general perspective on the so-called Moscow-Beijing-Teheran-Pyongyang axis or more particularly at particular regions of the globe". In Chapter 3, we argued that unsound US monetary policies have become a source of weakness for the West in confronting such geopolitical danger. Our monetary system has become a geo-political liability.

Bad money is a flaw in Western defences; clearly, the global financial crisis, product of our monetary regime, weakened Western democracies and caused their freedoms to erode—and one can only fear the continuation from the pandemic inflation and probable subsequent crisis. It is a mortal combat for Beijing because, as long as strong democratic states survive, the Chinese Communist Party will feel threatened. So it uses money to achieve its aims by:

– Buying national economies and governments of emerging markets, notably in Africa and parts of Asia and South America, and installing military bases in them;
– Enlarging network of client states—states that are not directly controlled by the CCP but which pragmatically accept their inferior, subsidiary status, notably though the BRI structure;
– Buying academic and diplomatic support in developed countries through bribery, corruption, sponsorship of university institutes, schools, etc;
– Demanding a restructuring of the international monetary system to give Beijing a much bigger vote;
– Responding to US deployment of the dollar's hegemony as a weapon of war by threatening anarchy. If access to dollar clearing in SWIFT is denied, China can, for example, close down HSBC and other Western financial institutions with massive exposure to and dependence on Chinese market (including Hong Kong);
– China could use competitive currency depreciation and a digital currency as other weapons.

Meanwhile, China is urging the IMF to address the "deficiencies" in the international monetary system and put it in a leadership role.

Liberty and Democracy depend on the "machinery of the economy" not being dislocated by bad money with woeful consequences for prosperity and social peace.

"Your Reforms Would Increase Instability"

In a free society, people will experience economic shocks, bumps, booms and crashes. Of course these are also experienced in potentially more devastating forms in totalitarian societies. But others' greater misfortune is and should be no comfort to us. The great economist Joseph Schumpeter talked eloquently about the process of "creative destruction" as being at the centre of capitalist progress—and he doubted whether it would prove acceptable in the long-run. We are still finding out whether he was right or whether people can live with these for the sake of all the benefits of liberty.

Yes, good money would reduce but not eliminate the system's liability to huge asset inflations and busts. Capitalism can perform its key economic functions together with security—insuring those who prefer stable income streams—if people learn how to protect themselves and their business enterprises. Yes, such protection has costs. Yes, it will require taking the long view, and yes, it will require placing ethics at the heart of business and finance. But uncorrupted market forces can guide economies through cyclical fluctuations. As regards financial crises, one way (in addition to having a good money regime in place) to reduce the risks and severity of these is for the state and its agencies to desist from constructing props which cause firms to skimp on their own defences. The age of endless bailouts must come to an end. The cost of insulating Big Finance from slumps is intolerable. Governments' power to raise massive taxation without legislative/democratic approval must also cease. Does society have to declare itself bankrupt before people understand such facts?

Reference

Pringle, Robert (2012): The Money Trap.

Schenk, Catherine R. (2013) The Global Gold Market and the International Monetary System. In: Bott, Sandra (ed.) *The Global Gold Market and the International Monetary System from the Late 19th Century to the Present: Actors, Networks, Power.* Palgrave Macmillan.

White, William, R (2009): Should Monetary Policy "Lean or Clean"?

14

Pathways to Good Money

The path to good money runs deeply through the forest of politics. Good money has to win a special place in the hearts and minds of men and women. It can only survive attack from the forces which would undermine it, whether cronyism or Big Government harnessing the money and credit system to its own ends, if it has solid, well-constructed defences. These should be founded on a belief, widely shared among citizens, in the values of human dignity and freedom as well as a shared intuitive understanding of the essential contribution good money makes to building and preserving these. While such belief or intuition is necessary, it is, however, not a sufficient condition for good money regimes to be installed and to endure. The idea that individuals could together construct a viable good money while bypassing the political process is wide of the mark. Yes, in principle that is possible. But before a good money system can establish itself anywhere, defend itself and evolve into a serious international money, the present state power which would thwart that has to be limited or at least used constructively and within constitutional limits. That requires winning the political struggle.

This view of good money rooted in strong popular conviction and belief is starkly different from the path of monetary evolution through the past 30 or 40 years. In broad terms, the driving "credo" has been that a group of well-intentioned and well-qualified monetary officials, provided with an appropriate super-econometric model, can safely bring about the best possible economic outcome in terms of the combined goal of low inflation and high employment by using an approved box of tools. These tools include

© The Author(s), under exclusive license to Springer Nature
Switzerland AG 2022
B. Brown and R. Pringle, *A Guide to Good Money*,
https://doi.org/10.1007/978-3-031-06041-0_14

both "conventional" instruments (setting short-term interest rates) and "non-conventional" instruments (quantitative easing, asset purchases to manipulate bond and credit markets, zero or negative interest rates, forward interest rate "guidance") as well as "macro-prudential" regulations, all to be used at their discretion, guided by a low inflation target. The message? Money may not be of the best but should be good enough for practical-minded men and women. The Global Financial Crisis (2007–2008) with its sequel in the European debt crisis (2010–2012), the Great Economic Sclerosis (2012–2020 with possible resumption ahead) and then the Great Pandemic and Russia War Inflation (2021–2022) should have been wake-up calls. Yet the monetary establishment is again at work issuing bland reassurances: "yes, there have been some inevitable forecasting errors, but do not be alarmed; grown-ups are in charge". So the official story would have it. As we, the authors, have endeavoured to demonstrate in this book, this Panglossian "all-is-for-the-best-in-a-challenging world" confidence is profoundly misplaced.

The Monetary Establishment

The monetary status quo is embedded in our societies. Its apologists have had stunning success in terms of self-preservation; they survive and indeed flourish, side-stepping any responsibility for successive economic disasters. The commanding communications strategy has worked like a dream: find scapegoats, vilify them and deny any links from the monetary regime to economic or social distress. The state's systematic build-up of its central regulatory power, ostensibly to ward of the danger of future crisis, is aimed in reality to prop up the status quo in the course of strengthening the state itself and its power over society.

Who are the constituents of the establishment built around the monetary status quo? As analysed in Chapter 10, the list is headed by the big banks, Big Tech and other monopoly capitalists who have enjoyed absurdly low-cost equity capital—and the private equity barons. We should also include finance ministries of governments seeking re-election, which justify programs of large tax cuts or expenditure increases, shamelessly exploiting the vast potential revenues from monetary taxation. Alongside these, a steady supply of new entrants trickles into the crony networks within the establishment. These entrants now include sections of the burgeoning crypto industry (see below).

Let's summarise. Latter-day Prince Metternichs do not look under threat; if there is to be a 2020s equivalent of the liberal 1848 revolutions against the reactionary regimes of that era, there are as yet no forward indications of it. Yet even at this dark historical moment, there are some grounds for optimism. There is public discontent with the evils of present monopoly capitalism—perhaps most of all in the abuses of Big Tech even as there are grounds for despair about the response so far in Congress or in legislatures outside the US. There is anger at the social and economic divisiveness of the establishment's favoured policies. And at falling living standards. These are topics which we have already discussed and to which we return in the next chapter. Also encouraging is the fact that an academic economic tradition of thinking about good money, liberty and prosperity has persisted outside the mainstream of economics, of which the present volume is one small example. If a Younger Pitt does seize the advantage of the next crisis (similar to that Prime Minister seizing a moment of popular dejection in Britain following the loss of its US colonies to rehabilitate Britain's finances and greatness) to make an assault on monopoly capitalism and bad money, there should be an academic script to inspire him or her—updated and expanded to be on the reading list alongside the "Wealth of Nations".

Digitalisation—How Regulators Stifle Initiative

In the established fiat money domain, regulation has stifled initiatives that might have lit up the journey ahead to good money. Take the illustration of JP Morgan Chase's endeavour to issue its own digital coin; this could have been the start of a more competitive era where banks and other non-financial institutions would issue their own banknotes, here in digital form, such as to appeal as super-money to a wide range of clients. Alongside, there could have been the development of clearing house system and exchange market where digital notes of the participating banks could be exchanged against each other at par. But the reaction of regulators was negative. They quickly pointed to every possible weakness or vulnerability for clients and stifled the innovation. Flitter (2021) recounts how "soon after the JPMorgan Chase (JPM) digital coin went live, regulators began calling ---; they worried that the movement of coins around the financial system could cause a build-up of risk because they were tied to the dollar. The bank had to cut back on the scope of JPM coin's use. Now JPM coins cannot be used to transfer value outside JP Morgan's internal systems. It is meaningless in the wider world".

Suppose instead several banks were able to offer virtual banknotes (digital coin) for dollar cash. In effect, they would specify that this virtual cash (based on say a 1000 dollar digital coin) was interchangeable between them and that each participating bank in the clearing house for these would back the digital coins 100% with Fed banknotes or Fed reserves (and in the event of insolvency, the digital coin holders would have first claim on that backing). Via the blockchain, individuals could make transfers of these notes into other digital wallets designed for them and banks would undertake on demand to change 1 to 1 coins issued by one participating bank into coins issued by other participating banks. They could also be redeemed on demand for cash (paper bank notes) at par. Blockchain fees would be levied per transaction and these would accrue to the participating banks. Specialist banks or agents would have emerged to whom individuals could sell one digital coin for another or to realise cash, leaving these to effect the closing transactions with the source banks. The flourishing of the digital version of cash, available say in a 1000 dollar unit, could put pressure on regulators and the Treasury to drop their opposition to the issuance of banknotes of similar size (rather than 1oo dollars maximum as at present).

The monetary establishment can be fierce and ruthless in suppressing innovation when it threatens their monopoly power or otherwise weakens their revenue-raising capability (for finance ministries a top concern here is that innovation should not reduce their power of compulsion in the levying of tax). Even so, the financial media is full of reports about the many opportunities which have opened up for private financial enterprises in the digital space that have nothing to do with Bitcoin. Some of these are now tainted by the crypto crash of spring and summer 2022 together with the related bubble-bursting in fintech and this will doubtless become a pretext for new innovation-suppressing regulations.

—And Gold Remonetisation

Competition from gold money could have been based on the growth of bullion banking. Banks and other financial institutions would issue deposits and sell loans in gold denomination, with clearing of balances for transaction purposes taking place in bullion transfers at a specified geographical location (say London, Zurich or New York) in a clearing house. Banks could include in their range of gold deposits an ultra-safe category, 100% backed by holdings of gold bullion. Alongside, banks could have applied digitalisation to the marketing of gold "coins" which would make use of blockchain technology for payments, backed by gold and convertible on demand into such safe gold deposits or directly into gold bullion. The backing of these gold "coins" (in effect stablecoins) would be vetted by an independent inspectorate. Some gold market practitioners and commentators attribute the lack of progress towards gold monetisation in private markets to the heavy hand of regulatory authorities—actual or potential. As a practical matter, dislocations to shipping gold during the pandemic also have hindered private gold money development. There are one or two examples of stablecoins issued in gold by small non-regulated financial institutions, but with little basis for holders to feel that these are safe (in comparison say with the main gold ETFs) they have made virtually no progress.

Suppose some banks or other financial institutions for example in Switzerland or the UK could overcome the regulatory hurdles and agree that their gold deposits could be cleared in physical gold deliverable in Zurich or London? For good measure, they could set up a digital gold wallet system interchangeable between them. Wallets would accept digital gold from any participating bank, with each digital coin issued by any of them. Individual holders of digital coins issued by any participating bank, say bank X, could present to any other bank Y and ask for conversion into a digital coin of Y. Digital gold coins issued by any bank would be backed 100% by gold bullion deliverable in the given centre and secured absolutely in the case of bankruptcy. Specialist banks or brokers would assume the role of converting digital coins of X into Y and dealing with the banks to effect this while paying out customers at par on the exchange. The participating banks would belong to a gold clearing house for settling in physical metal in the given centre balances between them.

In this way, in principle, gold could develop into a fully-fledged money again with deposits and loans denominated in the metal, bank notes both digital and physical issued by gold deposit banks and so on. None of this could take place without the blessing of the "authorities" at least in one centre, and these must have sufficient confidence and diplomatic ability to take on pressure from elsewhere. We should also note that there are trading businesses in the gold industry which make good profit in the climate of present restrictions and would not welcome a free for all spell of great monetary innovation. (Some bullion bankers in London, for example, have no interest in regulations changing to permit other banks and financial institutions to compete with them in the bullion banking business.) And there is still a question about how large and stable any transactions demand would be for gold money.

On that point, in every country there are sections of the population with a deep appreciation of the yellow metal's role as a historic store of value and money. This is especially true of the rising superpowers of Asia. Indians and Chinese are the largest private holders of gold in the world (notably in the forms of jewellery held as a store of value), probably totalling together between 40,000 and 50,000 tonnes, more than the total official world gold reserves of about 35,000 tonnes. China is also the leading producer of newly-mined gold. Other important powers with a cultural and historic attachment to gold as a private investment asset include the Germany, France, Italy, Turkey, Saudi Arabia and other Middle East states. Many people in these countries still believe that only gold is real money. Although, to repeat, there is no perfect anchor, the advocates of monetary reform based on gold can show how a machinery of money which functioned in the past with built-in stabilising mechanisms could function again in a comparable role, updated to suit modern conditions. True reformers would have to rebut the familiar anti-gold concerns—that gold has lost its main monetary role, that it has become a highly speculative asset, that the cost of re-anchoring monetary systems to gold could be so large as to offset any conceivable gains, and that instability in its real price could bring about large swings in its purchasing power. Although we have offered answers to all these concerns, they will certainly re-surface.

The question that complacent defenders of the status quo have to face is not what is best in theory but rather what works in practice. It is easy to point to gold's weaknesses as a standard. Gold, however, should be compared not to some ideal regime but rather to the money regimes that actually exist with all the inequities, waste, cronyism and costs that come with them. It is not what is best in some ideal world but what kind of money in practice has proved in the past—and may even now—relatively better than alternatives. Here, gold's star rises in the east as fiat money's star sinks in the west.

Engaging in Politics—The US

In sum, the case for radical reform of money must engage the political process. This is a story with many variations around the world. Let's take a look.

First, in the US, in recent decades the Republican Party has attracted a fringe of gold money advocates. But by the time of the November 2020 election defeats these had drifted away. The Trump administration followed inflationary policies, as the Republicans had under the first Administration of George W. Bush (2001–2004), under the second Administration of Ronald Reagan (1985–1988) and under Richard Nixon and then Gerald Ford in the early and mid-1970s. In the mid- and late 1970s, calls for monetary policy to combat inflation emerged on the right of the Democratic Party and recall President Carter's attacks on Republican monetary policies during the 1976 election campaign and subsequently his nomination of Paul Volcker as Fed Chief in 1978 on the clear understanding that he would pursue a tough anti-inflationary policy. So could the case for good money return to the mainstream of US politics? Yes, it could but events will be critical. If the Great pandemic inflation of 2021–2022 were to be followed by years of high consumer price inflation during which monetary tax collections remained heavy, pressures for monetary reform would surely grow, especially if there were no longer an offset in broad-based gains in asset markets. At some stage, the destruction of wealth through a process of asset price deflation coupled with a devastating downward trend in real middle-class incomes could well become a strong catalyst for monetary reform. High consumer price inflation would be particularly effective as a tool for argument against the present regime as it would be not difficult to attribute this to an ailing money (money printing according to the jargon). So would the growing feeling that the system "just ain't fair".

At the time of writing, there is a surge of consumer prices in the US and Europe which naturally is unpopular, notably where this goes along with a squeeze on aggregate real incomes. So far, there is, however, no evidence that the dislike of these income squeezes is fuelling a grassroots movement for monetary reform. For now, many voters might reasonably suppose that the income squeezes have more to do with pandemic and war-related dislocations including the Russia-US/EU economic war than with flaws in the monetary regime; they might become angry though when prices overall do not decline substantially once the shortages fade and their savings fail to recoup any of their lost real purchasing power. Yet as the episode of high inflation rolls on to asset deflation and financial crisis, there will be a multitude of scapegoats for the monetary establishment to target and it is far from clear that bad money will emerge as the lead culprit in popular perceptions. This is where the importance of thinkers and writers about money enters the stage—their scripts of how bad money is responsible should have been circulating well in advance of the crisis and some on the political stage could prepare themselves for the opening which would be provided by the crisis.

The backbone of the popular case for good money in the US will be that the present system is not only responsible for serious loss of prosperity across society as a whole but is also unfair and immoral. Outrage at growing wealth disparities could and should also contribute to support for good money, where such inequalities are, as at present, often the result of a bad money mechanism and have little or no connection to a person's real contribution. No, envy is never a sound basis for reform movements. But a money that cannot be manipulated serves as an impartial medium and measure, a money that binds generations across time and individuals across space in the same net of rules, that is a prize worth fighting for on moral as well as economic grounds. Indeed, voters should view the ugly symptoms of social and economic inequality and unfairness generated by bad money as having more in common with an Oriental Despotism (whether Russian or Chinese) than with market economies. Americans can call on traditions of protest against unfair taxation from the Boston Tea Party onwards (Europeans to the great reforms to root out corruption in public administration and strict guardianship of public finances in the nineteenth century).

If Americans further connect the current money system to taxation without representation, to unfair economic outcomes and to the vast growth in monopoly rents, then reformers will gain a hearing. The puncturing of popular illusions of wealth could be decisive. The advocates have to tell a convincing narrative and pin blame on the mistaken ideas, the cynicism and indeed the inhumanity of those responsible. They also must have a well thought-out program of monetary reform which is consistent with this advocacy. Under their new regime, the barons of Wall Street, and more broadly the cronyists, must be brought to heel. Much more importantly, the ordinary American must have reason (because of the monetary reform) to be more confident in future prosperity and their individual as well as common or social well-being and financial safety.

If indeed the US were to lead the way in establishing a good money regime, a key issue would be the selection of system type and solid anchor. Would it be a fiat money system or a money based on gold or real asset? We have already described in this volume the pluses and minuses of each including the solidity or otherwise of anchors. But we should also consider the particular issues related to anchoring a currency based on gold where the rest of the world is still on fiat money standards. These issues should be distinguished for the largest economy in the world, the US, whose currency is the international hegemon, from smaller economies.

Imagine the situation where unilaterally the US dollar becomes fully convertible into gold (including gold and digital gold coin). Suppose further that as part of the new arrangements the Federal Reserve no longer has the power to create money (in fact monetary base) on a discretionary basis. Rather, changes in the outstanding amount of notes and cash (including reserves of the banks at the Fed or clearing house) in aggregate could occur only exactly in step with their gold holdings.

All outstanding banknotes become claims against the US Treasury which in turn pledges to convert them into gold on demand at the new par. There would be a similar starting arrangement for bank reserves, slimmed down to a normal level by extensive open market operations in the lead-up to gold convertibility for the dollar.

In such a system, we could expect that the real value of the dollar (and now of gold) would be substantially less volatile than in the many decades during which no widely circulating national money has been convertible into gold. The huge monetary demand from the US would be a stabilising influence in the gold market (as regards the real gold price). Even so, the fluctuations in the real value of the dollar, most importantly in terms of the US shopping basket, but also in terms of the global shopping basket, would be substantially more volatile over short and medium-term periods than what would be the case under a full international gold standard.

This volatility may be a deterrent to the US giving up all discretionary control over the supply of core money assets in the new system. The arrangements could allow the US authorities to make additional issues of base money (in the form of banknotes or reserve deposits)—or sometimes to withdraw these—so as to achieve a smoother path for the real value of the dollar over the short and medium term. Realistically, adoption of a gold money regime by the US would not emerge as a black swan. There would be much discussion of benefits, costs, how and when to make the move. The legislative route would surely include a gold monetary stability act (or whatever the eventual title). Included in that would be clauses dealing with the minimum gold backing for Federal Reserve banknotes (this was 40 per cent in the 1913 Federal Reserve Act) and constraints/rules as to how the Fed would determine the supply of reserve deposits to the banks under the new regime, in so far as excess gold holdings relative to the minimum gold backing gave it scope for discretion. This would be subject to the over-riding condition that the dollar be freely convertible into gold at a par value to be determined. At a late point in the journey, plausibly just before the regime starts, the par value would be announced. Ahead of that, there would have been considerable speculation about where this would be. If the predominant view globally and in the US was that the return to gold convertibility for the dollar was indeed fully achievable, there would likely be a massive dishoarding i.e. sales of physical gold for dollars, which would now be "as good as gold" and earn interest. This dishoarding would increase the dollar monetary base (dollar banknotes and reserve deposits held by the banks as the Federal Reserve (acting for the Treasury) issued dollars in exchange for gold. To reduce inflationary risks, the Fed could offset some of these inflows from gold into the dollar monetary base by open market operations in government securities. In principle the Fed's scope to create additional dollar monetary base in this way would still be restricted by the possibility of dollar holders globally presenting dollar paper for redemption in gold. The legal minimum for gold backing of dollar banknotes and cash outstanding as established for the Fed at the start of the gold standard could become in this way an effective constraint.

True, once we open the door to such discretionary monetary interventions, progress towards a good money regime might be derailed. But, hey! the prize is worth taking risks for. With luck, also public opinion would already have swung behind the progress towards good money.

—The World Outside the US

Elsewhere widespread resentment at the inflationary monetary policies of the US and its negative consequences for prosperity could spur demands for regime change. True, the monetary establishments everywhere are signed up members of the "central bankers club" (see Chapter 3). But who knows what resentment is simmering below the surface? The case for good money might turn on how governments that moved to gold convertibility would manage the national currency's fluctuations against the dollar, and contain any surge, so as to protect the profits of groups to which they are close or form part (most of all the export industries); advocates, however, could also build on support of savers and much of the middle classes. Reform advocates would again use the natural appeal of gold, but the way forward on this would be different for small and medium-size countries.

A stark point of comparison here. If the dollar were again convertible into gold, monetary demand there would reduce the volatility of the real price of gold (whether in the US or globally) compared to what it is now. That is not the case for a much smaller economy unilaterally adopting gold convertibility. So there would be considerable pressure from within that smaller country for its monetary authority to adopt discretionary monetary policies so as to smooth out this volatility in terms of domestic real purchasing power of the new gold money. As we have seen, any such domestic anchoring is especially problematic for small open economies.

Don't Rule Out the EU Led by Germany and France

The nearest to the US unilaterally adopting gold as its money would be a group of European countries adopting a gold-based euro. How could the advocacy for gold develop at a European level? Fanning resentment at US inflationary hegemony as discussed above could be one element, but more powerful to latch on to could be anger in Northern Europe at how the ECB has plundered savings and wealth for transfers to weak sovereign and weak banks (their shareholders and creditors). That anger is not going to emerge during a period of asset inflation when many feel they are doing well thank you with their house prices booming and all well with their pensions and portfolio assets. The anger could emerge as or when all this crashes and/or there is a surge in goods and services inflation.

Proceeding down a pathway to a convertible euro would surely require joint political action in France and Germany. Both countries have in the past defied the US inflationary hegemon—France under the Presidency of De Gaulle as advised by Jacques Rueff and Germany under the regime of monetarism. Both have a deep affinity and cultural attachment to gold. Despite its critical commitment and dependence on the alliance with the US (via NATO) in the Cold War, Germany was still building up its gold reserves in the 1960s and hasn't sold an ounce.

Action led by France and Germany (or the two acting jointly without the other euro members) to make their common currency convertible into gold would encounter the same set of issues regarding stability as discussed above for the US. The most plausible work-around would be the same—residual discretionary monetary issuance by their authorities, albeit harnessed to an aim of price stabilisation and other ends. A money convertible into a real asset based around a German hegemon without France would be an alternative— at least it could bring a good money not only to an economic heavyweight but also its monetary satellites.

The Swiss also Like Gold

Think back to the early and mid-1970s when Switzerland instituted a strict monetarist regime and allowed its franc to float freely (see Kugler and Rich 2001). Could a good money regime be revived there? The last one was brought to an end by first a powerful rise of the franc through the mid-1970s and later a breakdown of Switzerland's then monetary base control system. The franc's explosive rise produced a backlash in the Swiss political scene culminating in heavy-handed foreign exchange intervention in the late 1970s inconsistent with keeping the spirit of the franc as a hard money. Advocates seeking to reincarnate Swiss monetary exceptionalism would have to confront the tawdry record of how the Swiss National Bank (SNB) has acted through the quarter century so far of the global 2% inflation standard. They would have to indicate persuasively how Switzerland could have defied the Goliaths of Bad Money (the ECB and Federal Reserve), especially their spells of monetary repression tax and virulent asset inflation.

Monetarism as practised in the 1970s might have provided a reasonable starting point for a Swiss pathway to sound money through the 1990s and beyond. If the SNB had broadened and deepened the demand for monetary base (sometimes described as high-powered money), there would have been grounds for confidence in the franc maintaining its purchasing power over the long-run founded on strict control of monetary base expansion within a low annual limit. One element of redesign would be to eliminate deposit insurance while simultaneously modifying regulations so as to permit banks to issue a new category of super safe sight deposits backed 100% by either banknotes or reserves (all non-interest bearing) at the central bank.

Under this re-designed monetary system there would be no carry trade boom in Swiss franc as occurred in 2000–2007, a testament to the SNB's inflationary stance at that time. The bust of the carry trade during the Great Crash of 2008 and then the European sovereign debt crisis of 2010–2012 generated huge upward pressure on the franc. The SNB responded to that by massive foreign exchange intervention which it justified as countering disorderly markets. When the crisis passed, the SNB should have brought its foreign exchange reserves back to normal level. Instead, the SNB turned itself into one of the world largest sovereign wealth funds, financing this by issuing franc certificates subject in effect to high monetary repression tax. This massive fund stands as an affront to economic freedom and symptomatic of a pernicious sustained currency manipulation. Persistently, the SNB has added to its mass of foreign exchange holdings (reaching near 140% of GDP in 2021) so as to continually "stabilise" the CHF/euro rate, moderating thereby the alleged overvaluation of the franc, albeit at times losing control.

Under the hypothetical sound money regime, the franc might well climb to lofty summits amidst much volatility, far above the 1.00 euro/franc peak of summer 2022. This would cause pain to certain businesses in Switzerland concentrated in the export sector or import-competing areas. Businesses there might well cut wages as quoted in nominal francs. In these early stages, import prices in francs would fall steeply; wages in francs as averaged across all sectors would also decline, but by less than prices in general. The internal and external purchasing power of franc-denominated assets would rise. In the long-run, these price falls in Switzerland would, however, go into reverse as the expansion of the monetary base continued.

Crucially, the huge surplus of Swiss savings would then seep into foreign assets acquired with the ultra-strong franc rather than flowing into the swollen coffers of the SNB debt at absurdly repressed sub-zero interest rates. With the Swiss currency at the mountain summits, the market would expect it to descend somewhat over the long-run. Hence, from the viewpoint of Swiss investors, the rate of return on non-franc assets, as on franc assets, would be higher than from the perspective of individuals in the interest-income-deprived universe outside Switzerland.

The franc itself would enjoy a renaissance as a global investment money, burnishing the Swiss financial sector. Foreigners who had adopted the franc early on would gain too. The Swiss would avoid the stress and toil of residential real estate inflation—with houses remaining much more affordable. Swiss households would shelter from the setback to prosperity which will surely follow the global asset bubble of the past decade. True, a sudden transition to sound money could trigger a fall in its real estate market, inflict losses at the SNB (in which the cantons are holders of equity) and destabilise sectors of the pension fund and wealth industry where the dominant strategy has been salvaging yield by buying foreign assets. But a return to sound money would bring dividends in the long-run far in excess of transitional costs. Meanwhile, we applaud its insistence on continuing to issue large denomination Swiss banknotes (1000 francs, currently worth about $1,100); the Swiss here makes a splendid gesture of defiance to those who would do away with cash.

Britain or Japan: As US Satellites?

The grip of the central bank/discretionary money model is nowhere stronger than in Britain, so it is unlikely to lead the radical reforms needed. But it could be a good disciple of the US. One formidable barrier is the extent to which middle-class wealth in the UK is concentrated in home-ownership often in highly leveraged form; the journey to sound money and positive real interest rates would inflict financial damage on a crucial political constituency. Today, there is no sound money tradition to speak of in the UK and it plays no role in the political economy of that country. As a practical matter, the selling off of gold reserves by the Blair administration in the early 2000s makes any gold-linked good money in the UK much less feasible than in several European countries (including Germany, France, Netherlands, Italy) or the US. But if the US for whatever reason returned to gold, the UK would be an early follower in a diluted form. As Britain will never be leader of the orchestra, it could enjoy playing second fiddle.

Could Japan find a pathway to a good money? The short answer is yes, but it would need a political earthquake. Important segments of Japanese voters are deeply committed to stability and uneasy with recent policies of continual stimulus, monetary repression and mountainous state debts. The collapse of the yen in the first half of 2022 - down by 25 per cent against the dollar - has surely added to their anxiety. But in essence a one party (LDP) democracy with deeply ailing public finances, where the dominating political party has deep financial roots in exporting firms and in a highly regulated banking sector, Japan is not a promising greenhouse for good money. There was a brief period in the late 2000s when the LDP temporarily lost power and Japan seemed about to embark on the early stages of a journey to good money. The BoJ Governor at the time, Masaaki Shirakawa, was a Chicago-trained PhD economist who in the weeks following his appointment re-read volumes of Milton Friedman (see Chapter 8). But even then there was a lack of strategic thinking—especially around the issue of finding a firm monetary anchor for a freely floating yen. That would have required a radical shake-up of Japan's oligopolistic banks. That was politically a non-starter. But, like the UK, Japan could follow an American lead.

—And Then There Is China

China is anxious to reduce its dependence on the US dollar. At present, its monetary leadership as in other countries usually follows the Fed's lead; but the limited convertibility of the yuan does provide greater scope for China not to follow suit without fanning economic tensions most of all in the export sector. And in any case such tensions manifest themselves in different form under a repressive political regime. Even so for now China is subject to US monetary hegemony in important respects. Analysts track the RMB's exchange rate against the dollar—it is the only exchange rate that matters to Beijing. China is highly vulnerable to US sanctions focusing on access to dollar markets, clearing of dollar-denominated transactions and flows of money from China into and out of dollars. Might a link to gold offer a way to reduce its vulnerability and dependence?

No, China cannot and will not return to a full gold standard in the traditional sense. One of the basic principles of such a standard as we have noted is complete freedom to import and export gold, including for residents. This is unthinkable for Chinese leadership at the moment—it would involve far too great a sacrifice of control by Beijing. There is no prospect either of Beijing encouraging the growth of free, private markets offering a range of instruments and facilities with clearly-defined property rights protected by trusted civil courts. Nor can China challenge America's monetary hegemony more widely.

Beijing might, however, see attractions in making the RMB convertible for external official holders of China's currency at a fixed rate into and out of gold. There are some evident hurdles here. Why make the currency attractive for foreign official holders rather than for its own citizens? (well, the US did for several decades). And how to prevent convertibility into gold for foreign official holders in fact becoming a conduit to more general convertibility for all foreign holders (private and official) as leakages grew between the official yuan exchange market and the private markets? But Beijing can count on strict enforcement of its exchange controls. Yes, it would be contrary to the IMF rulebook, which bans countries from linking their currencies to gold. But for the IMF to expel China for a technical breach of this outmoded rule would be unthinkable. The IMF's skilled senior bureaucrats would quickly find a way round the rule.

Anyhow, if this limited convertibility pledge ever became activated, it could instantly (if believed to be durable) give credibility to the currency. It would encourage other governments and central banks, especially in Asia and among China's growing number of clientele states with close financial and investment links to hold working balances in Chinese currency. Political regimes around the world fearful of US asset freezes could see considerable advantage in holding the new golden yuan and Beijing might be able to use this to its geopolitical advantage. Hong Kong might be designated as the market centre. (The Hong Kong dollar could eventually switch its anchor from the US dollar to gold, keeping the rest of the currency board apparatus unchanged.) China would then gradually reduce its dependence on the dollar, e.g. by investing more of its reserves in gold and developing clearing facilities in the RMB. This act would also greatly strengthen domestic confidence in the currency, given China's deep historical and cultural attachment to gold (China is the world's fastest-growing gold market). It could issue gold bonds.

Such a gold link would also strengthen the attraction of China to foreign investors, in terms of both portfolio and direct investment. While China's financial, economic and wider political repression is a severe handicap to the international growth of its currency, the destruction that Western financial sanctions have wrought on Russia's economy and the wealth of its ruling elite will have jolted China's ruling oligarchs severely. They will surely speed up efforts to establish alternative currency payments and clearing systems if only as a fallback in future emergencies. Though not an immediate challenge to

American hegemony, a gold link would put down a marker that Washington could not ignore. It might strongly attract countries including not only Russia but also India and those in South-East Asia with ancient gold cultures and massive private gold holdings to be drawn into Beijing's monetary orbit and loosen their dependence on the dollar. It is unlikely that the US with or without its allies would seek to frustrate such a policy, e.g. destabilise the gold market by selling gold from it stocks or otherwise manipulating the price.

Good Money's Appeal to All Savers

Reformers who champion a replacement of unsound money with good money are often lampooned as cranks. But not so fast…Good money has occasionally won elections—think of the SPD in Germany 1968–1970s and de Gaulle in the mid-1960s with Jacques Rueff. A popular backlash against inflation was a powerful factor behind the elections of Mrs Thatcher in the UK in 1979 and Ronald Reagan in the US in 1981 (though Reagan abandoned hard money later) and both espoused versions of monetarist doctrine. Mrs Thatcher had a famous fight with the Bank of England over base money control but backed down.

The party of the savers, the middle class, the pensioners, those who would gain from falling prices and greater competition, naturally favour good money; forces are joined here with those who hate monopoly and Big Government. The movement to monetary reform will probably be led by the (reconstituted) right wings of social democratic parties. This could emerge in a new formulation that cuts across the traditional right-left line—a party which champions competitive market economies to bring lower prices and bolster real living standards of the many while confronting monopoly power, and free individuals from the terrors of inflation and/or manipulated low interest rates, a strengthening of worker rights, an end to surveillance capitalism where individuals have little if any defence over their private data being pillaged by the tech monopolists and Big Government, more competition and choice in health care without reducing overall coverage for the less well-off, etc. Antagonism to cronyism and pseudo-globalism in the shape of dodgy UN organisations could bring in some populist elements.

And to Greens

The Greens are a natural ally of good money. For this alliance to become real Greens must see that the long-term horizons for investment which good money stimulates and the sober-rational market-pricing of long-run risks including environmental which it fosters would be positive to meeting environmental challenges. A problem here is that some self-styled fellow-travellers of the Greens, for example in the electric vehicles sector, have done well from asset inflation and crony capitalism.

Good money should therefore not be seen, as is sometimes alleged, as a project of libertarian free market fringe groups. It is a regime that appeals to people with many different political viewpoints. Whereas parties representing big exporters, big banks and big business typically oppose good money, ordinary people want it; to them, it is associated with honesty and fair dealing. Yes, it is naturally linked to competitive banking/money systems, but these should bring benefits across the social spectrum.

The Pandemic and End of Regime

The "inflation shock" of the pandemic may well be seen historically as the historical moment when a sense of impending "end of regime" started to grow. The policy toolkit of the bad money establishment appears to be close to exhaustion and has evidently failed in the case of the pandemic inflation. It is no exaggeration to say that the "2% inflation standard" has collapsed amidst the inflation shock of the pandemic, though this may be far from apparent in some conventional readings of long-run inflation expectations. Monetary weapons are blunt and have increasingly unacceptable side-effects—including inequalities. The frantic search for yield by interest income famined individuals is another symptom of monetary sickness. Huge runs into and out of different asset classes broken by occasional bouts of panic demand for safe havens fuel massive global capital flows with disruptive effects. People feel anxious and vulnerable. Support for state money is variable and fickle with a deep-seated sense of unfairness.

Further Objections to Our Proposals—Our Answers in Brief

Along the pathway to good money, there are surely likely to be bouts of doubt. Some of this might come in response to temporary economic setbacks or from swings in the political pendulum. Determined reformers hoping to point the way to a better monetary future should anticipate possible objections which could well surface before the journey starts or well into the journey (these supplement those in the previous Chapter 13). They should have readymade answers available to politicians in the front line advancing a good money agenda.

Below is a list of possible objections ("O") and criticisms, drawn up in short form such as can be applied in public debate and our answers ("A").

No to Laissez-Faire?

O: A laissez-faire money system could not meet today's challenges. The system is enormously complex. This calls for a body continuously gathering information, understanding it, ensuring market integrity, etc., as well as or in addition to anti-cartel watchdog.
A: Free markets require legal watchdogs or guardians. That is clear. And yes, the sustaining of competition and prevention of monopoly creation require a tough legal regime which is enforced. As to the point though about information gathering, the best assembler and user of massive and highly decentralised information is the market itself, not a central planning authority.

Economies Are Not Self-Stabilising?

O: You assume free enterprise economies are self-stabilising. This is contrary to all experience—capitalist economies are inherently unstable. Economies can reach equilibrium at high levels of unemployment.
A: We reject the view that free competitive market economies under sound money regimes are inherently unstable. This view of endemic instability has its origins either in Marxist doctrine about the inevitable rise of monopoly capitalism or in Keynesian doctrine about a multitude of malfunctionings largely centred around money illusion and absolute liquidity preference, the latter supplemented by the zero rate boundary problem and pessimism about investment opportunity. Certainly, monopoly is a threat; but this is not endemic to capitalism. It arises where legal systems and their applications fail to deal with the problem and where unsound monies fuel the growth of monopoly.

Turning to the Keynesian critique, the great recessions which according to this have been so problematic for free market competitive capitalism have all emerged from episodes of highly unsound money. The severity of these great recessions has been further amplified by extraordinarily destabilising twists in monetary or other policies (e.g. the Fed's sharp tightening of policy in Summer 1931 in response to a drain of gold prompted by sterling's devaluation, or the encouragement of cartel formation and wage protections as promoted by the Hoover administration). Keynesians make no mention of the potential for pro-cyclical flexibility in prices under sound money regimes to promote recovery from recession (prices fall to a lower than normal level during the weak business cycle phase and expectations of a subsequent recovery means businesses and households bring forward spending).

Regulation Is Needed to Counter Tendency to Excess Leverage?

O: Actors are under huge competitive pressure, and the incentive to take excessive risks is likely to remain high. Detailed and comprehensive regulation is required to combat this or we will always be heading for another global financial crisis.

A: There is no innate tendency in competitive financial markets under sound money to over-leverage and engage in other bad practices. It is unsound money which stimulates such behaviour—driving some combination of desperation for yield and irrational exuberance based on positive feedback loops from capital gains to over-confidence. How monetary inflation via asset inflation creates dangerous illusion-making has been a key subject in our book.

Markets Need Central Banks as Lenders of Last Resort?

O: Lender of last resort is critical in a crisis and the private sector cannot replicate it. Private money fanatics always drone on about Scottish banking in the eighteenth century or US experiments with free banking that are completely inappropriate to today's world.

A: Lender of last resort function grew out of an essential ambiguity and related legal unclarity in the evolution of deposit banking. Holders of deposits with banks came to expect (and were encouraged to do so by the banks) that their deposits were always convertible into cash (or equivalent) on demand even though the banks were not holding 100 per recent cash reserves against these. This certainty is built on myth. Yes, a highly capitalised bank is likely able to deliver on such a promise, more so than a weak competitor, but not always so. Governments (including banking authorities) joined in the ambiguity by unofficially promising to supply liquidity to deemed sound institutions at times of crisis. We have detailed the cronyism to which this gave rise. Eventually, governments responding to financial crises introduced new expedients to resolve the problem—deposit insurance and too big to fail—which by setting up perverse incentives required ever more regulation alongside. In our volume, good money would be rid of all this luggage. The only totally safe and liquid deposits would be those backed 100% by cash. Alongside there would be a whole gradation of bank liabilities distinguished by the ratio of their cash backing (if any) and equity backing. In addition, good money would have a high-powered money component which was elastic in supply so as to meet short-term surges in demand for this without big swings in money rates.

Markets Cannot Regulate Behaviour?

O: Investors/depositors cannot discipline the system whatever the incentives they face short of frequent massive disruptions that are politically unacceptable. As the monetary system is the base/foundation of the whole economy, no government will or could adopt the "hands off" attitude that we recommend.

A: If price signalling in asset and credit markets is not corrupted by unsound money, then this brings about a pruning or permanent shrinking of activities/businesses/state entities well before they have the potential to explode the system. We can see this in the example of the European sovereign and banking debt crisis of 2010–2012; it was the deep corruption of market signalling during the monetary inflation of the late 1990s and into the first half of the 2000s that allowed the future problems to fester.

System Needs 24-Hour Standby Liquidity Support?

O: Even the payment system needs constant short-term liquidity support to ensure it functions 24-hour without a hitch. The money supply is endogenous so it is historically illiterate to use it as an anchor.

A: Yes any functioning monetary system has to include a clearing house/system for settling balances between institutions which are prominent in effecting money transactions for their clients. It is not clear why this clearing system has to be state-run including a central bank, though historically this has become the case. State or supranational institutions that control the clearing house for payments might be able to achieve other objectives; for example, in the European Monetary Union, large transfers from Northern into Southern Europe have been made, camouflaged as balances outstanding to central banks (positive and negative) within the central bank's clearing system. As regards the broadly defined money supply (say M3), yes this is only very loosely related to the supply of high-powered money—the ratio of the first to the second at any time determined by a whole range of factors which are endogenous. These include banks' success or failure in making their deposits more or less attractive relative to close substitute financial instruments outside the banking system By contrast, a solid anchor can effectively exercise constraint with respect to the supply of high-powered money—exogenously within a fiat money system and in combination with feedback loops from demand in combination with real supply conditions (e.g. in the mining industry for gold) in the case of a real asset-based money. That is why monetary base (which overlaps considerably super-money) is a good candidate for a key role in anchoring the monetary system but broad money is not.

The Monetary Base Is Irrelevant?

O: The monetary base plays no role in determining the money supply or GDP and thus is a completely irrelevant target.

A: It may play no pivotal economic role in the present dysfunctional monetary system and we doubt it would bear a tight and predictable relationship to broad money even under a sound money regime as discussed. But we can and indeed should design a system where monetary base does play a very important role. This is in the sense that a solid anchor can be attached to monetary base and exercise effective constraints (in a general setting which takes account of shifts in underlying demand) such as to mean that money does not become the monkey wrench in the economic machinery. Further, monetary base is an explicit target only under monetarism, not under a full gold standard. Under the latter demand and supply of monetary base are critical in determining the monetary path, but supply is not targeted—its supply, constrained by geology, is endogenously determined.

O: You want a monetary base made up of assets with "super-money qualities" but have no discussion of its function apart from vague references to it as a pivot. You talk about high-powered money, but there is no mention of the money multiplier, without which the term "high-powered" makes no sense. If you did it would make no difference anyway as the money multiple is not a useful concept.

A: For us, the key concept here is super-money—components of the broader defined money supply which are especially money-like. In the case of a good money, the assets which make up the monetary base (high-powered money) have super-money qualities. Our ideas about the importance of a well-developed super-money are key to designing a solidly anchored monetary system, but in no way do these imply a stable multiplier between monetary base and the broader money supply.

O: A good system depends on trust not only in money but also in the institutions of government and the state which stand behind money and protect people, for example, from bank defaults.

A: Good money does not mean general protection against bank defaults except for holders of safe money deposits or cash as described. Good money does not depend on institutions of government—but a constitutional including legal framework which protects and defends the ideally working machinery of money from attack, including by governments and crony capitalists. Bureaucrats are nowhere pulling the levers or watching the control posts; rather, there is an intricate system of automatic mechanisms.

We Ignore the Fact That Money Is a Public Good?

O: Money is a public good, so that the state has to take ultimate responsibility.

A: Money's description as a public good is often mentioned as if it were a conclusive point while actually being more or less meaningless. Money is a consumer good yielding various services—and under a good monetary system, market forces can determine good outcomes. Nowhere, do we have to introduce concept of public good. Yes, society and economic prosperity will gain from good money in the same way as it gains from a well-functioning legal system which protects liberty. So what?

References

Flitter, Emily (2021) "Banks Tried to Kill Crypto and Failed. Now They're Embracing It (Slowly)" *New York Times*, November 1.

Kugler, Peter and Rich, Georg (2001) "Monetary Policy Under Low Interest Rates: The Experience of Switzerland in the Late 1970s" SNB Working Paper, April 9.

15

Criticism, Realism, Idealism and Reform

Introduction

We the authors have had many discussions between us about the ideal kind of money for the modern world.

Money takes its place along with the rule of law, representative government and property rights, as one of the basic institutions essential to human freedom and social peace. Potentially, money supports the functioning of the market economy in so many ways that a severe ongoing deterioration in its quality such as we have experienced (not continuously but in a series of painful lurches) in modern times and in particular in the past quarter century poses existential threats to social harmony, freedom and to the generation of widespread prosperity. And the quality of money does not need to fall to the point of triggering currency collapse or hyperinflation to raise substantially the threat level, which can occur gradually. Indeed, as we have shown in previous chapters, these ill-effects can materialise when recorded consumer price inflation seems quite modest.

We have identified in this volume asset inflation as a monetary source of destruction, whether of prosperity or freedom—see especially Chapters 6, 8 and 9. This is a topic that even today does not receive the critical attention it deserves. Sharpened awareness of the disease of asset inflation would raise the prospects that the voyage to better money could begin. Another catalyst could be sheer public revulsion at the dishonesty, incompetence and inequity of the current system - all on view during the Great Pandemic and Russia War Inflation.

© The Author(s), under exclusive license to Springer Nature Switzerland AG 2022
B. Brown and R. Pringle, *A Guide to Good Money*,
https://doi.org/10.1007/978-3-031-06041-0_15

We are concerned that, when such revulsion occurs, conditions should be conducive to better money emerging as the journey proceeds. This explains the emphasis throughout this work on the two-way links between good money and competition, within an orderly, law-based system, applying to financial intermediation and more generally. Pervasive regulations and the failure to tackle monopoly power, especially here in the context of financial markets and institutions, smother the chances of any serious competitor to bad money emerging, even when conditions are ripe, whether in the US, Europe or anywhere else. Regulations, monopoly power and cronyism form the apparatus of power that latter-day Metternichs use to defend the bad money status quo.

The deterioration in the capacity of money to fulfil its basic functions has gone so far that only radical reform will save us. Many people will go along with the criticisms of recent policies but stop short of calling for a reform of money itself. They will say that the bad effects we point to were the result of mistaken judgements; that the Fed or ECB or Bank of Japan or Bank of England "made the wrong call" (e.g. in raising or lowering policy rates) at a certain date and that if such mistakes were avoided all would we well (implicitly, they often clam that blunders would have been avoided if only "I" the writer had been running policy!). Yet, it should be obvious from the cacophony of clashing voices that the problem is structural.

How to fix it? Well, however much modern mainstream economists may hate to admit it, historically gold money has come the nearest to approaching the ideal standards of good money. And, though more than a century has passed since the end of the classical international gold standard, during which time a forest of opposition to any return has grown, we should not join the chorus that says that a second era of gold is impossible. Many apparently indestructible barriers protecting repressive regimes have proved to be fragile—including, for example, the Berlin Wall. The practical men who scorn idealism often turn out to be on the losing side of history—and so it will be with those who counsel that bad money is here to stay. Recognising that fact, our book on good money will not trim to "the myth of impossibility" or bow to the force of "the practical".

On the other hand, this is not a work of monetary messianism. Even if gold were to stage a come-back as international money, nothing in this book is likely to add to the reader's knowledge as to when this will happen. Many of the benefits of the classical gold standard depended in significant degree on the fact that for nearly half a century all the leading economies were on gold. The road back to gold monies circulating across a large part of the globe is at present largely invisible amidst the fog and darkness. Other conditions that allowed the international gold standard to function well—albeit far from perfectly—before World War I may also not be replicable or replaceable in the contemporary world. Just two illustrations here—not necessarily the most important: would a large-scale demand for gold coin re-emerge as pre-1914 supplemented this time by a gold digital coin? And would the anchoring of the gold money system be sufficiently solid to ensure that the purchasing power of money would be sustained over the long-run?

It would be great for good money if these and other questions could be answered in the affirmative. But we cannot do so without running an experiment first. Experiments in monetary economics do not have a good record. Sometimes, big changes in monetary regime have occurred without there being any provision for an experimental phase at all; sometimes they stay on even after results from actual implementation are bad—one can think here of European Monetary Union and the 2% inflation standard. Experiment should however help societies in choosing the good money regime of the future. Ideally, there should be a first phase, before the old bad regime is finally toppled, where the new money is tested, whether it be a gold money, an equity-based money (the Ikon), a fiat money or anything else. The idea of a test tallies with our dislike of monetary statism. The new money should emerge from a process where it first earns popularity in private market and in doing so we can learn much about its potentials, possible flaws and how the latter can be addressed. Of course this type of testing cannot be comprehensive as private monies with substantial circulations but lacking the scale and status of, say, the dollar or euro cannot reveal all the qualities and flaws they could have in a larger role.

We are not in a position amidst all the unknowables of a new monetary regime and without any relevant experiment yet having taken place, to categorically decide in favour of one new potential money over another as the best candidate for good money. We have presented a range of options—including a re-born gold standard, a re-constructed constitutional fiat money and an equity-based anchor. We explored in Chapter 5 the anchoring of fiat money based on constitutional rules which would constrain the money issuer from sliding into monetary inflation (the supply of money veering ahead of underlying demand on a sustained basis). There were experiments in the laboratory of history for this during the 1970s and 1980s, all of which were aborted, each for a variety of different reasons—in the US, Republican political strategy ahead of the 1986 and 1988 elections; in Germany, on the journey to European Monetary Union. But that should not be the final word on the matter. We saw that the most promising and effective implementation of a monetarist approach requires root and branch reform of the monetary system such as to allow the super-money qualities of the monetary core to prosper. None of this happened last time round. The triumph of good money broadly depends on this occurring as an essential element of a much larger drama about the renaissance of freedom and the dawn of real prosperity across society as a whole. (An example of a reform agenda put forward in this spirit is a paper written by Cogan and Warsh for the Hoover Institute in early 2022, see Cogan & Warsh, 2022).

On its own, there is nothing new in the advocacy of a solid anchor in the pursuit of good money. But earlier generations of economists who made the case in their day faced in some respects a simpler task than we do today. Now, "tolerable" bad money has been around for many decades. After World War II, mainstream media and academic opinion formed the view that such money is in fact the best of the second best or even the first best. That opinion remains dominant. Money's failures are interpreted as calling for more of the same - more intervention, more quasi-official regulation, and with these, more moral hazard (In the next section, we review and combat some such views).

Sound money advocates in the eighteenth or nineteenth century often had recent history of periods off gold to make their case—whether the debasement of coinage by eighteenth century or earlier monarchs, or the experience of the continental currency during the American Revolution or the Assignat during the French revolution; later, the greenbacks during the US Civil War. Into the early twentieth century, there were the examples of hyper-inflations in Central Europe following the World War I. At the same time, they did not have the wealth of material and evidence about what can go wrong, with apparently only "moderately bad" money, that we now have.

Today, in making the case for good money, we should consider a range of serious alternatives. We have discussed and reviewed these in this volume—including a fiat money with a putative solid anchoring system based on constitutional rules which are actively enforced; or a real asset-based money which is convertible into units of business capital stock as proxied by a type of equity ETF. Other options reviewed here particularly for small economies have included an anchoring system based on foreign money. All of these deserve serious consideration in any real world opportunity for the building of a good money regime and our purpose here has been to present them as live options for that time. We are not saying gold is always best in all circumstances in all societies. There will always be known unknowns whenever society makes the choice.

Getting to grips with the destructive power of money when misused, especially in fomenting asset inflation during the past half century and more, increases our appreciation and understanding of what makes good money. In turn, an understanding of how a good money system would work helps us to dissect the flaws in the current regime. That dissection is valuable not only in galvanising the forces of reform but also in helping us as individuals navigate our economic and financial affairs. To be sure, the evidence of recent history is less dramatic than these older examples in terms of goods and services inflation. The case against bad money is in that sense more difficult to make. That renders it all the more urgent to expose the false claims of bad money regimes.

So let us navigate our way through these final concluding thoughts of our volume.

The Moat of Consensus

The authorities running our moderately bad fiat monies enjoy protection; a deep moat of consensus surrounds their castle of power. This consensus permeates the political bodies with which the authorities interact, whether in the executive, legislative or court branches of government. Dissenters from this consensus are few and far between; they do not get even near the outer gates of the castle. The academic defenders of the monetary status quo support policy-makers in claiming that money management has never been as good (though the consumer price "bulge" in 2021–2022 presented new challenges to their well-honed communication skills). Recorded consumer price inflation has by and large been kept "low" in these last thirty years. Even if the arithmetic of consumer price averages is on their side, however, we have demonstrated in this volume that the cost of these moderately bad fiat monies has been high and rising, and that is without taking into account yet the denouement of this story. No solution is in sight; more sticking plaster, Band Aid, but no cure.

This consensus relies on a belief in the power of activist, discretionary policies. We have traced the origins of this belief back to the early twentieth century, shown how it gripped educated opinion and why it survived despite being exposed and challenged by successive crises. We have recognised that a break from gold money—and indeed, away from any fixed standard—may have been unavoidable given the political/economic/social chaos of the early and mid-twentieth century. But people (the citizens) learn from experience (unlike the Bourbons in the castle who learnt nothing and forgot nothing according to Talleyrand's famous observation), as Milton Friedman pointed out. As they learn, they take avoiding actions (e.g. in anticipating rising prices), and as a result the purported benefits of activist policies decline while their costs rise. People on the inside are quick to learn how to game the system; people on the outside suffer relative deprivation. It is no accident that elites (including intellectuals) back policies that benefit them, not only in terms of influence and prestige but also in terms of monetary rewards, even as they (whether sincerely or not) defend such policies as being in the general interest. This battle for an inside track round the source of the money supply is inevitable when money is placed at the service of the state/government rather than of the community. Back in the 1990s, there was hope that the new vogue for central bank independence would protect societies from this danger; despite some initial success, these hopes have not been realised.

To topple the consensus of ideas we must understand the interests that support them. In earlier chapters, we revealed reasons why the present system is entrenched, including a calculus of winners and losers in which winners are more powerful than losers; costs are disregarded or minimised by governments and officials.

Illusions of Prosperity

The process of asset inflation such as we have seen in the past quarter century gives rise to illusions whereby many people feel they are better off than they really are. For example, individuals may gain when they hold investments benefiting from the flight of capital out of assets subject to monetary taxation (notably government bonds and money). This will include speculative shares, real estate, commodities, artworks, cryptocurrencies and other assets in whose markets bubbles can form. Separately, individuals may benefit from wealth gains that have their source in the advance of monopoly capitalism, the decline of free markets and an abrogation of freedom—in short individual gain is matched by loss of prosperity and freedom at a society level.

Although these illusions of wealth at an individual level are not sustainable, the ways in which reality will assert itself are multifarious and unpredictable. For example, the premium on assets that (investors may hope) is not subject to monetary taxation might suddenly collapse. As the latest set of momentum traders bail out, the quasi-ponzi schemes collapse. A sharp rise in rates may make the burden of debt unsustainable for many sovereign countries and corporate borrowers. At the same time, the earnings growth that underpins sky-high equity markets might suddenly undergo a reality check—either via the unannounced arrival of an economic downturn or via the cumulative drag of mal-investment as driven by monetary inflation. One way or another, the illusions created by markets long driven by frantic investors in search for yield will be shattered.

Equally, the social costs of the rise of monopoly profits, the trampling on property rights and predatory actions/abuses against potential competitors, the invasion of privacy and widening disparities of wealth could reach a point at which people say "enough of this". By this route, the political process could produce a renaissance of liberty/free society, especially if all this goes along with stagnation or an actual fall in living standards.

There is no inevitability here, especially where monopoly power works behind the scenes. The money establishment takes care that their predatory activities do not take the form of spectacular action to raise particular prices in the forefront of public attention. Platform monopolists use the allure of free access to soften up those who in aggregate are to be plundered to the point where many who enter do not care about or do not realise the plot. Sadly, also, as the experience during COVID-19 has vividly shown, there is widespread tolerance of inroads into personal freedoms. Even so, one should not lose hope.

In the US, we can discern forces at work which might one day come together with others to achieve meaningful action—whether cross-aisle support for strengthening of anti-trust legislation for the new age of digitalization or media success in exposing abuse of democratic standards. Historically, there are grounds for hope; one can reflect, for example, on how the US political system tackled the scourge of slavery. Like the present Big Tech monopoly, at an economic level slavery engendered a combination of high profits and income at the top of the scale both in the Northern and Southern states of the US while contaminating liberal democracy and the free society; the growth of general prosperity was cramped. However, the two decades of the 1870s and 1880s that followed the Civil War, featuring in the first a return to gold, were the most prosperous in the history of the US. Monetary reform today alongside the implementation of a wide agenda for restoring freedom could usher in a similar long economic miracle. If there are grounds for despair it is in the apparent lack of connection anywhere being made in the political scene between bad money and illusions as described at the society level.

The Costs of the "Silent Killer"

Many ills of modern society can be traced to flawed monetary arrangements—fragile long-term economic outlook, economic sclerosis including long spells of low capital investment, crony capitalism, great inequality stemming from an abusive corruption of capitalism. Much of our book has been devoted to explaining the links connecting poor money to poor outcomes; so there is no need to restate the evidence. The challenge is how to use it effectively as a force for change.

For good money to become a mainstream political cause, it has to become clear to a large number of people not only that present bad money is indeed the source of much malaise, but also why and how it affects them negatively both at the level of society and as individuals. Gifted and idealistic politicians can play a key role in that awakening; thinkers formulate the ideas and arguments that get passed on between people and become part of the lead discussion.

Steering a Course to Better Money

How could the journey to good money get under way?

Good money can become a popular cause when joined with an idealism that transcends monetary matters. The underlying themes are that the money system should serve the community as a whole, without fear or favour, guided by the interplay of competitive free-market forces, not the state or government of the day; such guidance works best when the system and the markets which form part of this enjoy a status within constitutional law which makes assault in various forms by government illegal. True, we have to be careful not to have an elitist disregard for "politics"; but having said that the market processes in which good money is delivered to the public have to be protected from abuse—just as the processes which deliver bread to the customer. And even more so given the huge importance of money. The doctrine of central bank independence makes a gesture in this direction, but in practice money remains deeply vulnerable to corruption whether by Big Government or Big Finance or other harmful influences.

Good money also has to earn respect and "esteem" (Jevons). It does this best when convertible into commodities/real assets that are themselves desired and esteemed. The anchor and its crucial role should be widely understood; convertibility can be key here. It may be readily understood even by a child. Trust laws, not wise princes, even when they follow Machiavelli's advice to choose good advisers. As Locke wrote, liberty is "not to be subject to the inconstant, uncertain, unknown, arbitrary will of another man", even when, or especially when, she is all dressed up as a regulator supposedly acting purely for the public good.

Might a severe crisis provide a catalyst to meaningful reform? It's possible but far from certain. As authors, we hope that reform materialises before the next devastating consequence of bad money and succeeds in pre-emption, though there would be the costs of anchoring an unanchored monetary system. During a crisis and its immediate aftermath, there is a hunt for scape-goats, along with much obfuscation. True, there are historical examples of money suddenly becoming apparently sound due to crisis—one thinks of the end of the German hyperinflation, for example, in 1923—but that is the exception to the rule. The return to gold in the US in 1878, the hardening of the franc and campaign for gold under De Gaulle in France, the birth of the hard DM, and the short-lived Volcker "monetarist experiment" in the early 1980s all occurred as part of a confluence of economic and political forces as well as changing ideas. Radical reform may avert rather than require a devastating societal and economic crisis.

Blueprints for monetary reform are not the stuff of successful election campaigns, unless there is a vivid symbolic key to them which can impress popular imagination, or unless they seem to offer an instant cure to a widely perceived ill. On its own, monetary reform is unlikely to be the decider of election outcomes. As we have seen, monetary reformers must form winning coalitions with other causes.

As illustration, monetarism as an abstract dogma of monetary control could not have won the 1969 General Election in Germany; but mone-tarism presented as meaning an immediate revaluation of the DM against the dollar which would bring a rise in living standards for the middle classes—and by the way bring an end to hated consumer price inflation, that was a different matter. De Gaulle in his pursuit of a gold international order and by promising the French to replace the duplicity of the dollar with the yellow metal could capture a national imagination—and even so only as part of a more general strategy of restoring French independence of a US hegemon, not just in money but also in defence.

By contrast, good money has not entered any US election as an unam-biguous winning theme in modern history (since the nineteenth century). Yes, Carter attacked Republican monetary policies in the 1976 elections and won, but no-one sees that as his winning campaign promise; and before he brought Volcker into the Fed on the understanding that he would apply monetarism to ending the high inflation, Arthur Burns had been able to deliver his second big inflationary dose to the US economy (1976–1978);Carter likely carried the blame somehow with the electorate—not to mention the disaster of the Iran hostage crisis. Somehow, Reagan managed to present himself as the candidate of sound money based on monetarism alongside his other campaign promises. At the forefront of the economic programme were big personal tax cuts endorsed by supply-side economics as popularised by his advisor Professor Arthur Laffer.

So how could good money win elections in the US or Europe or Japan looking into the future from the viewpoint of the early 2020s? It is implausible to expect that in the US or Europe the case for gold would emerge spontaneously in such a strong form as to catapult immediate reform. There are, it must be acknowledged, unknown and potentially burdensome costs to anchoring a poorly anchored or non-anchored monetary system. These might, however, become palatable if the costs of continuing with the present money systems are widely understood. This is precisely what happened in England at the start of the eighteenth century. Governments had often debased the coinage. Suddenly, the public was ready to listen to the pleas of Locke and others for a moral and quasi-constitutional restraint on the powers of the sovereign to manipulate the currency. Without the trust of creditors, they will not risk their money. With it, banking, investment and stock markets would flourish.

A Reform Agenda

Monetary reformers driven by the ideal of good money are likely to make headway by appealing to the concepts of a competitive and fair economy, fighting monopoly capital and cronyism, attacking the undue power of the financial/banking world and giving individuals greater freedom to choose their preferred money.

This could all translate into such measures as removing regulatory or tax obstacles to the private development of any competing money (including Ikons as discussed in Chapter 12), whether by banks or other financial intermediaries; removal of too big to fail protection and vigorous pursuit of re-vamped anti-trust agendas; radical reform of legal tender laws to remove obstacles to making payments in a whole range of possible monies; abolition of deposit insurance and instead providing "weights and measures" inspectors to validate financial intermediary promises of producing super-safe deposits backed 100% with cash or the commodity base of the given money; allowing digitalization as pioneered and developed by private sector institutions to spread to all the different money forms—not as at present impeding the spread in many conventional areas (banks issuing digital coins e.g. whether in gold or in dollars or any other fiat money); allowing competition in the issuance of banknotes, with issuers free to make these in any denomination of their choosing.

By allowing monetary competition in this way, as we have shown, the demand for high-powered money in its various expanded forms, largely overlapping what we have described as "super-money", would become broader and more stable, a key development along the way to providing a solid anchor to the monetary system.

Money in Its Proper Place

Finally, suppose the case for good money does indeed win political allies and the journey towards this starts. What should be the ideal constitutional order in which the journey would continue? More specifically, what would be the essence of constitutional amendments to set the guardrails in the future for the state's role in the realm of money? We need to conjure up a vision of a brighter future and why it can be made appealing and practical. End result, money finds its rightful place in our lives at the individual level and in society.

There are perils in money constitution writing as any serious look at history suggests, most recently including the Maastricht Treaty, but extending back to central bank independence in the Weimar Republic and US money clauses in the founding US Constitution. In particular, constitutions can become reinterpreted along the way by Big Government, and the courts can approve these changes. The constitution may end up giving unforeseen advantages to a broken fiat money status quo, inhibiting rather than helping the journey towards a better monetary future.

So, here are some suggestions as to what should be in the constitution regarding money's place (let's think of the US or Europe).

The state should allow free competition between alternative monies as issuers seek to best provide citizens with top quality monies. The state should not create and/or tolerate monopolies in monetary services, allowing, for example, free competition in the provision of banknotes and other types (including digital) of payment, while blocking the transgressions of the big payment and credit card companies. The state's role in all of this is primarily as guardian of the market-place—with its legal system capable of clamping down on abuse and deceptions. In its role as market-place guardian, the legal authorities should scrupulously be guided by the principle that all institutions of whatever size are treated equally; none are too big to fail, none enjoy privileged access to central bank financing. If indeed gold monies were to emerge in the ascendant in the competitive market-place, the state's weights and measures inspectorate specialist division in money would ensure standards there. The state should use its authority within the legal system to prevent abuses (including false claims) especially in the areas of deposit money creation, ensuring by inspection that claims as to liquidity, cash or commodity backing for safe deposits, and solvency were genuine. A comparable role would also be needed if another type of real asset-based currency emerged as the choice of society, as we have described (e.g. to monitor the suitability and integrity of a market index).

As regards the legacy fiat money regime which subsists from before this monetary constitution was enacted, the state and its institutions would henceforth have no authority to set interest rates, which should be wholly market-determined. The guiding principle of official policy should be to provide good money with its core of super money to citizens. (We set out the principles of good money in Chapter 3). The authorities would aim to anchor this legacy fiat money by convertibility into a real asset.

As already mentioned, money also should be respected and "esteemed". Although fiat money can in principle be adequately anchored, as just explained, experience shows this is extremely challenging and the results in the medium and longer term generally poor. Money is more likely to be respected and admired when convertible at par into a commodity or bundle of commodities/real assets that are themselves desired and esteemed. This shows that a monetary unit that is defined to satisfy purely statistical criteria of long-term price stability will not be able to do the "heavy lifting" needed of it. It would not be able to carry a money from here to eternity (the belief of citizens in Victorian Britain, widely shared beyond, that their money would endure for ever was important to its success). When these commodities/real assets enjoy considerable non-monetary demand that adds to their quality as a potential solid monetary anchor. This shows the central role of an anchor that is widely understood; and why convertibility is key. The intrinsic value of such a money can be readily understood even by a child.

No, money is not wealth, as Adam Smith reminds his readers—he attacked mercantilism for its obsession with the national accumulation of money (then gold). Rather we should view money as indispensable to the operation of markets in the goods, services and assets that comprise the items traded in a modern economy. The wonders of efficient price-signalling across the whole range of markets essential to prosperity "of the many, not the few" and ultimately political liberty, are critically dependent on good money. A money that imposes the same disciplines on every citizen, without fear or favour, even if these may sometimes appear harsh, is to be preferred to one that seems to be your friend, but that has favourites, that favours some groups at the expense of others and that can be manipulated because it is weak. All of this is a tough case to make in the sense that the enemy is formidable—ubiquitous, highly self-motivated, heterogeneous, plausible and with no obvious control centre. The enemy has no respect for the precious prize of freedom and views its essential grounding in good money as an obstacle to its purposes. These are defined by personal greed and lust for power unrestrained by what Adam Smith described as "moral sentiments".

In striving to build and safeguard healthy markets founded on good money we should not fall into the trap of embracing the ready-to-hand slogans of "neo-liberalism". We do not assert that good money is possible only in a state with small government; on the contrary it is fully consistent with maintenance of a mixed economy, protection of minorities, ethnic and religious diversity and the full range of social services characteristic of modern democracies. Instead, our focus should be on the need for a constitutional order full of checks and balances and containing specific legal impediments to corruption—whether the abetting of protectionism, monopoly power, surveillance capitalism or more broadly the entire apparatus that enables and nourishes crony capitalism. We do not claim that markets are everywhere and at all times efficient but only that as a rule, with some clearly understood conditions and exceptions, they do a better job in fulfilling consumers' demands, steering resources to their best uses and providing people with the type of money they want, than committees composed at best of busy-bodies and at worst packed with cronies of the prime minister. They form an essential element in our system's defences against imminent threats to our security and freedom, notably from the growth of the surveillance state at home and the existential challenge from totalitarian states such as China abroad.

The freedoms that citizens enjoy within a society, including the freedom to make mistakes and lose money, depend ultimately on the vigilant upkeep of the institutions that safeguard them and repel and weaken their enemies— as described in this volume. A Good Money regime, once founded, has to be resilient. Vigilance can come only after there has been an Act of Creation or some would say Re-Creation. This book has been about both vigilance and creation. A spark from the eternal candle of liberty must fire the spirit of human imagination and societal aspirations. These must rise above the illusions and contaminations of asset inflation—the disease that bad money regimes have spread so viciously and that can paralyse its opponents.

Reference

Cogan, John F and Warsh, Kevin. (2022). *"Re-invigorating Economic Governance: Advancing a New Framework for American Prosperity"*. Hoover Institution Press, May.

Glossary

Asset Inflation
Currency Wars
Economic Sclerosis
Goods Inflation
Mal-Investment
Monetary Anchor
Monetary Inflation
Monetary Deflation
Monetary Taxation
Natural Rhythm of Prices
Super-Money
Bibliography

Asset Inflation

Asset inflation is a corruption of the price signalling function in asset markets induced by monetary inflation. This concept of asset inflation follows the lead of Austrian school economists (see Brown 2017) rather than monetarist economists (see Schwartz 2003), who describe the concept in terms of "rising asset prices". A key area of corruption is the long-term interest rate market. Rather than the rate reflecting a percolation of decentralised information stemming from decisions of individuals (millions or even billions) about how

B. Brown and R. Pringle, *A Guide to Good Money*, https://doi.org/10.1007/978-3-031-06041-0

much to save, consume and invest, taking account of investment opportunities which they perceive, it becomes heavily influenced by the inflationary objectives of the government acting together with the monetary authorities. More generally, today we can say that asset inflation is the result of monetary inflation inducing market behaviour which runs counter to prices of assets fully reflecting information on an efficient basis, a key feature of well-functioning markets. For example, investors seeking yield in the face of negative returns on monetary assets and so-called safe bills or bonds denominated in money may easily develop a distorted vision of the future, failing to give due weight to a wide range of possible scenarios based on a careful and full assessment of the future.

This results in "mal-signalling" i.e. misleading price signals—another Austrian School concept. In this situation, prices of many assets reflect a widespread distorted vision of the future. Investors and other market participants pass judgements about the future, for the purpose of assessing value, which are inconsistent with what one might describe as "sober-rationality" taking full account of normal scepticism. Some commentators would describe this situation as one where asset prices are widely above their underlying value; we do not favour that definition here as "underlying value" is not an empirically actionable concept. It is not a variable we can look up anywhere.

The hypothesis that price signalling in asset markets becomes distorted under conditions of monetary inflation stems from clinical research by psychologists. Notably, Daniel Kahneman reports evidence from experimental data (see Kahneman 2011) that individuals if offered a choice between certain loss or a bad bet whose actuarial outcome is worse but which offers a small chance of gains, choose the bad bet. That is inconsistent with rational behaviour (maximisation of expected utility) as assumed in traditional price theory. Going beyond Kahneman's work, let's think about what this means for behaviour under monetary inflation. Here most individuals expect certain real loss on monetary assets. Hence, they choose to take on bad bets which nonetheless offer a significant chance of gain. Accordingly, prices of assets become distorted relative to where they would be if normal rationality was dominant across the market-place.

We can gain further insights into the nature of these price distortions under conditions of monetary inflation from other empirical research in behavioural finance (see Shiller 2000). The original clinical work was unrelated specifically to monetary factors, but we can infer implications. For example, take the finding that individuals become influenced by positive feedback loops, where a stream of positive gains makes them irrationally form more favourable judgement of the asset's prospects. Such streams are a feature of monetary inflation. Also, we can extend Shiller's research regarding how narratives spread (see Shiller 2019) into questions about how this process is influenced by an environment of certain loss on monetary assets where many individuals are accepting bad bets: do they become prone to the cognitive bias of seeking to turn these bad bets into good bets by asking fewer questions than normal about speculative narratives which seem to justify their position and which have been consistent with capital gains until this point? Also in our experience of asset inflation during the past thirty years, as historically, we see a boom in financial engineering, which involves essentially designing securities in which leverage is partly or wholly disguised (though not from investors prepared to dig into the prospectuses). Market practitioners seek to boost returns on fixed-interest assets by being ready to take on substantial credit risk even when the premium (additional yield) for doing so has become unusually low (see Stein 2013).

Asset inflation, as a malign phenomenon, can persist beyond the monetary inflation from which it stemmed. The distortions in market-pricing described do not instantaneously come to an end. The positive feedback loops, the speculative narratives, the illusions which have built up, do not necessarily fade away quickly. That might happen in some situations—but considerable variation is possible. For the record, the great asset inflation of 1995–2007 may have continued for at least two years beyond the end of the monetary inflation. We say "may" here, because although the Greenspan/Bernanke Fed had driven up short-term rates by 400 bp in a short period of time (less than two years) from late 2004, the US monetary system was not operating in a way which permitted anything like a precise judgement to be made about whether the growth in money supply was coming more into line with the growth of demand.

Under conditions of economic sclerosis (see glossary entry below) virulent asset inflation can co-exist for many years with an only moderate goods and services inflation. Interest rates well below where they would be on average under a good money regime induce a range of distortions and severe mal-signalling.

In the longer term, asset inflation imposes economic costs in terms of low growth and lost prosperity. In severe cases, these losses materialise in market collapse and a great depression. True, in the years running up to that, there will have been sustained periods of rising asset prices. These periods, however, are not the defining characteristic of asset inflation. Finally, high and rising asset prices can be a natural and healthy phenomenon at times of economic miracles or what the Germans describe as "Wirtschaftswunder" under good money regimes. They do not in themselves constitute asset inflation. Rather than simply looking at prices, in diagnosing asset inflation, we should focus on the mal-signalling.

NB Asset classes include equities (stocks), fixed income bonds, property including housing, gold, commodities, financial derivatives such as futures and options, art works, super-yachts, NFTs and cryptocurrencies.

Currency Wars

Currency wars are economic conflicts between countries that seek to achieve advantage at the cost of others by manipulating their exchange rates. Currency wars are a feature of a global economy where governments can pursue discretionary policies with respect to the international value of their national currencies. They do not occur where a global currency standard operates. Under the present system of floating exchange rates among the main currencies, countries wage currency war when they harness their monetary policies to the objective of devaluation.

Illustrations of alleged currency warfare have included episodes where the US has pursued monetary inflation and the dollar has fallen sharply in consequence. Sometimes, there is no doubt about the intent of policy; indeed, US administration economic officials sometimes have complained of the dollar's "overvaluation". At other times, the US, or any other country, may engage in aggressively easy monetary policies ostensibly for purely domestic objectives. "Intent" in such circumstances is difficult to prove but the belief that a country is attempting to gain a competitive advantage in this way can become a sore in international economic and even geopolitical relations. An example of such alleged currency warfare was the aggressive use of quantitative easing during the mid-2010s by Europe and Japan coupled with negative interest rates. The Trump Administration on occasion accused those countries of depreciating their currencies to stimulate their economies at the cost of other countries.

The US Treasury Department prepares a semi-annual report summarising which countries (if any) it assesses to be manipulating their exchange rates (i.e. engaging in currency warfare). Its criteria, however, are deeply flawed. They do not include any measures of domestic monetary policy, focusing on non-monetary indicators of little relevance (to the charge) such as bilateral trade balances with the US.

Economic Sclerosis

Economic sclerosis is a decline in the dynamism of a capitalist economy which results from long and sustained asset inflation. This is distinct from an illness diagnosed by some Keynesian economists—described as secular stagnation as popularised most recently by Summers (see Summers 2015) —though some of the symptoms can be similar. Hallmarks of economic sclerosis are weak competition, the growth of monopoly power, reluctance of investors to engage in long-gestation investment and a popular bur flawed diagnosis of "savings glut". The description here of economic sclerosis fits the observed malaise in the US, Japanese and European economies during the second half of the 2010s.

Under what conditions does asset inflation cause economic sclerosis to form? A link between asset inflation and economic sclerosis becomes apparent when a long and sustained asset inflation induces a financial and business climate inimical to the normal dynamism of a capitalist economy. Perceived long-run business investment opportunities shrink when would-be investors worry about how the asset inflation will end. The forces of competition which promote investment—for example, by new entrants challenging established firms—become enfeebled as monopolist predators, strengthened by monetary inflation, establish for example a "death zone" where they wipe out new entrants or take them over.

The link just described (from asset inflation to economic sclerosis) is not inevitable. Sometimes, asset inflation coincides with a burst of productivity growth, driven by rapid technological change. Here, the source of the monetary inflation is likely to be the monetary authority seeking to prevent a fall of goods prices as would occur in a benign process of firms competing and passing on lower costs to the consumer. Such episodes culminate in economic damage but not economic sclerosis in the form described here.

Under conditions of asset inflation, individuals will chase apparently high-return business opportunities often created by financial engineers painting a rosy picture of the prospects for some project based on taking on more debt in relation to equity (i.e. leverage). They will be blind to the elevated risks. The illusions lead to bad decisions, waste and inefficiency in how capital becomes allocated. Living standards suffer. The tentacles of monopoly capitalism increase their reach.

Such asset inflation, if long and sustained, curbs the growth of productivity, in turn feeding back to decreased investment opportunity and pessimism. Slow-growing or stagnant household real incomes, accompanied by concerns about pension insufficiency and fears of an eventual crash, enfeeble consumer spending.

Goods Inflation

Goods inflation is the manifestation of monetary inflation in the goods and services markets. It resembles but is not to be identified with popular measures of inflation as taken from official data on consumer prices (Mises 1979). Goods inflation, for example, can be present even if we do not observe a rise in the consumer price data. Such might be the case where there is a spurt of productivity growth, for example. If the machinery of money were under control, or equivalently there were no malaise of monetary inflation, then prices in general would be falling at such a time. If we observe prices flat or rising very slowly, then that would indicate the presence of goods inflation. We can make a similar statement about the failure of prices to fall during a business recession due to an excess of money—another case of monetary inflation in goods markets which does not show up as rising prices.

Mal-Investment

Mal-investment is the misallocation of capital that occurs under monetary inflation which corrupts prices and /or interest rates. Capital is misallocated when it flows into firms of sectors of the economy that do not in fact offer the best, i.e. most productive, investment opportunities. Our concept of mal-investment as used in this volume has its origins in the Austrian School (see Sechrest 2006). The waste can involve both over-investment and a bad distribution of investment. Mal-investment results in a loss of economic prosperity—albeit that this loss may become evident only after long periods of time. It is often not possible in real time, i.e. during a spell of asset inflation, to point out mal-investment with confidence. As Warren Buffet noted, we find out who was swimming naked when the tide goes out. In principle, mal-investment is likely to be found in areas where monetary inflation has distorted prices most, as will often be the case where particular asset prices have been influenced by speculative narratives.

The source of mal-investment is our inability to foresee future market conditions correctly. This inability is part of the human condition. But accurate price signals provide crucial information channel through which entrepreneurs can identify investment opportunities. These price signals are distorted by monetary inflation.

When investigating a historical episode, the diagnosis of mal-investment may turn on making a plausible counterfactual hypothesis. Sometimes mal-investment turns out to have been prevalent in what was the leading frontier of technology—for example, the railroads in the mid-nineteenth century (see the counterfactual historical analysis of Fogel 1964. This author argued that the investment in railways was excessive and could have yielded better results if more capital had gone into building canals). In the modern world, especially in the context of the Great Pandemic, it is likely that mal-investment has been occurring through underestimating the risks involved in digitalisation.

Monetary Anchor

A monetary anchor is a device that constrains the supply of money so as to prevent the emergence of monetary inflation. A "solid" anchor is one that is effective in that purpose. The concept of monetary anchor as developed in this volume has its origins in an older use of the term as found, for example, in Flood and Mussa (1994) but is different. In that original literature, an anchor was defined as the nominal variable which the central bank targeted; the guiding idea was that by choosing appropriately one such variable, the central bank policy-makers could firmly guide the broad path of prices. We modify that definition here: the choice between several possible good money regimes (which the reader of this volume is invited to make) depends critically on their relative success in preventing the emergence of monetary inflation (see entry in this glossary). To assess this, we consider how anchoring works under each alternative anchor—hence our focus on anchoring as a system device. Under a fiat money regime, the anchoring device takes the form of controls on money supply issuance which prevent its total supply veering out of line with the path of underlying demand for money (ideally this is in the context of super money which means that high-powered money can be tied directly to the anchor).

Monetary Inflation

Monetary inflation takes place when the supply of money continuously tends to run ahead of demand for money over a sustained period. It is a process that causes inflation in asset markets (see "asset inflation") and in markets for goods and services (see "goods inflation"). The excess supply of money is continuously worn down by price rises, but the supply of money rises still further ahead, so the gap between the two does not close as long as monetary inflation persists. We follow here the insight of Milton Friedman (see Friedman 1942) who likens the monetary "inflation gap" to a mirage in the road; we can see the pool of water out there in the bright sunshine ahead but when the car gets to that point, there is nothing. It was an optical illusion. And so, it is with the gap between supply and demand for money; as money holders try to spend their excess holdings, continuously prices move upwards, prompting the public to raise its desired level of money holdings in nominal terms (and in the short-term interest rates also play a role). Looking ahead the gap remains, however, so long as further monetary injections mean that money supply continues to veer ahead of demand.

For readers who may be puzzled by the term "money supply veering ahead of demand", here is a different way of looking at that situation.

The amount of money an individual will hold—in digital or physical form—will depend to a large extent on his/her income and wealth. If money has the super qualities we describe, this amount will be relatively stable in the short or medium term. If the amount of money rises above the level that people as a whole are comfortable with, they will tend to spend it either on goods and services or on buying more assets or both. In the case of a shortfall of money supply, they will tend to sell goods or assets or postpone purchases in order to restore money holdings to a comfortable level. The process will change the value of money in terms of goods, services and assets. A key dynamic in the process of asset inflation is the influence of excess money in depressing interest rates and so leading to a distortion of price signals whilst simultaneously stimulating "hunger for yield" and "positive feedback loops" from capital gains to over-confidence (see "asset inflation" in this glossary).

Direct and early diagnosis of the condition monetary inflation is possible where a group of core money assets has super-money qualities and where these overlap the aggregate that economists call high-powered money or the monetary base. And even at a later point in the process, a diagnosis of monetary inflation can be made from its typical symptoms with more confidence, while rejecting at the same time a collection of "real factors" (such as institutional changes, bottlenecks, etc.) as possible explanations. Such symptoms of monetary inflation *in asset markets* include a boom in financial engineering, featuring camouflaged leverage, rapid contagion of hot speculative narratives, suspected manias, abnormally low credit spreads; *in goods markets*, the symptoms include rising prices and shortages.

The presence of super-money qualities at the core mean that the statistics of high-powered money should provide some useful indication of whether or not a process of monetary inflation is under way. This indication would be in the form of large growth in supply of high-powered money which has no obvious parallel in a sudden sustained increase in demand for this.

Under a fiat money regime, the issuer would ideally respond to such indications, which always are judgemental in part, by slowing the growth of or actually cutting the supply of high-powered money.

Under an international gold standard, monetary inflation could occur where the above-ground supply of gold is running ahead of demand on a sustained basis. The main historical example of this is the inflation (including strong asset inflation) in early/mid-seventeenth-century Holland due to gold inflows to Amsterdam from Latin America.

In general, where demand for high-powered money is broad, stable and strong as is the case where its components overlap core components of money with super-money qualities, we can say that monetary inflation describes the situation where the supply of high-powered money runs ahead of demand for it. That definition can fit both fiat money regimes and real asset/commodity-based monies including gold monies. The monetary inflation gap causes goods inflation by driving individuals, who find themselves with money in excess of their optimum holdings, to spend this excess on buying goods and services; it also empowers asset inflation. It does this by stimulating directly the purchase of some assets—for example houses, by depressing interest rates, and by creating a climate of concern about loss of purchasing power of money.

In such ways, monetary inflation leads to a fall in the value of money. Note that in the case of a bad money regime (where there is no core money with super-money qualities), a diagnosis of monetary inflation based on assessments of demand running ahead of supply of high-powered money is very difficult and may be even impossible to make with any significant degree of confidence. This does not mean that monetary inflation is banished! Rather, until we have any confidence in such a diagnosis, the symptoms must already be loud and clear, whether in goods markets, or asset markets or both.

Sharp rises in consumer prices do not necessarily indicate monetary inflation. For example, a sudden resource shortage—whether driven by war, pandemic, oil producers forming a cartel or business cycle boom (non-monetary in source)—might drive prices under a good money regime to well above their long-run mean (coupled with expectations of these falling back subsequently). The diagnosis of monetary inflation in goods and services markets requires much more than merely reading the monthly consumer price index reports.

Monetary Deflation

Monetary deflation takes place when the supply of money runs below demand for a sustained period. As for monetary inflation, prices move—in this case generally downwards—so that that the gap between demand and supply continuously tends to close; as Friedman observed (see monetary inflation), the gap is always in the future rather than the present. Our concept differs from that used in popular economic discourse, where deflation refers to a sustained fall in consumer prices. Prices of goods and services can fall under sound money with no monetary deflation and are a natural phenomenon as described, for example, by Bagus (2015). Under monetary deflation, a fall in consumer prices can be induced by the continuous shortage of money. It is also possible for monetary deflation to be present even though prices are not falling. This would be the case if simultaneously there are non-monetary forces upwards on prices as induced, for example, by resource shortage (as during pandemic or war or when an oil cartel flexes its muscles). Reversely, there are many situations where a falling consumer price index is absolutely not an indicator of monetary deflation.

Under a well-anchored money regime, where money sustains its purchasing power over the long run, we should expect an equal number of periods during which prices are rising and falling. The periods of price decline are equally benign to the period of price rise. In this volume, we have described at a number of points the critical mechanism in a competitive capitalist economy under good money where prices falling to a lower level (below the long-run expected mean) plays a critical role in enabling the invisible hands to function. This is the case for example in a business cycle downturn, where the fall of prices to a low level coupled with expectations of price rebound in the future, induces some spending in the present. It could also be the case where there is a transitory fading of investment opportunity or rise in personal savings; the invisible hands cope with this by virtue of a fall of prices in general in the present coupled with expectations of a recovery in the future.

Finally, as a historical observation, monetary deflations are rare in modern monetary history (since the collapse of the international gold standard in 1914). In the case of the US, the only clear period of monetary deflation was during the Great Depression.

Monetary Taxation

Monetary taxation describes the collection of revenue by government arising from monetary inflation and the resulting losses of capital or income suffered by holders of monetary assets. These tax collections are used directly to reduce government indebtedness and debt servicing costs real terms. There are two types of monetary taxation—inflation tax (IT) and monetary repression tax (MRT). The concept of inflation tax is well-established in monetary economics (see Kimborough 2006), though in this volume we adopt an extended definition. We consider the tax as levied both on holdings of cash (banknotes) and bank reserves at the central bank (in the case, where these are non-interest bearing), on the one hand (this is the traditional meaning) and on government bonds and bills outstanding on the other (this is our extension of the concept). In the case of banknotes and reserves, the tax rate equals the inflation rate—inflation reduces their real value. In the case of interest-bearing liabilities of government, including bonds and bills, the inflation tax is the amount by which actual inflation is greater than expectations already built into the nominal interest rate markets.

Turning to the monetary repression tax, a concept not found as yet broadly in the monetary economics literature, this is equal to the amount by which market interest rates are suppressed in real terms below the level which would prevail under a good money regime. For example, at the time when non-monetary disinflationary forces are strong, as during a productivity spurt, or in the context of economic sclerosis as induced by a long-running asset inflation, it is possible for the central bank to administer a stimulus (e.g. through what seem like artificially low interest rates) without this inducing a rising reported consumer price inflation rate. Yet, this would still raise MRT tax revenue.

Note that governments do not in general plan a given amount of monetary taxation ahead—in any case, the outcomes would usually defy their predictions. Rather, they take policy actions which are likely to lead to substantial tax burdens under one or other heading (IT or MRT), even though in their projected central scenarios high inflation would not figure.

We should also note that alongside the government's collection of monetary taxation, the monetary inflation process permits some groups of private individuals and private sector entities to raise quasi-monetary taxation from their creditors which they apply directly to reduce the real value of their outstanding debts.

Natural Rhythm of Prices

Even if money supply is well anchored, there will be episodes of rising and falling prices. These can be quite long-lasting and take place without any monetary inflation or monetary deflation being present - i.e. without any corruption of price signals. The interval between episodes is variable and in general unpredictable. They reflect a series of market adjustments that we term a "natural rhythm". Let us explain.

Individual businesses set prices in response to economic developments such as a spurt in productivity growth or a shortage of natural resources. The fluctuations in prices on average that correspond to a multitude of such behavior at an individual level can easily be interpreted by commentators or officials as indicating "the emergence of inflation" when prices rise, as in the opposite case of falling prices as a "worrying deflation". But they may be no cause for concern at all—but rather evidence that the price mechanism is working well. Here are some illustrations to demonstrate how this can give rise to a natural rhythm of prices under a good money regime.

Let's continue first with the case of a natural resource shortage—take for example the supply disruptions that resulted from the pandemic of 2020-22 and then from the economic war with Russia. Under a good money regime, yes, there will be price spikes in the areas affected by disruptions and shortages and these will broaden out as businesses find themselves under cost pressure. Most people's money incomes would not rise in step with higher prices; this squeeze on real incomes (including also income loss due for example to the extinction of employment opportunity) would reflect the overall impoverishment due to the disasters of war and pandemic. Hence demand for money probably would not rise in consequence of disruptions (strictly, a rise in transaction demand in line with higher prices being offset by a decline in general savings-type demand for money in consequence of lower real incomes in aggregate). And so, with money supply unchanged in the short-term (in line with very slow growth in the long run as for a solidly anchored money), no monetary forces would emerge to thwart an upward trend of prices as driven by shortages.

In practice, however, the rise in prices on average recorded in the US and Europe during and in the aftermath of the pandemic and war surely exceeded the natural rhythm upwards of prices which would have occurred under good money. This excess stems from monetary inflation - the large injections administered during 2020-1/2 as explained in chapter 11. As pandemic and war recedes we should expect an episode where the natural rhythm of prices is downwards, but this may well not show up in practice in the recorded behavior of the consumer price index due to further monetary inflation.

For our next illustration, consider the case of an economic miracle - when, for example, a cluster of scientific/technological breakthroughs spurs productivity growth. Many individual businessed find that their costs are falling and competitive pressures lead them to cut prices. The overall fall in prices at the same time as real incomes are accelerating in line with raised productivity growth mean that demand for money would not veer ahead of supply where the latter remains on an unchanged very low upward trajectory. There would be no monetary deflation, but there could well be a quite prolonged spell of falling prices. Note however that a good money regime might indeed include feeback loops in the long-run from spurts in productivity growth to money supply - as for example under a gold regime where productivity gains in the gold mining industry would mean a long-run increase in gold production; in effect the gold money regime of the gold standard would generate some mild monetary inflation meaning that the natural rhythm downward of prices would eventually reverse but at a very slow pace.

A final illustration of natural rhythm comes from the case of business cycle downturn. At such a time many businesses will come under pressure to cut prices whether in response to weak demand and excess capacity or excess inventories which have built up. Diminished real incomes and lower prices mean a reduced demand for money. But the fall in demand could be offset by the tendency during weak economic and financial conditions amidst rising default risks for individuals to build up money holdings as a safe store of value. Interest rate movements will underpin this tendency - with lower interest rates as typical during recession meaning an increase in demand for money (especially base/high-powered money which in good money regimes does not pay interest). And so money demand might well continue to be in line with supply - no monetary inflation or deflation - despite the widespread price-cuts. Again we should note as in the previous example that automatic mechanisms might come into play, meaning there will be some rise in base money over the medium term in response (here to recession, above to miracle); under a gold regime, for example, lower mining costs would lead to higher production of gold.

There is an economic elegance in the natural rhythm of prices which is typical of a good money regime. The direction of price change is intuitively in line with the need for broader economic re-balancing over time. The price rises which occur, for example, during a famine encourage households to postpone consumption; the price falls which occur during business downturns encourage households and businesses to bring consumption forward.

The price cuts during an economic miracle mean that real interest rates will rise more than nominal rates (if these rise at all) as individuals expect price declines to continue; this calmness of long-term nominal rates is positive for money's function as a denominator of contracts in long-term loan markets. Finally monetary regimes which attempt to suppress this natural rhythm of prices do so at great peril. In order to prevent a downward rhythm during a productivity spurt the authorities would inject money inflation into the economy; yes, this could result in stable prices or low consumer price inflation for some considerable time but would generate asset inflation. Likewise, the authorities by inducing tight money to block an upward rhythm (as during natural resource shock) might ensure stable prices or stable low inflation, but produce undesirable asset deflation.

Super-Money

This refers to a property ideally possessed by a group of assets at the core of the monetary system having an especially high degree of "moneyness", i.e. they are strongly demanded and indeed desired as money (Yuran 2014). Individuals wish to hold large amounts of such core monetary assets on a long-term basis (i.e. not making big changes for example in response to interest rate fluctuations) even though they earn no interest. These super-money assets have a strong appeal as a medium of exchange and store of value. They can emerge in both fiat money and commodity or real-asset money regimes. Examples of such core monetary assets with super-money qualities under a fiat money regime should include cash (banknotes) and reserve deposits at the central bank; their super-money qualities depend on confidence that the given money will retain its excellence in fulfilling monetary functions in the long run. The importance of the super-money concept to our understanding of good money regimes turns on the fact that demand for such monetary assets is broad, strong and stable.

The concept of super-money, which we develop in this book, is related to the conventional inverted money pyramid presented in banking and money textbooks where the bottom layer is so-called high-powered money. Take the case of a fiat money regime. When we juxtapose that property of demand for those assets which in aggregate largely overlap high-powered money with the supply of this being directly under the control of the authorities, we have a firm basis for good money fulfilling its promises.

This key and central role of high-powered money in a good money regime may seem at odds with the tendency among monetarists to favour broad rather than narrow money as the target (see Brunner and Meltzer 1998). We should note, however, that this importance of high-powered money is in the context of a hypothetical good money regime where its component core monetary assets have super-money qualities. By contrast, the monetarist debate about which money supply aggregate to target was largely coloured by empirical research in terms of the contemporary monetary system, where these super-money qualities had faded away to a considerable degree. The two schools of thought in dispute about whether to focus on the monetary base or broad money inhabit different monetary worlds and so make implicitly quite different assumptions.

Bibliography

Bagus, Philipp (2015) *In Defense of Deflation*. Financial and Policy Studies, No. 41 Springer.

Brown, Brendan (2017) A Modern Concept of Asset Inflation in Boom and Depression. *Quarterly Journal of Austrian Economics*, Spring, pp. 29–60.

Brunner, Karl and Meltzer, Allan H. (1998) *Money and the Economy: Issues in Monetary Analysis*. Cambridge University Press

Flood, Robert P and Mussa, Michael (1994) "Issues Concerning Nominal Anchors for Monetary Policy", NBER Working Paper Series 4850, May 1.

Fogel, Robert W (1964) *Railroads and American Economic Growth*. John Hopkins University.

Friedman, Milton (1942) Discussion of the Inflationary Gap. *American Economic Review*, Vol. 32, No. 2, June, pp. 314–20.

Kahneman, Daniel (2011) "Thinking Fast and Slow" Farrar, Straus and Giroux.

Kimborough KP (2006) Revenue Maximizing Inflation. *Journal of Monetary Economics*, Vol. 53, No. 8, pp 1697–1709.

Mises, Ludwig van (1979) *Economic Policy Thoughts for Today and Tomorrow*. Regnery/Gateway Inc., Chicago.

Schwartz, Anna (2003) Asset Price Inflation and Monetary Policy. *Atlantic Economic Journal*, Vol. 3, No. 1, March, pp. 1–14.

Sechrest, Larry J. (2006) Explaining Mal-investment and Overinvestment. *Quarterly Journal of Austrian Economics*, Vol. 9, No. 4, Winter, pp. 27–38.

Shiller, Robert (2000) Irrational Exuberance Princeton University Press.

Shiller, Robert (2019) Narrative Economics Princeton University Press.

Stein. Jeremy C (2013) "Overheating in Credit Markets: Origins, Measurement, and Policy Responses" A speech at St. Louis Federal Reserve Bank Research Symposium February 7

Summers, Lawrence H. (2015) "Reflections on Secular Stagnation" Speech at Julius-Rabinowitz Centre, Princeton University, February 19.

Yuran, Noam (2014) *What Money Wants: An Economy of Desire*, Stanford University Press.

Index